GREAT SMOKY MOUNTAINS NATIONAL PARK

JASON FRYE

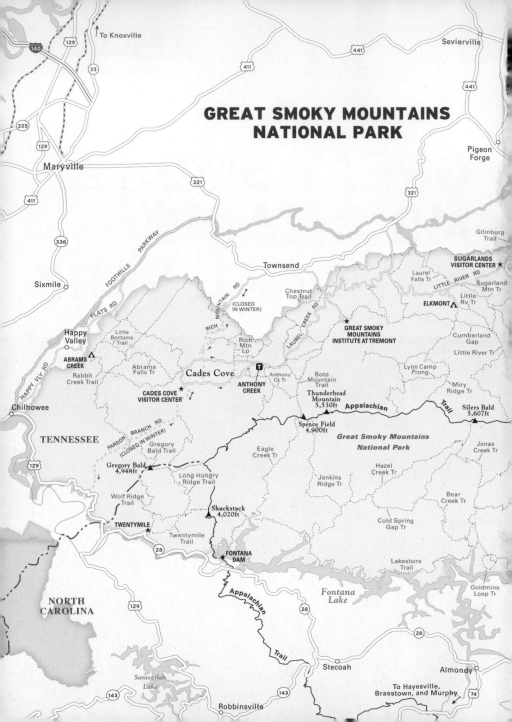

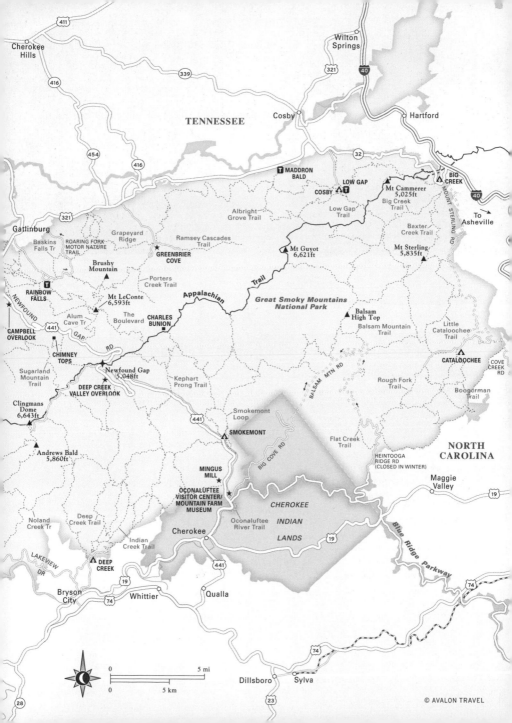

Contents

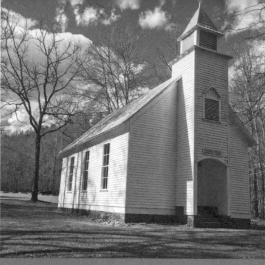

Great Smoky Mountains National Park

The national parks are called "America's Great Idea," and I think Great Smoky Mountains National Park is the best of the bunch. But I may be biased.

My earliest vacation memories are of these green mountains in summer and their blazing color in fall, of mountain streams and bears and the fields of Cades Cove filled with deer. On one morning ride across Newfound Gap Road, I learned why these mountains are called the Smokies. The mist rising from the coves and hollows and hidden places in the hills looked like smoke: tendrils of it rose like the sure sign of a chimney or a campfire; drifts of it formed miniature cloudbanks.

The Smokies are a colorful place. In the summer, the mountains are emerald green. In the fall the leaves are a riot of color. Spring is a time when wildflowers blanket high mountain meadows and secret glades. Thickets of rhododendron, galax, mountain laurel, and flame azalea bring flowery breath to the trails and paths throughout the park. In the winter, there's the beauty of a red fox running across a field white with snow, the crystalline shine of ice at the waterfalls, the jewel-like glint of snow in the morning sun.

There's a smell to this place, too—rich, wet, and fertile, the smell of dirt and

---

Clockwise from top left: Clingmans Dome; Palmer Chapel in Cataloochee; crossing a foot log; horse at the Cades Cove riding stable; old cabin on Roaring Fork Road; Sparks Lane in Cades Cove.

decades of leaves. Moss tinges the air near the springs, seeps, and waterfalls. In the autumn, the faintly cinnamon smell of leaves perfumes the breeze and the sound of those leaves underfoot announces your passage.

Birds, cicadas, the rush of water, and the sigh of wind create a layer of sonic landscape. When the elk bugle and call to one another, when a turkey gobbles, or when a hawk keens, it punctuates the soundtrack of the Smokies.

There's other music—banjos and dulcimers and guitars and song. That music sounds so at home it feels like it's been here as long as the stream or bird or wind, but it's just evidence of us. We drive the roads and hike the trails, fish in the streams, take photos of the sunsets and vistas, adding our voices to the music of the place.

When we leave, this song stays with us. We hum it to ourselves, recalling the place, the breeze, the sun on our faces, and the smell of fall on the air. We sing because this place is songworthy, a place like no other.

This is why we go back: to revel in the mountains, to learn a new verse, to find a place or experience missed on a previous trip. I go not to lose myself in the wilds of the Smokies, but to find myself there.

Clockwise from top left: Cades Cove; rhododendron bloom on the Appalachian Trail; the John P Cable Grist Mill; finishing the glaze on pottery in Dillsboro.

Planning Your Trip

Where to Go

Great Smoky Mountains National Park

Great Smoky Mountains National Park is the **most-visited national park** in the country. The scenery and **wildlife** are incredible: rounded peaks and jagged mountaintops, crystal-clear trout streams and white-water rivers, elk and bear, morning mist and **evening firefly shows** all delight millions of visitors every year. Crisscrossed by more than 800 miles of **trails** and studded with **waterfalls,** this is a hiker's paradise.

NEWFOUND GAP

Newfound Gap bisects the park and connects Cherokee, North Carolina, with Gatlinburg, Tennessee. It's a beautiful drive, and easily

the **most-visited part** of the park. From the **overlooks** that give big views of the eastern and western Smokies to **Clingmans Dome** to **short day hikes** to some stellar fall color, it's where you can say, "I went to Great Smoky Mountains National Park and it was great."

WESTERN SMOKIES

In the Western Smokies you find some busy spots like **Cades Cove, Fontana Lake,** and **Deep Creek** (a little less visited, but still busy), and a few places, like **Abrams Creek,** where visitors are infrequent. **Fly-fishing** is outstanding here as the creeks flow into various rivers and into Fontana Lake. Long-distance hikers come here for the **Appalachian Trail, Lakeshore Trail,** and other big backpacking adventures.

sign marking intersections on the Appalachian Trail

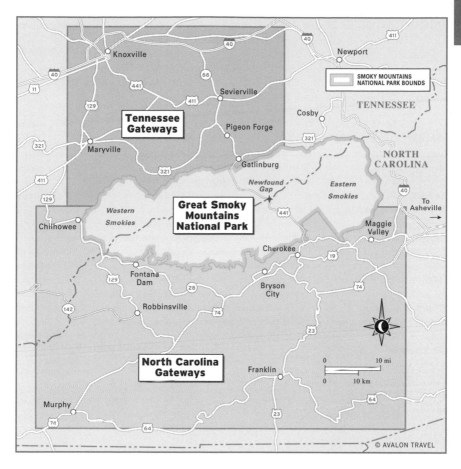

The map shows the Great Smoky Mountains National Park region with labels including Knoxville, Newport, Sevierville, Cosby, Pigeon Forge, Gatlinburg, Maryville, Chilhowee, Newfound Gap, Eastern Smokies, Western Smokies, Maggie Valley, Cherokee, Fontana Dam, Bryson City, Robbinsville, Franklin, Murphy, and To Asheville. Labeled areas: Tennessee Gateways, Great Smoky Mountains National Park, North Carolina Gateways. Legend: SMOKY MOUNTAINS NATIONAL PARK BOUNDS. Scale: 0 10 mi / 0 10 km. © AVALON TRAVEL

EASTERN SMOKIES

The Eastern Smokies are less-visited, but spots like **Cosby** and **Cataloochee,** as well as **Balsam Mountain** and **Greenbrier,** offer the remoteness and rugged beauty that characterize this park. **Camping, day hikes,** and **backpacking** adventures are the norm here. While many casual visitors don't frequent this region, serious outdoorspeople do. This region is worth the visit for the **wildlife-viewing** alone.

Tennessee Gateways

Gatlinburg is the western gateway to the Smokies, while nearby **Pigeon Forge** is home to **Dollywood,** the mountain-themed amusement park from the country music legend. **Knoxville,** a bigtime college town and one of Tennessee's music cities, offers a taste of city living at the edge of the Smokies. All three towns are tourist draws in their own right, and their blend of Southern hospitality, humor, and mountain culture makes quite the impression.

North Carolina Gateways

Cherokee, North Carolina, is where **Newfound Gap Road** begins. Cherokee is the ancestral home of the Eastern Band of the Cherokee Nation who celebrate their history and culture, past and present, on the **Qualla Boundary.** Between Cherokee and Asheville, small appealing towns like **Dillsboro, Waynesville,** and **Sylva** are rich with history and culture.

Located between the Blue Ridge and Smokies, with easy access to the mountains, **Asheville** is home to the lauded **Biltmore Estate,** some of the best **restaurants** in the South, and a number of cool **inns** and **B&Bs.** Only 90 minutes away, staying here makes getting to Great Smoky Mountains National Park easy.

When to Go

High Season
SUMMER (JUNE-AUG.)

Summer draws a **big number of visitors** escaping the summer heat at these cooler high elevations and spending their vacation days in a beautiful part of the world. Beat the heat by tubing in **Deep Creek,** going **white-water rafting,** or heading to spots like Cades Cove for **early morning bike rides** or even **hikes at higher elevations** throughout the summer. Plan for **warm weather** and pack shorts and light tops, plenty of water, as well as sunscreen and bug spray.

AUTUMN (SEPT.-MID-NOV.)

Autumn is the obvious season to visit the mountains. With leaves showing their last—and brightest—bit of **fall color** from the end of **September** through **October,** you can have as long a season of leaf-peeping as you want. This is prime time to hit some of the park's **backroads—** Balsam, Heintooga Ridge, Little Greenbrier, Parson Branch, Rich Mountain, and Heintooga-Roundbottom Roads—for great views before the **routes close (early- to mid-Nov.).**

Most days are warm and sunny in the daytime, chilly in the evening, and even cold at the

the first leaves of autumn

If You're Looking For...

- **Backpacking:** Make overnight reservations in advance to backpack to Mount LeConte or hike a section of the Appalachian Trail.

- **Bicycling:** Get up early to rent a bike from the Cades Cove Stove and ride the loop car-free in summer.

- **Camping:** The Cataloochee Valley offers solitude; or time it right to see fireflies at Elkmont Campground.

- **Hiking:** Follow the easy Hen Wallow Falls Trail to a lovely waterfall or take in the views from the top of Andrews Bald. Adventurous souls can step foot on the Appalachian Trail.

- **Historic Sites:** Watch living history demonstrations at the Mountain Farm Museum or explore the chapel and cemetery of Cataloochee's former communities.

- **Scenic Drives:** Cruise along Newfound Gap Road for epic views and scenic overlooks.

- **Solitude:** Camp at Abrams Creek or Cosby Campgrounds, drive along Balsam Mountain Road, or take a midday hike in the Cataloochee valley.

- **Waterfalls:** Hike to Grotto Falls, or head to the Roaring Fork Motor Trail for an easy drive with plenty of falls along the way.

highest elevations. You'll be fine in long sleeves and a vest or light jacket most of the time, but you'll want something a little heavier if you're visiting late in the season.

Low Season
WINTER (MID-NOV.-FEB.)
Winter in this region varies by elevation. At the highest points, the temperatures drop—plummet even—and the chance of snow or ice is real. It's a little warmer at the lowest elevations, but make no mistake, it's still winter. **Clingmans Dome Road** and **Roaring Fork Motor Nature Trail close** in late November when inclement winter weather has the potential to arrive.

Expect snow several times throughout the season, with a few significant snowfalls; come with some warm layers, a hat, and gloves.

SPRING (MAR.-MAY)
Spring rains bring **wildflowers** and **waterfalls** back to life. Though trails can be muddy, it's a fabulous time to visit, especially for **wildlife-viewing.** In **Cades Cove** and **Cataloochee** you'll see bear cubs, deer fawn, and elk calves trailing their mothers at the woods' edge. The park's back roads—Balsam, Heintooga Ridge, Little Greenbrier, Parson Branch, Rich Mountain, and Heintooga-Roundbottom Roads—as well as **Roaring Fork Motor Nature Trail** and **Clingmans Dome Road reopen.**

Spring temperatures are similar to fall, with warm days and cooler or even cold evenings, so pack accordingly, just remember to throw in a rain jacket.

Campgrounds in GSMNP are spacious and reasonably private.

Before You Go

Park Fees and Passes

Great Smoky Mountains National Park (www. nps.gov/grsm) is **free** to visit. Backcountry campgrounds require permits and reservations through the **Backcountry Information Office** (Sugarlands Visitor Center, 865/436-1297, https:// smokiespermits.nps.gov, 8am-5pm daily, $4 pp/ night) up to 30 days in advance.

Entrance Stations

There are three main entrances to Great Smoky Mountains National Park. Each entrance is easily accessed from a nearby gateway town:

- From **Gatlinburg, Tennessee,** follow US-441 south 2 miles into the north entrance to the park.

- From **Cherokee, North Carolina,** drive 2 miles north along US-441 into the south entrance to the park.

- From **Townsend, Tennessee,** take TN-73 east for 3 miles into the park near Cades Cove.

Reservations

Reservations are recommended at **campgrounds** in the national park and along the Blue Ridge Parkway, especially during the peak seasons of summer and fall. Reservations for **hotels and B&Bs** in the gateway towns of Cherokee, North Carolina, or Gatlinburg, Tennessee, are recommended during summer and fall.

In the Park

Visitors Centers

The busiest information center in the park is **Sugarlands Visitor Center and Park Headquarters** (1420 Old TN-73 Scenic, 865/436-1200, www.nps.gov/grsm, hours vary seasonally), located in Gatlinburg, Tennessee, at the north entrance to Newfound Gap Road.

If entering from the North Carolina side, **Oconaluftee Visitor Center** (1194 Newfound Gap Rd., 828/497-1904, www.nps.gov/grsm, hours vary seasonally) is just 2 miles north of Cherokee at the south entrance to Newfound Gap Road.

Where to Stay

LeConte Lodge (865/429-5704, www.lecontelodge.com, Mar. 21-Nov. 22) is the only true lodging in the park, accessible via a 5-6.8-mile hike. Even though there is no running water or electricity, the lodge books quickly. Reservations are via lottery up to **one year in advance.** For more amenities, plan to stay in the gateway towns of **Cherokee, North Carolina,** or **Gatlinburg, Tennessee.**

There are 10 developed campgrounds in the park. **Campground reservations** (877/444-6777, www.recreation.gov, $17-25) are accepted up to **six months in advance** for the following sites:

- **Elkmont Campground** (220 sites, Gatlinburg, TN, Mar.-Nov.), located west of Sugarlands Visitor Center, is the largest of the campgrounds and one of the most visited.

- **Smokemont Campground** (142 sites, Cherokee, NC, year-round) is just off Newfound Gap Road, 3.2 miles north of the Oconaluftee Visitor Center.

- **Cades Cove Campground** (159 sites, Townsend, TN, year-round) is a popular spot located on the east side off Cades Cove Loop.

- **Cosby Campground** (157 sites, Cosby, TN, Apr.-Oct.) is the park's third-largest campground, located in the quiet northwest corner of the park.

- **Cataloochee Campground** (Cataloochee, NC, Mar.-Oct.) has only 27 tent and RV sites in a valley on the west side. Reservations are required.

All other developed park campgrounds are **first-come, first-served** and are usually open April-October.

Getting Around

There are no park shuttles or public transportation available within the park—you will need **your own vehicle.** There are also **no gas stations** in the park; fill up first in Cherokee, North Carolina; Gatlinburg, Tennessee; or Townsend, Tennessee.

Best of the Smokies

Many visitors are puzzled by what to do in Great Smoky Mountains National Park. Most of the park is wild, and hiking trails rather than roads lead into every holler, corner, and cove. Here's an idea on how to spend a week here, and to spend it well.

Day 1
NEWFOUND GAP ROAD

Base yourself in **Gatlinburg,** Tennessee, where you'll have all manner of accommodation options and tempting entertainments easily at hand. Begin your exploration of Smoky at the **Sugarlands Visitor Center,** a mere two miles from Gatlinburg at the northern end of Newfound Gap Road.

Drive **Newfound Gap Road** south through the park. Hit the trail to **Alum Cave Bluffs,** a steep and strenuous five-mile hike that rewards you with a view many visitors never see.

As you come to the crest of the mountains on Newfound Gap Road, take the time to visit

Clingmans Dome, the highest peak in the park. From the viewing platform at the top (an easy walk), you'll have an unparalleled view of the surrounding country. There's a lovely hike to **Andrews Bald** nearby, a moderate 3.5-hour trek to a high mountain meadow that's often ablaze with wildflowers.

Newfound Gap Road ends at the **Oconaluftee Visitor Center** in Cherokee, North Carolina. Stop here to peruse the historic structures at the **Mountain Farm Museum** before returning to Gatlinburg for dinner with a show at the **Dixie Stampede,** a sort of Southern feast combined with a live-action play with horses, gunfire, and all sorts of excitement. Afterward, hit **Sugarlands Distilling** for a little moonshine to calm your nerves.

Day 2
ROARING FORK

In the morning, have breakfast at the **Pancake Pantry,** and then head for the **Roaring Fork**

Clingmans Dome

If all you have is one day to spend in Great Smoky Mountains National Park, don't sweat it. You can still see a lot (and plan a return trip as soon as you can).

Start the day in **Gatlinburg** with a stop at **Sugarlands Visitor Center** to pick up maps and find out about special events. Follow **Little River Gorge Road** west toward Cades Cove. You never move too fast on this curvy road, so slow down and take your time to soak up the views.

At **Cades Cove,** grab a map and a driving guide for the scenic 11-mile **Cades Cove Loop,** one of the most popular drives in the park (so you'll find you're not alone). Though there may be company—crowds even—this wide, verdant valley ringed by tall peaks is the very picture of calm, rural beauty. Stop for a walk to **John Oliver Place,** the **Methodist** or **Primitive Baptist Church,** or one of the many **cabins** that showcase the history of settlement here.

At the midpoint of Cades Cove Loop, stop for a hike to **Abrams Falls,** a pleasant 5-mile round-trip hike to a 20-foot waterfall. The entire hike should take 3 hours or less to complete, giving you plenty of time to complete the Cades Cove Loop before returning to grab lunch in **Gatlinburg.**

Newfound Gap Road connects Gatlinburg, Tennessee, to Cherokee, North Carolina. Follow Newfound Gap Road south up and over the Smokies. In 23 miles, you'll reach the turnoff to **Clingmans Dome,** the highest peak in the park. If the weather is good, you'll be able to see the observation tower at the summit as you drive up Newfound Gap. After the 8-mile drive to the parking area, make the short, steep hike to the top. If the summit is shrouded in clouds (and it may well be), continue south along the crest of the Smokies.

Mountain Farm Museum

Stop at **Newfound Gap** to check out the **Rockefeller Memorial,** the place where president Franklin Delano Roosevelt dedicated the park in 1940. As you continue east toward Cherokee, stop at any of the **scenic overlooks** along the way—you can't go wrong.

You'll draw close to the **Oconaluftee Visitor Center** in North Carolina by the end of the day. Perfect timing, as every evening **elk** make an appearance in a field adjacent to the visitor center and the **Mountain Farm Museum.** While checking out the collection of historic structures at Mountain Farm, keep an eye out for elk; they will often cross right through the middle of this re-created farmstead on their way to dinner.

Motor Nature Trail for today's hike. Depending on how adventurous you feel, this can be a half-day exploration of a waterfall or two, or a strenuous 14-mile trek to **Mount LeConte** and back. Either way, start off by hiking to **Rainbow Falls,** an 80-foot waterfall on LeConte Creek. For a short hike, turn around and hoof it back

to the trailhead. To reach the summit of Mount LeConte, continue on the trail but be ready for a long, hard day of it. **Baskins Falls** is a smaller waterfall—only 30 feet—but few people make the tough hike in to see it, so it's a bit of a hidden gem.

Since you've earned your supper, go for some

traditional, stick-to-your-ribs country cooking at **Mama's Farmhouse** in Pigeon Forge.

Day 3
COSBY

Head east to **Cosby** for a night of camping at **Cosby Campground,** where you'll have your choice of beautiful day hikes. **Hen Wallow Falls** and **Albright Grove** offer easy, wildflower-filled hikes. The trip to the stone fire tower at the top of **Mount Cammerer** is a long, tough day on the trail, but well worth it. If you've brought your fishing gear (and license), catch dinner in **Cosby Creek.**

Day 4
CATALOOCHEE

In the morning, break camp and head north on Highway 32 for breakfast in Cosby at **Janice's Diner.** From Cosby, follow Foothills Parkway east to I-40 and take the scenic route south to **Mount Sterling Road,** a drive of about an hour. Along Mount Sterling Road, roll down the windows, relax, and breathe deep—you're

almost at one of the most secluded areas of the park.

In **Cataloochee,** register at the campground (reserve a site in advance), set up your tent, and enjoy a picnic lunch before lacing up your boots and heading into the valley. Look for **elk** in the field across from **Caldwell Place,** or hike to **Palmer Chapel, Little Cataloochee Church,** or the **Woody House.** Anglers can wet a line in one of the nearby creeks and try to catch dinner. Sunset signals time for chow and **stargazing**—there's so little light pollution that the celestial show is breathtaking. Sit back and enjoy.

Day 5
CADES COVE

Today, we head west to **Cades Cove,** a mountain community that was one of the first places settled on the western side of the Smokies. The 11-mile **Cades Cove Loop** leads through the former settlement and a collection of homes and structures. Take a moderate hike to **Abrams Falls,** a 20-foot waterfall or follow the **Rich Mountain Loop** (it's a big day hike). A scenic drive north along **Rich**

elk grazing in a field in Cataloochee

Family Fun

Great Smoky Mountains National Park is an ideal place to show kids the wonders of the great outdoors and the importance of our national parks. In addition to the Junior Ranger Program and ranger-led activities, there are several places that are perfect for kids.

- **Mountain Farm Museum:** This life-size model of a working mountain farm gives kids a feel for life here years ago.

- **Synchronous Fireflies:** These rare fireflies blink in unison, and make an appearance near the Elkmont Campground just a couple of weeks a year.

- **Elk Watching:** Visit Cataloochee to see the elk herd there or stick around the Oconaluftee Visitor Center while they make a dusk appearance.

- **Morning Bike Ride:** Head to Cades Cove bright and early (Wed.-Sat. May-Sept.) when the road is closed to cars, but open to bicycles and foot traffic. Rent a bike and spend the morning pedaling around in relative solitude.

- **Big Creek Trail:** This gentle hike includes wildflowers galore, a stream to wade in, and a 35-foot waterfall cascade.

cycling Cades Cove Loop

- **Go Fish:** Try your hand at fly-fishing. Cherokee, North Carolina, has weekly fishing contests for kids and adults. Fontana Lake is full of fish in the deep water and feeder streams. Along Little River, you'll find plenty of places to wet a line.

Mountain Road winds over the mountains to Townsend, where you can easily circle your way back to Cades Cove. Pitch a tent in **Cades Cove Campground** (reserve in advance) for the night. Be sure to take a walk and admire the stars.

Day 6
FONTANA LAKE AND DEEP CREEK
The next day, follow **Parsons Branch Road** south out of Cades Cove to its junction with Highway 129. You'll skirt the southern edge of the park heading east, crossing the border into **North Carolina** at **Deals Gap.**

After Deals Gap, follow Highway 28 east along Cheoah Lake and past **Twentymile**

to Fontana Village. To stretch your legs, turn north toward **Fontana Dam,** at the western end of Fontana Lake, and the trailhead for **Shuckstack Mountain,** a strenuous hike along the **Appalachian Trail.**

Or stay on Highway 28 east all the way to **Bryson City.** Stop for lunch at the **Cork & Bean Bistro** before turning north for your overnight at the **Deep Creek Campground.** For a short hike, follow the trail to **Juney Whank Falls,** or head to **The Road to Nowhere,** an abandoned highway project that terminates with a tunnel through the mountain and hike alongside Fontana Lake.

After a long day, relax at the campground in Deep Creek, which offers a relaxing treat:

The park can attract a crowd, especially at certain times of the year or along popular trails. Avoid the throngs by planning a wintertime hike, or explore the seldom-seen regions of the park.

- **Balsam Mountain Road:** The road's location off the Blue Ridge Parkway means people tend to forget this beautiful corner of the park. Head here in the fall to immerse yourself in foliage and be safe from the typical leaf-peeping traffic.

- **Mount Cammerer:** This strenuous hike is avoided by many, but rewards with an unparalleled view. The few folks on this trail are here to be surrounded by the Smokies—and to dodge the crowds.

- **Lakeshore Trail:** Start this trail from Fontana Dam to avoid trail traffic. You'll see the dam and have a tough uphill right off the start, but the western end of the trail is a beautiful one.

- **Big Creek:** An almost-forgotten campground and some awesome hikes in a corner of the park most casual visitors forget? That's Big Creek. Camp here, backpack to Mount Sterling, or check out the suited-for-everyone Big Creek Trail.

- **Abrams Creek:** This seasonal campground is

Abrams Creek trail

rarely full; even if it is, several great hikes originate here. Hit the Rabbit and Abrams Creeks Loop or hike the easy (and wildflower-rich) Little Bottoms Trail.

tubing. Wash away the sweat and trail dust with a float trip and some splashing in the creek.

Day 7
CHEROKEE, NC

For your final day, head to Cherokee, the ancestral heart of the Cherokee Indians and home of the Eastern Band of Cherokee Indians. The drive from Deep Creek is a short one, so you'll have a full day to explore. Start by visiting the **Museum of the Cherokee Indian** where you'll learn the Cherokee creation story, hear songs and legends, and discover the heartache of the Trail of Tears. Across the street at the **Qualla Arts and Crafts Mutual** browse the traditional arts and crafts made by Cherokee artisans and craftspeople, then head up the hill to the **Oconaluftee Indian Village** to see how the tribe lived in the 1700 and 1800s.

Grab a belly-busting country buffet lunch at **Granny's Kitchen** then drive to **Soco Falls** for a short hike to stunning twin waterfalls. In the evening, head to **Harrah's Cherokee Casino** where you can entertain yourself by dropping $20 on table games or slots before dining at one of the on-site restaurants. The casino has overnight accommodations or you can spend a quiet night at **Panther Creek Cabins.**

In the morning, it's a 1.5-hour drive to the airport in Asheville and the flight home.

Best Hikes

This is a beautiful country to tour by car, but you're not doing the landscape justice if you only experience it through your windshield. Here are some fantastic chances to get out and be surrounded by nature.

Andrews Bald

At **Clingmans Dome,** a few miles off Newfound Gap Road, this **3.5-mile round-trip** trail is one of the loveliest and most rewarding hikes you'll find.

Grotto Falls Trail

This popular hike to a picture-perfect waterfall off the **Roaring Fork Motor Nature Trail** is only **2.6 mile round-trip.**

Hen Wallow Falls Trail

In **Cosby,** a few miles northeast of Gatlinburg, you'll find this **4.4-mile round-trip** hike to a delicate waterfall some 90-feet high.

Mount Cammerer Trail

It's a tough **11.2-mile round-trip** hike to the summit, but you're rewarded with some of the best views in the park, courtesy of a **stone fire tower** built in the 1930s.

Little River Trail

Keep this trail short and sweet as you follow an old logging road alongside Little River and through the home of the **synchronous fireflies,** or follow all **12.3 miles** for an out-and-back day hike.

Lynn Camp Prong

At first glance, this **21-mile round-trip** lollipop loop looks like a huge hike, but you can take as much time as you want on this trail—or even turn it into an overnighter. Whatever you do, hike to the lovely **Indian Flats Falls** before turning back.

Abrams Falls Trail

A hike suited to just about anyone? That leads to a great waterfall? This **5-mile round-trip** hike is the one—and it's in **Cades Cove,** so you know you'll drive right by the trailhead.

Rich Mountain Loop

This **8.5-mile round-trip** loop in **Cades Cove** is one of the most fabulous hikes in the park.

Great Smoky Mountains National Park

G reat Smoky Mountain National Park wears a well-earned title: Great.

In its lifetime the park has seen more than 510 million visitors, with 10.7 million visiting in 2015 alone. Why do they come? The mountains, the sky, the wildlife, the waters, the peaks, the stories—all of it. The Smokies are laced with trails; rivers, streams, and waterfalls trace their courses through the wrinkled mountains; and wildlife from rare salamanders to huge elk to black bear call this place home.

Straddling the North Carolina/Tennessee state line, Great Smoky Mountains National Park's 522,427 acres are nearly equally split between the two states. On the slightly larger North Carolina side of the park, the mountains pile up against one another, making for tall peaks, steep slopes, and deep coves. It's wild here and more sparsely populated than on the Tennessee side, but throughout the park you'll find places so remote and so isolated they've remained undisturbed by humans for impossible stretches of time, or at least they feel that way. As wild and secret as these mountains are, you'll also find places like Cades Cove where the first pioneers to crest the mountain range

and push into Tennessee found a wide, fertile valley—the perfect place to settle. Today the remote places are still remote, requiring sometimes considerable effort to reach, but Cades Cove is a sightseer's delight with its preserved historic churches, schools, and homesteads, and in the fall, droves of visitors come for one of the most impressive color shows in the eastern United States.

The park comprises more than 800 square miles of cloud-ringed peaks and rainforest. The park was designated an International Biosphere Reserve in 1976 and a World Heritage Site in 1983, and researchers, like the nonprofit organization Discover Life in America (www.dlia.org), come here to study the flora and fauna. Tens of thousands of species of plants and animals reside here, with 80 species of reptiles and amphibians alone, which is why the park is sometimes called the Salamander Capital of the World. More than 200 species of birds nest here, and 60-plus mammals—from mice to mountain lions (though the mountain lions are unofficial denizens, you can hear tales of a sighting now and again)—roam these hills. Discover Life

Previous: on the trail from Andrews Bald; on the summit of Mount LeConte. **Above:** fall colors on the Chimney Tops trail.

Look for ★ to find recommended
sights, activities, dining, and lodging.

Highlights

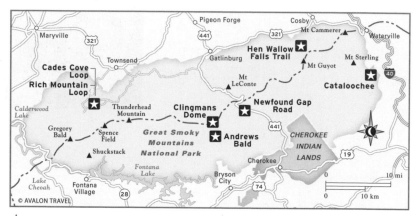

★ **Newfound Gap Road:** Bisecting the park, this 33-mile route offers plenty of long views, short hikes, and streamside driving (page 33).

★ **Clingmans Dome:** From this third-highest peak in the eastern United States, you'll have an astounding view of up to 100 miles on a clear day (page 36).

★ **Andrews Bald:** Hike to one of the prettiest high-altitude meadows in the Smokies (page 39).

★ **Hen Wallow Falls Trail:** An easy out-and-back day hike leads to one of the loveliest waterfalls in the park (page 52).

★ **Cataloochee:** Camping in this secluded valley—with its Milky Way views, solitude, and frequent elk sightings—is bliss (page 58).

★ **Cades Cove Loop:** The most-visited spot in the park offers plenty of wildlife viewing and its largest collection of intact historic structures (page 68).

★ **Rich Mountain Loop:** Hike up, up, up into the hills for a gorgeous view of Cades Cove (page 72).

in America's All-Taxa Biodiversity Inventory (a census of all nonmicrobial life forms) of Great Smoky Mountains National Park has turned up 970 species of plants and animals previously unknown to science.

The deep wilderness here makes an awesome refuge for outdoor enthusiasts, and the accessibility of the park's absolutely ravishing scenery makes it ideal for visitors of all ability levels and nearly all interests.

PLANNING YOUR TIME

Many visitors devote a single day to the park, driving Newfound Gap Road, taking a short hike along the way, and circling Cades Cove before moving on. To give the park a fair shake, devote at least **three days** to exploring. Spend a day in the north end of the park in Cataloochee Valley, then devote another day to savoring the sights of Newfound Gap Road including a stop by Clingmans Dome and time to drive Cades Cove, on the third day pick a waterfall to visit or trail to hike—on the Roaring Fork Motor Nature Trail you'll find both.

Within the park, **lodging** is limited to camping—unless you want to pack your sleeping bag and hike to the rustic LeConte Lodge just below the summit of Mount LeConte—so your best bet for hotels, motels, inns, cabins, and B&Bs are the Tennessee towns of **Gatlinburg, Pigeon Forge, Townsend,** and **Knoxville;** or the North Carolina towns of **Cherokee, Bryson City, Maggie Valley, Sylva, Dillsboro,** or **Asheville.**

When to Go

Seasonal considerations have a big influence on park visitation. Crowds arrive for the blooming of **spring** wildflowers and each **autumn** the park is crawling with visitors for a good long look at the mountains blazing with red, yellow, and burgundy leaves. **Summer** brings visitors for hiking and that cool mountain air, while **winter** finds the park more empty than full, but no less beautiful.

Weather can vary wildly across the park in any season, due in part to the elevation, which ranges from 900 feet at the lowest point to more than 6,600 feet at the highest. Clingmans Dome, the highest point in the park, has an average high temperature of only 65°F in July; the only time you're guaranteed *not* to see snow flurries are June-August. In contrast, you will find temperatures in the upper 60s on Clingmans Dome the same day, and it can be in the low 90s with some contentious humidity in Cades Cove.

If ever there was a place for wearing layers, this is it. Be sure to pack long sleeves or a light jacket and your rain gear, regardless of the season. Keep these extremes in mind in terms of safety as well: a snowstorm can bring two feet of snow to the highest elevations and leave ice on the curvy mountain roads while temperatures at the foot of the mountains are considerably warmer and snow-free. Thick fog and isolated storms are also a possibility year-round.

SPRING

Spring wildflowers begin to appear in late **March** and peak in mid- to late **April.** This time of year rain is common and there's a chance of a spring snowstorm (especially at higher elevations, but even at the base of the mountains) or a strong spring thunderstorm. It's a muddy time to hit the trail and you'll want to pack layers and foul-weather gear if you plan on heading into the woods. Temperatures begin to climb in spring, working toward summer's warmth, but doing so in fits and starts, another reason to keep a sweater or jacket handy when visiting in the spring.

The wildflower show bleeds over into early summer as azaleas, mountain laurels, and rhododendrons put on their best show just after the season transitions to summer, but due to the park's extensive microclimates, it's possible to see flame azaleas blooming early, peaking **April-July.** Mountain laurel comes next, blooming **May-June,** and rhododendron comes last with a burst of color

Great Smoky Mountains National Park

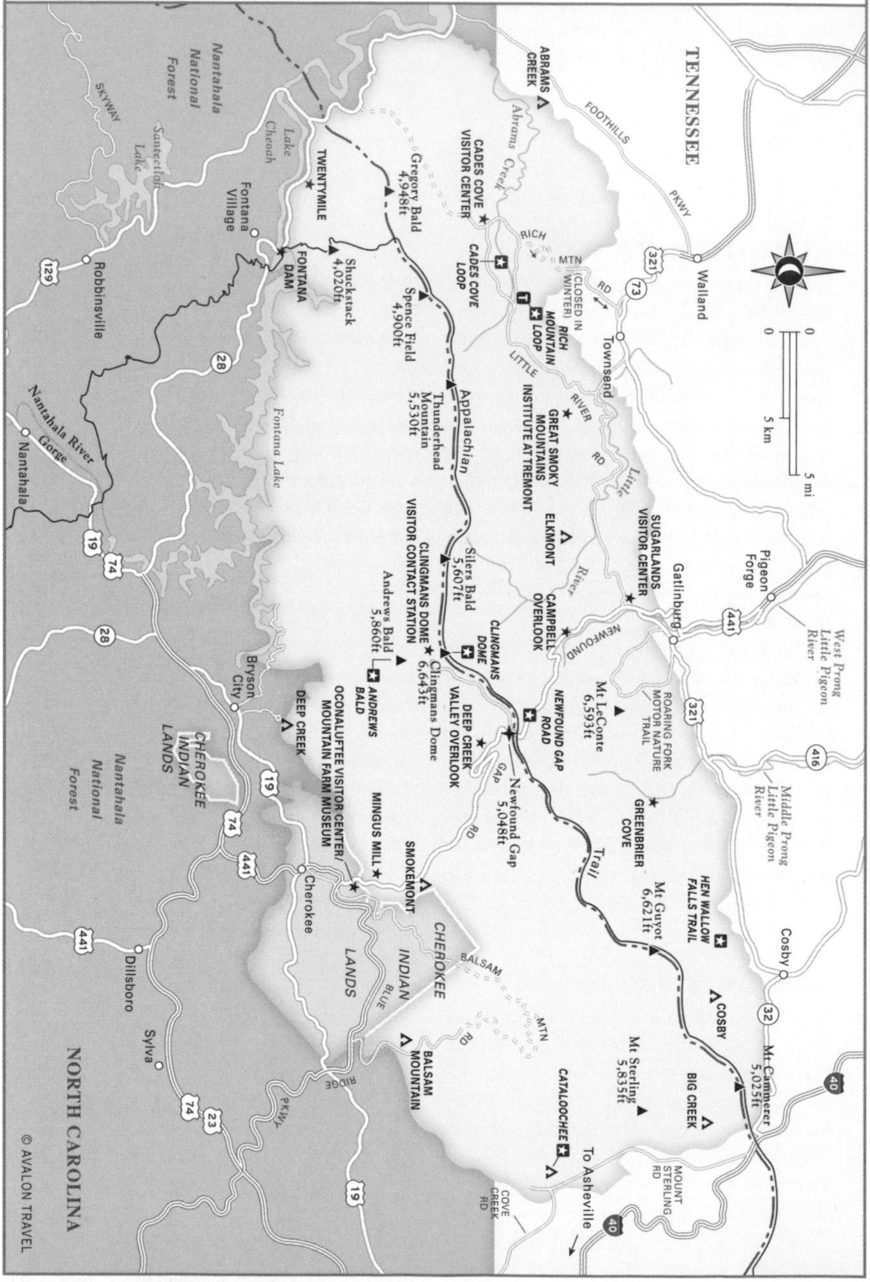

in **June** and **July.** You'll find the wildflowers bloom from the bottom of the mountain to the top, with patches of color and reports of blooms occurring first at lower elevations and ending at the high balds and ridgelines.

SUMMER AND FALL

Summer and fall constitute the park's high season; the busiest times to visit are **mid-June to mid-August** and throughout **October.** In summer, the most popular hiking trails don't quite resemble a queue, but you're guaranteed to encounter many groups of hikers of all ages and ability levels coming and going. In fall, these same trails are busy with picture-takers; if fall color is on your agenda, consider spending more time on the gravel roads and long hikes and in seldom-seen corners of the park's extreme north and south ends.

Fall color is on everyone's mind when they visit in October. The mountaintops are the first to show signs of the season's best and brightest show as they begin to turn in early October. Colors bleed down the mountain, descending until early November, when the trees from the foot to the crest of the mountains are aflame with color. Note that the color's arrival and departure isn't set, summer heat can alter the schedule for wildflower blooms and fall color, and rainfall can do the same. It's best to call the park or check regional websites to see how fall color is progressing. It's a safe bet to visit in **mid-October** for a solid color show.

Temperatures throughout summer and fall can get as high as the low 90s (F) at the lowest elevations, though high temperatures and humidity are relatively rare. There is an extreme of temperature to consider, though. Spots like Clingmans Dome can be chilly even in the summer, with as much as a 30°F difference from peak to valley floor. Those temperature extremes also give rise to the park's namesake "smoky" effect as layers of fog can fill valleys or wrap the peaks. If you visit Clingmans Dome and find it enshrouded in fog, try again in an hour or two, or even the next day, and the weather will likely reward you.

WINTER

Winter can be a fantastic time to visit the park, especially if you're there for a bit of snow. The crowds are nearly nonexistent and maintained roads like Cades Cove Loop and Newfound Gap are starkly beautiful. Along the mountain ridges, trails, and streams, as well as among the historic structures, you'll find lovely, lonely sights.

Temperatures can hit highs of 50°F, but more often than not it's cold with nighttime temperatures at or below freezing (32°F, and colder at high elevations) and daytime temperatures in the 40s. Snow is possible, with most significant snow occurring in **January** and **February.**

Several roads in the park are closed in the winter, though closing dates vary. Among these are Balsam Mountain, Clingmans Dome, Little Greenbrier, Rich Mountain, and Heintooga-Roundbottom Roads, and the Roaring Fork Motor Nature Trail. The **Blue Ridge Parkway,** which starts (or ends) in Cherokee, North Carolina, also closes in the winter. **Newfound Gap Road** remains open in all but the most serious of weather; however, road crews work to maintain it in the winter. Before you set out, check current road conditions (865/436-1200, ext. 630).

Exploring the Park

Great Smoky Mountains National Park (GSMNP, 865/436-1200, www.nps.gov/grsm) was the first—and the largest—of three National Park Service units established in the southern Appalachians. The park was founded in 1934, followed in 1935 by the Blue Ridge Parkway and in 1936 by Shenandoah National Park. These sister facilities include some 600 miles of contiguous roads and close to 800,000 acres of land, all of it acquired from private landholders, and all of it standing testament to the wild, rugged beauty of the Appalachian Mountains and the people who helped to tame these places.

Great Smoky Mountains National Park is the most-visited national park, with visitor numbers approaching 11 million each year. In the 522,427-acre park, there are 850 miles of hiking trails, including 71 miles of the Appalachian Trail; 16 mountains over 6,000 feet; 2,100 miles of mountain streams and rivers; and an astoundingly diverse set of flora and fauna.

More than 17,000 species have been documented here, including more than 100 species of native trees, 1,500 flowering plant species, 200 species of birds, 66 types of mammals, 67 native species of fish, 39 varieties of reptiles, and 43 species of amphibians. And that's not even counting the mushrooms, mollusks, and millipedes. Researchers believe an additional 30,000-80,000 species may exist. No other area of a similar size in a similar climate can boast a higher number of species. A multitude of factors are believed to have contributed to this astounding number, including the wide elevation range (875-6,643 feet), which provides a large variance in temperature, as well as the fantastic growing conditions created by summer's high humidity and abundant rainfall (apart from the Pacific Northwest, these are the rainiest mountains in the country). Plus, as some of the oldest mountains in the world—it is believed they were formed some

200-300 million years ago—the Smokies have seen a number of dramatic climactic changes. During the last ice age (10,000 years ago), the glacial intrusion into the United States didn't reach the Smokies, making them a refuge for species of plants and animals displaced from homes farther north.

VISITORS CENTERS

Begin your exploration of Great Smoky Mountains National Park with a stop at one of the park's four visitors centers. You'll find rangers who know the trail and road conditions as well as what's blooming where. You can also grab detailed maps and trail guides.

Sugarlands Visitor Center

The busiest information center in the park is also the first stop for visitors entering the park from Tennessee. **Sugarlands Visitor Center and Park Headquarters** (1420 Old TN-73 Scenic, Gatlinburg, TN, 865/436-1200, www.nps.gov/grsm, 8am-4:30pm daily Dec.-Feb., except Christmas Day, 8am-5pm daily Mar. and Nov., 8am-6pm daily Apr.-May, 8am-7:30pm daily June-Aug., 8am-6:30pm daily Sept.-Oct.) is located just inside the park, only 2 miles from Gatlinburg. Here you'll find the usual visitors center information as well as a 20-minute film introducing you to the park.

The **Backcountry Information Office** (865/436-1297, https://smokiespermits.nps.gov, 8am-5pm daily) is located at the Sugarlands Visitor Center. This is the place to get backcountry permits, as well as thru-hiker permits for the Appalachian Trail. Facilities include restrooms, snack machines, and a **Great Smoky Mountains Association** (www.smokiesinformation.org) bookstore and shop.

Oconaluftee Visitor Center

If you're entering Great Smoky Mountains National Park from the North Carolina

Blooms and Foliage

You'll find the most abundant display of spring wildflower blooms in mid- to late April. Keep in mind that the dates for wildflower blooms and fall color displays are only guidelines. A number of factors contribute to peak timing of blooms and changing leaves. Check with park officials for the best times and places to experience the finest each season has to offer. At the highest elevations, leaves begin to change during the first two weeks of October, creeping down the mountains and ending in late October or early November.

- **Catawba rhododendron:** Grows at elevations above 3,500 feet; blooms in June.

- **Flame azalea:** This wild shrub blooms at lower elevations in April and May, at higher elevations through June and early July.

- **Mountain laurel:** Blooms from early May through June.

- **Rosebay rhododendron:** Blooms in lower elevations in June and July.

side, **Oconaluftee Visitor Center** (1194 Newfound Gap Rd., Cherokee, NC, 828/497-1904, www.nps.gov/grsm, 8am-4:30pm daily Dec.-Feb., except Christmas Day, 8am-5pm daily Mar. and Nov., 8am-6pm daily Apr.-May, 8am-7:30pm daily June-Aug., 8am-6:30pm daily Sept.-Oct., closed Dec.-Mar.), just 2 miles north of Cherokee on US-441/ Newfound Gap Road, is the best place to begin your tour.

You'll find public restrooms, snack machines, and a bookstore and shop operated by the Great Smoky Mountains Association (www.smokiesinformation.org). Adjacent is the **Mountain Farm Museum,** a collection of log structures including a farmhouse, barn, smokehouse, and other homestead structures; demonstrations of early farm life are held here regularly.

Clingmans Dome Visitor Contact Station

Along Newfound Gap Road is the turnoff to Clingmans Dome and the **Clingmans Dome Visitor Contact Station** (Clingmans Dome Rd., off Newfound Gap Rd., 25 miles from Cherokee, NC, and 23 miles from Gatlinburg, TN, 865/436-1200, www.nps.gov/grsm, 10am-6pm daily Apr.-June and Aug.-Oct., 10am-6:30pm daily July, 9:30am-5pm daily Nov.). Clingmans Dome is the highest peak in Great

Smoky Mountains National Park and features a fantastic viewing platform. At the visitor contact station, you'll find information on the park, a bookstore operated by the Great Smoky Mountains Association (www.smokiesinformation.org), and restrooms.

Cades Cove Visitor Center

In Cades Cove, about halfway around the ever-popular Loop Road, is the **Cades Cove Visitor Center** (Cades Cove Loop Rd., 865/436-1200, www.nps.gov/grsm, 9am-4:30pm daily Dec.-Jan., except Christmas Day, 9am-5:30pm daily Feb. and Nov., 9am-6:30pm daily Mar. and Sept.-Oct., 9am-7pm daily Apr. and Aug., 9am-7:30pm daily May-July). Indoor and outdoor exhibits illustrate Southern mountain life and culture, and there are a number of historic structures to photograph and explore. You'll also find a Great Smoky Mountains Association bookstore (www.smokiesinformation.org) and shop, as well as restrooms at the Cades Cove Visitor Center.

Backcountry Information Office

The knowledgeable folks at the **Backcountry Information Office** (1420 Old TN-73 Scenic, Gatlinburg, TN, 865/436-1297, https://smokiespermits.nps.gov, 8am-5pm daily) are

By the Numbers

Great Smoky Mountains National Park puts up some impressive numbers, from the staggering number of visitors—10,712,674 in 2015—to the incredible biodiversity—970 plant and animal species new to science have been discovered within the park. Its other numbers are just as impressive.

- Size: 522,427 acres

- Elevation: From 875 feet at the mouth of Abrams Creek to the towering summit of Clingmans Dome at 6,643 feet

- 16 peaks stand at more than 6,000 feet elevation.

- 850 miles of hiking trails, including 70 miles of the Appalachian Trail

- More than 400,000 hikers lace up and hit the trails annually.

- There's only 384 miles of roadway in the park; 146 miles are unpaved.

- 730 miles of fish-bearing streams

- And all this with only 240 permanent employees

a good first resource when planning a hiking or backcountry camping trip. There are more than a dozen shelters and approximately 100 backcountry campsites sprinkled throughout the park at convenient intervals. Those on multiday hikes or interested in backcountry camping can **reserve tent sites** and shelter space (www.smokiespermits.nps.gov, permits $4 per person per night) up to 30 days in advance of their trip. Hikers, campers, anglers, and equestrians are asked to follow Leave No Trace practices.

Field Schools

Two Tennessee-based organizations affiliated with Great Smoky Mountains National Park offer ways to get to know the park even better. The **Smoky Mountain Field School** (865/974-0150, www.outreach.utk. edu/smoky) teaches workshops and leads excursions to educate participants in a wide array of fields related to the Smokies. One-day classes focus on the history and cultural heritage of the park, the lives of some of the park's most interesting animals, folk medicine and cooking of the southern Appalachians, and much more. Instructors also lead one-day

and overnight hikes into the heart of the park. This is a great way to discover the park far beyond what you would be able to do on your own, so check their schedule and sign up for a class that interests you.

The **Great Smoky Mountains Institute at Tremont** (9275 Tremont Rd., Townsend, TN, 865/448-6709, www.gsmit.org) teaches students of all ages about the ecology of the region, wilderness rescue and survival skills, and even nature photography. Many of the classes and guided trips are part of Road Scholars, kids' camps, or teacher-training institutes; however, there are also rich opportunities for unaffiliated learners.

PARK ENTRANCES

Great Smoky Mountains National Park is unusual among the National Park System in that it has **no entrance fee,** so if you see a Friends of the Smokies donation box and you're so inclined (or so moved by what you see around you), toss a few bucks their way.

Main Entrances

There are three main entrances to Great Smoky Mountains National Park that access

The 2016 Wildfire

On November 23, 2016, a wildfire was reported on Chimney Tops off Newfound Gap Road. Due to drought conditions and high winds, it spread quickly and affected lands inside and outside Great Smoky Mountains National Park. Inside the park, nearly 18,000 acres burned, causing the temporary closure of dozens of trails, roads, campsites, and facilities. Fortunately the park suffered little permanent damage aside from the burned acreage. Outside the park, the towns of Gatlinburg and Pigeon Forge in Tennessee suffered devastating losses. All told, more than 2,400 homes, businesses, and other structures were destroyed; 175 people were injured; and 14 people lost their lives. Damages exceed $500 million and rebuilding efforts are ongoing.

All temporary trail and campsite closures are expected to be open and operational for the 2017 season, though you should be aware that many trails—Chimney Tops, Road Prong, Sugarland Mountain, Rough Creek, Twin Creeks, Baskins Creek, Bull Head, Rainbow Falls, Trillium Gap, and others in the vicinity of Chimney Tops and Roaring Fork Motor Nature Trail—will show signs of extreme fire damage and trail crews as well as Park staff and foresters may be closing trails for repairs and reclamation work during 2017. Speak with rangers at the Visitors Centers or visit www.nps.gov/grsm for updated trail closure information.

Campers in frontcountry and backcountry sites should be aware of the seriousness and potential dangers of campfires. A stray spark could have started this fire and an improperly-extinguished fire could have done the same, and even the most seasoned camper could make a mistake with tremendous consequences. Be mindful of the fire regulations when camping in the park and be attentive to your campfire if you have one.

the busiest parts of the park. Each entrance is easily approached from a nearby gateway town:

- From **Cherokee, North Carolina,** drive two miles north along US-441 into the park.
- From **Gatlinburg, Tennessee,** follow US-441 south two miles into the park.
- From **Townsend, Tennessee,** take TN-73 three miles east into the park.

Remote Entrances

There are 17 additional points at which you can enter the park via automobile. The majority of these are gravel roads in varying states of maintenance that require different degrees of driving confidence and skill. If you're up for an adventure, these roads can lead you into some beautiful corners of the park that few others experience.

Note that though these secondary entrances enter the national park, they don't provide access to the extensive trail systems

and historic and recreational opportunities provided by the main entrances.

ROARING FORK MOTOR NATURE TRAIL

From **Gatlinburg, Tennessee,** turn off the main parkway in Gatlinburg at traffic light #8 and follow Historic Nature Trail Road to Cherokee Orchard and the entrance to the national park (about 1 mile from Gatlinburg). Soon after you pass the Rainbow Falls Trailhead, you can enter **Roaring Fork Motor Nature Trail** (open Mar.-Nov.) or turn back to Gatlinburg. All told, it's a drive of 3.7 miles.

Roaring Fork Motor Nature Trail is located in the western-central part of the park, to the east of Newfound Gap Road. From here, you can access several trails to waterfalls as well as trails leading to **Mount LeConte;** you'll also find several historic structures and homesteads along this one-way road that give visitors a taste of the wild, rugged nature of these mountains.

RICH MOUNTAIN ROAD

From **Townsend, Tennessee,** follow TN-73/West Lamar Alexander Parkway to Old Tuckaleechee Road, then turn left on Dry Valley Road/Old Cades Cove Road and follow it to where the pavement gives way to a gravel road. Soon after, it changes to a gravel road; you'll find a small parking area and signs indicating a one-way road. This is Rich Mountain Road coming in from **Cades Cove.**

This entrance is only 7 miles from Townsend, 0.5-mile from the nearest house, and just inside the national park boundary, but it will feel much more isolated because the forest is thick and wild here. From the parking area, you can access both **Ace Gap Trail** and **Rich Mountain Trail.**

HAPPY VALLEY ROAD

From **Walland, Tennessee,** follow TN-73/East Lamar Alexander Parkway to Foothills Parkway; take the Foothills Parkway south, then turn left onto Butterfly Gap Road, right on Flats Road, then follow Happy Valley Road to the unpaved **Abrams Creek Road,** a trip of 17.1 miles.

This entrance takes you into the southwestern portion of the park, just over the mountain from Cades Cove into the headwaters of Abrams Creek. The **Abrams Creek Campground** (late-May-mid-Oct., $14) has 16 first-come, first-served campsites and can accommodate RVs up to 12 feet.

DEEP CREEK ROAD

From **Cherokee, North Carolina,** follow US-19 south to Bryson City, then turn right on West Deep Creek Road until you enter the park and reach the Deep Creek Campground. At **Deep Creek Campground** (877/444-6777, www.recreation.gov, Apr.-Oct., $17) there are 92 campsites that fill up fast, so make reservations early if you want to explore the trails and waterfalls of the southeastern edge of the park. This 12-mile drive is easy on main roads.

LAKEVIEW DRIVE

From **Cherokee, North Carolina,** follow US-19 south to Bryson City; the road changes its name to Old River Road then Deep Creek Road. Turn left on Ramseur Street and then right on Depot Street, finally turn onto Everett Street (which changes to Fontana Road). Follow **Fontana Road** to the end, where there is a parking area a short walk from a tunnel through the mountain.

This 18.5-mile drive is known to locals at the **Road to Nowhere** (or, more properly, Fontana Road) for its strange intrusion into the national park. The road earned this name when the national park scrapped plans to build Lakeview Drive, a 26-mile parkway along the shores of Fontana Lake. The project built this first part of the road and completed a tunnel through the mountain before stopping. Today hikers, mountain bikers, and anglers use this point to access the streams and trails along the shores of **Fontana Lake.**

HEINTOOGA RIDGE ROAD

From the **Blue Ridge Parkway,** turn onto paved Heintooga Ridge Road (open May-Nov.) at Milepost 458.2. You'll be in the Blue Ridge Parkway for the first 4 miles, but will abruptly enter Great Smoky Mountains National Park at **Black Camp Gap.** The road continues 5 miles, passing **Balsam Mountain Campground.** It terminates at the **Heintooga Overlook.**

Look for the one-lane gravel road at Heintooga Overlook and you've found **Heintooga Round Bottom Road** (May-Nov.). This gravel track takes you on an hour-long, 14-mile trip along **Balsam Mountain** and down into Straight Fork Valley on the lands of the Eastern Band of the Cherokee Indian (the Qualla Boundary). Keep an eye out for wildlife along this seldom-traveled road, or stop for a short hike along the trails that branch off the road. This road is closed to vehicles longer than 25 feet or passenger vehicles towing trailers.

COVE CREEK ROAD

From **Asheville, North Carolina,** follow I-40 West to exit 20, then follow Highway 276 to Cove Creek Road into the Cataloochee Valley, a trip of 42 miles.

From **Knoxville, Tennessee,** follow I-40 East to exit 20, then take Highway 284 to Cove Creek Road into the Cataloochee Valley, a trip of 80 miles.

Cove Creek Road skirts the edge of the **Cherokee National Forest** before plunging into the park. The road is narrow, but paved for half of the drive; it changes to a well-maintained gravel track that while still narrow is open to two-way traffic. The road enters **Cataloochee Valley** in the extreme northern end of the national park where there is camping, plenty of hiking, wildlife viewing (including herds of elk), and historic buildings.

MOUNT STERLING ROAD

From **Cataloochee Valley, North Carolina,** take the gravel Mount Sterling Road north and west out of the valley to I-40, a drive of 16.4 miles. The road is narrow but well maintained, and it winds its way out of the **Cataloochee Valley** up toward **Mount Sterling,** then back down to cross the Tennessee state line where you access I-40.

COSBY PARK ROAD

From **Gatlinburg, Tennessee,** take US-321/TN-73/East Parkway northeast to Cosby, then turn right on TN-32 and right again onto Cosby Park Road to the **Cosby Campground** (471 Cosby Campground Road A, Cosby, TN, 423/487-2683, www.recreation.gov, Apr.-Oct., $14), a trip of 21 miles. Cosby Park Road provides access to the campground in the northwestern quadrant of the park, but also to the hiking trails and waterfalls nearby.

GREENBRIER ROAD

From **Gatlinburg, Tennessee,** take US-321/TN-73/East Parkway northeast 5.4 miles, then turn right into the park. This narrow but paved two-lane road leads to the **Ramsey Cascades** trailhead, some excellent wildflower viewing, and trout fishing. The paved road eventually gives way to a maintained gravel road, which leads to additional trailheads.

DRIVING TOURS
★ Newfound Gap Road
33 MILES

While many visitors use this 33-mile road that bisects Great Smoky Mountains National Park as a mere thruway, it's actually one of the prettiest drives you'll find anywhere. This curvy road alternates between exposed and tree-enclosed, and a number of **scenic overlooks** provide spectacular views of the Smokies. Stop at one that has a **trail** (more than half of them do) and take a short walk into the woods, or eat a picnic lunch at one of the mountainside overlooks. Whatever you do on this road between **Cherokee** and **Gatlinburg,** take your time and enjoy the ride.

Cades Cove Loop
11 MILES

This 11-mile loop around a broad and picturesque valley ringed by high peaks is about as pretty as it gets. The fields, forests, those high peaks, wildlife, and historic structures are just some of the highlights the **Cades Cove Loop** (closed to vehicles until 10am Wed.-Sat. May-Sept.). One of the most popular spots in the park in any season, expect crowds, especially in the fall. To avoid the crowds, show up early. Hikes include gentle strolls to homesteads, cabins, and churches, or longer hikes to **Abrams Falls.** The road is paved, and very well maintained, and though it's **one-way** there are two points where you can cut across the valley to shorten the drive (or circle back for one more look, whichever strikes your fancy).

Rich Mountain Road
8 MILES

Rich Mountain Road (open Apr.-Nov.) is a photographer's dream. Running north from Cades Cove over Rich Mountain to

Tuckaleechee Cove and **Townsend,** this **one-way gravel road** provides a few stunning views of Cades Cove and Tuckaleechee Cove. You're likely to see bear, deer, turkey, and other wildlife along the way. The road is typically in good condition and isn't too challenging as far as backroads go, but I'd avoid tackling this drive in a low-clearance vehicle or your economy rental car; instead, go with a truck or SUV (no four-wheel drive necessary). Know that the road gets a little steep once it passes outside park boundaries, but it's nothing too hair raising.

If you're stuck with a rental or you aren't confident in your off-road driving abilities, you can always enjoy similar views on the 8.5-mile Rich Mountain Loop hike, a great way to see Cades Cove without the high-season gridlock.

Heintooga Roundbottom Road/Balsam Mountain Road
14 MILES

This 14-mile one-way gravel road goes by two names—**Heintooga Roundnottom Road** and **Balsam Mountain Road** (open May-Nov.)—but they're one in the same. Accessed from Blue Ridge Parkway Milepost 458.2 (just a few miles from the Cherokee, NC,

entrance), this is an often-overlooked road through a high and wild part of Great Smoky Mountains National Park. In the spring and summer you'll find wildflowers blooming, and in the fall you'll find the road awash in color. The drive takes a little more than an hour from the **Blue Ridge Parkway** back down into **Cherokee;** as off-roading experiences go, it's an easy one. The road is well-maintained and generally in good condition, but don't try it in your low-clearance rental or the family minivan. You'll be fine in a truck, or even a small SUV.

Roaring Fork Motor Nature Trail
5.5 MILES

The 5.5-mile **Roaring Fork Motor Nature Trail** (open Mar.-Nov.), just a few miles from the heart of Gatlinburg, has everything Smoky Mountain visitors are looking for: rushing creeks, waterfalls, hikes, historic structures, and plenty of photo opportunities. This **one-way road** stays busy, but is seldom bumper-to-bumper, though some of the parking areas may make you feel differently. If you're looking for an **easy drive** with some **short walks** to homesteads and waterfalls (which make them perfect for those with mobility difficulty),

Newfound Gap Road draws motorcyclists to its curves and vistas.

this is the one you need. Head there just after a rainfall to see an impressive roadside waterfall called **Place of a Thousand Drips.**

Foothills Parkway
17 MILES
It's not technically in the park, but the **Foothills Parkway** is a great scenic drive that gives you high-elevation views without the same traffic on more popular routes in the park proper. The Foothills Parkway is reached via US-321, 5.5 miles from **Townsend.** The 17-mile road has plenty of places to pull off to picnic or take in the view. There's one short hike here at **Look Rock,** a 0.5-mile stroll to an observation tower.

Newfound Gap Road

Easily the most heavily traveled route in the Smokies, Newfound Gap Road (US-441) connects Cherokee with Gatlinburg and sees thousands of visitors a day. Newfound Gap Road is the perfect introduction to Great Smoky Mountains National Park: Contour-hugging curves, overlooks with million-dollar views, easy hikes right off the roadway, and a 3,000-foot elevation change give you a great overview of these mountains and this spectacular park. During peak times in the summer and fall, it's not uncommon to encounter a traffic jam or two along this 33-mile scenic route, especially when bears are taking their time crossing the road.

Newfound Gap Road earned its name in 1872 when Swiss geographer Arnold Henry Guyot determined that a newly found gap was the lowest pass through the Great Smoky Mountains. Lower in elevation and easier to access than the former passage at Indian Gap, 1.5 miles away, the name Newfound Gap was soon used to refer to the entire route.

SIGHTS
Oconaluftee Visitor Center
As you begin your trip along Newfound Gap Road from the North Carolina side, your first stop will probably be the "Welcome to Great Smoky Mountains National Park" sign, but the **Oconaluftee Visitor Center** (1194 Newfound Gap Rd., Cherokee, NC, 828/497-1904, www.nps.gov/grsm, 8am-4:30pm daily Dec.-Feb., except Christmas Day, 8am-5pm daily Mar. and Nov., 9am-6pm daily Apr.-May,

8am-7:30pm daily June-Aug., 8am-6:30pm daily Sept.-Oct.), just 2 miles north of Cherokee on US-441/Newfound Gap Road, will likely be the second stop you make. You can pick up a park map, grab the schedule of ranger-led programs, and see exhibits on the people who called these hills home long before the park was in existence. The visitors center and adjacent comfort station are LEED Gold certified.

Mountain Farm Museum
Next to the visitors center is **Mountain Farm Museum** (sunrise-sunset daily year-round, free), which showcases some of the finest farm buildings in the park. Most date to the early 1900s and among them are a barn, apple house, and the Davis House, a log home built from chestnut wood and constructed before the American chestnut blight decimated the species. This collection of structures is original to the area and dates back to the turn of the 20th century. Though the barn is the only structure original to this site, the other buildings were moved here from inside and adjacent to the park and arranged much like the typical farm of the era would have been laid out. If you visit during peak times, you'll see costumed living-history interpreters demonstrating the day-to-day chores that would've occurred on this farm: preparing meals, sowing seeds, maintaining and harvesting the garden, taking care of the hogs, and the like.

Mingus Mill
A half-mile north of the Oconaluftee Visitor

Center and Mountain Farm Museum you'll find **Mingus Mill** (9am-5pm daily mid-Mar.-mid-Nov. and Thanksgiving weekend). This historic grist mill was built in 1886; rather than use a water wheel to power the machinery and mill in the building, it uses a water-powered turbine to generate power. This cast-iron turbine still works! A miller is on hand to demonstrate how the machinery turns corn into cornmeal (for sale on site). Walk along the millrace (the wooden trough that carries water to power the turbine), check out the abundant seasonal wildflowers, and take a good look at how well the parks service restored the structure—it looks like it was built just a few years ago.

Deep Creek Valley Overlook

The **Deep Creek Valley Overlook,** 14 miles from the Oconaluftee Visitor Center (and 16 miles from Sugarlands Visitor Center if coming from the other direction), is one of the most popular overlooks in the park for good reason. From here you'll have a long view of the mountains, which roll away from you for as far as you can see.

Oconaluftee River Valley Overlook

Halfway through Newfound Gap Road is the **Oconaluftee River Valley Overlook,** a spot where you can spy the deep cut of the valley formed by the Oconaluftee River. This place is ideal for a picnic, so if you're hungry and you've brought your blanket and something to eat, spread out and relax for a few minutes.

Newfound Gap

One of the most-visited overlooks is at **Newfound Gap.** This is the highest elevation on Newfound Gap Road, at 5,048 feet, and though the views here are fantastic, the first thing you'll probably notice is the Rockefeller Memorial, a simple stone terrace that straddles the Tennessee/North Carolina state line and commemorates a $5 million gift made by the Rockefeller Foundation to

acquire land for the park. In 1940, President Franklin D. Roosevelt dedicated the park from this site. Plan to spend a little time here, especially early in the morning or near sunset. At sunset, you can see the Smokies' namesake haze settling into the folds and wrinkles of the mountains, and in the early morning, the mountains emerge from a blue haze in a subtle display of color that's been the subject of many a postcard and computer desktop background.

★ Clingmans Dome

At 6,643 feet, **Clingmans Dome** is the third-highest mountain in the eastern United States, and the highest in the Great Smoky Mountains. A flying saucer-like observation tower at the end of a long, steep walkway gives 360-degree views of the surrounding mountains, and on a clear day that view can be as far as 100 miles. More often, though, it's misty up here in the clouds, and Clingmans Dome receives so much precipitation that its woods are actually a coniferous rainforest. The road to the summit is closed December 1-March 31, but the observation tower remains open for those willing to make the hike. To get to Clingmans Dome, turn off Newfound Gap Road 0.1 mile south of Newfound Gap, and then take **Clingmans Dome Road** (closed in winter), which leads 7 miles to the parking lot. The peak is near the center of the park, due north from Bryson City, North Carolina.

Campbell Overlook

The **Campbell Overlook** is only 3 miles from the Sugarlands Visitor Center, and it is home to one of the best views of Mount LeConte you'll find along the road. LeConte is an interesting mountain. At 6,593 feet, it's the third-highest peak in the Smokies, but it's the tallest mountain east of the Mississippi in that it rises more than a mile from the foot of the mountain to the summit.

Sugarlands Visitor Center

The **Sugarlands Visitor Center** (1420 Old

TN-73 Scenic, Gatlinburg, TN, 865/436-1200, www.nps.gov/grsm, 8am-4:30pm daily Dec.-Feb., except Christmas Day, 8am-5pm daily Mar., 9am-6pm daily Apr.-May, 8am-7:30pm daily June-Aug., 8am-6:30pm daily Sept.-Oct., 8am-5pm daily Nov.) is the most popular visitors center in the park due to its proximity to Gatlinburg. There's the usual visitors center stuff—maps, guidebooks, a few gift items, some snacks—and it's also the origination point for the 1.9-mile Gatlinburg Trail.

RECREATION
Hiking

Great Smoky Mountains National Park contains hundreds of miles of hiking trails, ranging from family-friendly loop trails to strenuous wilderness treks. Before embarking on any of these trails, obtain a park map and talk to a park ranger to ascertain trail conditions and gauge whether it's suited to your hiking skills.

No dogs or other pets (other than service animals) are permitted on park trails, except the Gatlinburg Trail and Oconaluftee River Trail, though they are allowed in front-country campsites and picnic areas, so long as they remain on-leash.

OCONALUFTEE RIVER TRAIL

Distance: 3 miles round-trip
Duration: 45 minutes
Elevation gain: 70 feet
Difficulty: easy
Trailhead: Oconaluftee Visitor Center

This trail by the Oconaluftee River runs 1.5 miles from the **visitors center** to the outskirts of Cherokee. Flat save for a bridge or two and a few gentle rises, the Oconaluftee River Trail is a lovely walk. In the spring the banks of the Oconaluftee are blanketed with wildflowers, and throughout the year you may see a herd of elk crossing the river at any number of places. Bring bug spray because it can get a bit buggy right by the river on a still day. This is a great option for walking or jogging, and is one of only two paths in Great Smoky Mountains National Park where you can walk your **dog** or ride your **bike.**

KEPHART PRONG TRAIL

Distance: 4 miles round-trip
Duration: 2 hours
Elevation gain: 840 feet
Difficulty: easy
Trailhead: 6.9 miles north of Oconaluftee Visitor Center along Newfound Gap Road or 8.7 miles south from Newfound Gap. Trail begins on the east side of the road.

GREAT SMOKY MOUNTAINS NATIONAL PARK
NEWFOUND GAP ROAD

From Clingmans Dome, the highest point in the park, you'll have 100-mile views.

Kephart Prong offers an easy trail experience for those looking to stretch their legs a little or get more familiar with hiking in the Smokies. The trail crosses the Oconaluftee River, then follows the Kephart Prong (stream) for most of the hike, crossing it four times on log bridges. This hike ends at the Kephart Shelter, where the trail meets the Sweat Heifer Creek Trail and Grassy Branch Trail.

Begin by crossing Oconaluftee River via a **footbridge** and follow the wide, nearly flat trail. (Once this was a Jeep road, so you may spot bits of old asphalt along the way.) At 0.25 mile into the hike, you'll pass through a **Civilian Conservation Corps Camp** where you'll encounter ruins such as foundations, chimneys, and other evidence of the camp's use in the 1930s. Continue along the path and cross **Kephart Prong,** then begin to climb, passing the remains of a fish hatchery in 0.6 mile. Three more crossings of the Kephart Prong await, and you can ford the stream (use caution) or use the **log bridges** (they're narrow, use caution) at each crossing. As you continue the hike to **Kephart Shelter,** you'll pass evidence of a long-gone logging operation in the form of narrow-gauge railroad tracks. When you reach the shelter, catch your breath and get ready for the easy hike back.

The Oconaluftee River Trail

APPALACHIAN TRAIL TO MOUNT LECONTE

Distance: 15.6 miles one-way
Duration: 7-8.5 hours
Elevation gain: 3,000 feet
Difficulty: strenuous
Trailhead: Appalachian Trail trailhead at the Newfound Gap Road Overlook

This is a tough hike. The trail largely follows the crest of the mountains, and thus rises and falls several times with some significant elevation gains and losses.

From the start, the trail climbs for 2 miles. You'll be on a steady incline, but there are views aplenty to give you a little boost. At 1.7 miles, just before the junction with **Sweat Heifer Creek Trail,** you'll have a good look at Mount LeConte to the north. At 2.8 miles, **The Boulevard** forks off to the left.

Continue along The Boulevard, ignoring the sign for the Jump-Off Trail (you can hike that one-mile trail on the return trip if you want). Soon you'll drop down to an elevation around 5,500 feet, after which the trail bounces back and forth between 5,500 and 6,000 feet until you begin to properly climb **Mount LeConte** and make your way to the lodge there and the 6,593-foot summit.

CHARLIES BUNION

Distance: 8.1 miles round-trip
Duration: 7-8.5 hours
Elevation gain: 1,700 feet
Difficulty: strenuous
Trailhead: Appalachian Trail trailhead at the Newfound Gap Road Overlook

Originally named Fodderstack, the rock formation of Charlies Bunion earned its new name when two men, Charlie Conner and Horace Kephart, were hiking here. According to legend, they stopped to rest at Fodderstack

Clingmans Dome and Andrews Bald Trails

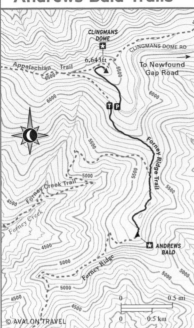

★ **ANDREWS BALD**

Distance: 3.5 miles round-trip
Duration: 3 hours
Elevation gain: 1,200 feet
Difficulty: moderate
Trailhead: Clingmans Dome parking area at the end of Clingmans Dome Road

The highest grassy bald in Great Smoky Mountains National Park, Andrews Bald is a beautiful sight at the end of a nearly 2-mile hike from Clingmans Dome. Balds are meadows found higher up on the mountain, and this one is absolutely lousy with flame azalea and rhododendron blooms in the summer. Note that Clingmans Dome Road is closed in the winter.

Before recent trail renovations, the Andrews Bald hike had some of the most rugged sections of rocky trails in the park. Thanks to the Trails Forever program, work crews fixed drainage issues, rebuilt parts of the trail, and even built a few stairways from native rocks and trees. Now the hike is easier and safer and leads to a spectacular view of the Smoky Mountains. A bonus: The hike is just long enough to discourage some potential hikers, but it's still short enough to be doable by everyone in your party.

The **Forney Ridge Trail** starts in a spruce-fir forest that was once beautiful, but is now unfortunately dead or dying. That's because the forest has been ravaged by a tiny bug—the balsam woolly adelgid—which devours Fraser firs. However, there is a certain beauty in the white bones of the tree trunks jutting up from the land. Don't worry though, the views get considerably better in a short time. Around 1.6 miles into the hike you'll reach the edge of **Andrews Bald,** where the forest opens up into a fantastic panorama. In spring and summer, there is a proliferation of wildflowers, flame azalea, and rhododendron.

SILERS BALD

Distance: 9.8 miles round-trip
Duration: 6-7 hours
Elevation gain: 2,100 feet
Difficulty: moderate to strenuous

and Conner removed his boots and socks, revealing a bunion that Kephart felt resembled the rocks around them. Impressed, Kephart promised Charlie that he'd get the name of this place changed on official maps in honor of the bunion.

The first leg of this trail follows the **Appalachian Trail** and **The Boulevard** to **Mount LeConte.** The trail climbs for 2 miles. At 1.7 miles, you'll come to the junction with Sweat Heifer Creek Trail. At 2.8 miles, The Boulevard forks off to the left; continue straight to reach Charlies Bunion.

The **Icewater Spring Shelter,** aptly named for the cold spring that flows out of the mountain here (treat the water before you drink it), is just 0.25 mile from the junction and is a good spot to rest. From the spring, continue a little less than a mile to a short **spur trail** on your left that leads out to the rock outcrop known as **Charlies Bunion.**

Trailhead: Clingmans Dome parking area at the end of Clingmans Dome Road

This hike is a highlight for many (even though Andrews Bald is the showier of the high-altitude meadows) because it offers a nice day hike along the **Appalachian Trail.** The hike begins at the parking area for Clingmans Dome, the highest peak in Great Smoky Mountains National Park; on the way back, you can divert your path just a little and pay a visit to the summit here. While the Clingmans Dome parking area is a big lot, it can get crowded. Get here early, especially in peak seasons. Note that Clingmans Dome Road closes in winter.

Begin at the far end of the Clingmans Dome parking area and descend along **Forney Ridge Trail.** Follow this rocky path 0.1 mile to a junction: Forney Ridge leads to the left, Clingmans Dome leads to the right. Take Forney Ridge left for 0.6 mile to **Mount Buckley** and the **Appalachian Trail.** Here you can turn right to reach the summit of Clingmans Dome (which you can do on the return trip), or continue left (west) to Silers Bald.

As you continue west along the Appalachian Trail, you'll pass through wildflowers and flowering shrubs mixed with a fir and spruce forest until you reach a **clearing** 0.9 mile into the hike. The clearing has good views, so catch your breath and keep following the ridgeline. Descending, the trail passes through clearings and back into the woods. At 2.6 miles, you'll reach the junction with **Goshen Prong Trail** (which descends toward Elkmont); continue straight along the AT.

At **Double Spring Gap,** in 3.4 miles, there is an **Appalachian Trail shelter** and springs (two, hence the name). The gap is the low point on the trail, so begin climbing into a forest where the fir gives way to beech trees. Top out at **Jenkins Knob,** then descend through another gap. At 3.9 miles, the trail crosses an open ridge and grassy area that again provides some great views of the Smokies.

Continue along the trail to a section known as **The Narrows** (4.2 miles), and push on

your final ascent toward Silers Bald. Pass the **Welch Ridge Trail** at 4.5 miles, then climb steeply to **Silers Bald,** 4.9 miles into the hike. Enjoy the view and catch your breath— or continue along the trail another 0.3 mile to the **Silers Bald Shelter** and a spring alongside the AT.

Despite the blooming wildflowers and shrubs along the path, Silers Bald receives some deserved criticism. The once wide-open bald is shrinking as the forest seeks to reclaim it. There's a small debate on what to do—let the forest take it back or maintain it as a bald—but it's a beautiful spot and a worthwhile hike no matter what.

When ready, reverse course and head back to Clingmans Dome. To divert to the summit and add 0.7 mile or so to your trip, continue along the **Appalachian Trail** when you reach **Mount Buckley.** The trail gets steep here, but it leads to a spot 50 yards or so from the ramp to the lookout tower at the summit of **Clingmans Dome.**

ALUM CAVE BLUFF TO MOUNT LECONTE

Distance: 5 miles one-way
Duration: 3-3.5 hours
Elevation gain: 2,560 feet
Difficulty: moderate with strenuous sections
Trailhead: Alum Cave Trailhead

As one of the most popular hikes in the park, this trail receives a lot of wear-and-tear, which can leave the trail in bad shape. Fortunately, repair work completed in 2015 and 2016 have left the trail in fantastic condition. Repairs focused on the lower portion, then the upper sections of the trail. Hikers will find sturdy handholds along the stone stairs and narrow, exposed sections at the upper end of the trail.

The trail starts off fairly gently as it climbs up to Arch Rock. **Alum Cave Creek** runs alongside the trail for a while, and here you'll have the chance to snap pictures of several cascades and beautiful rhododendron thickets (which bloom in late June and July). You'll reach **Arch Rock,** which is less arch and more natural tunnel, around 1.5 miles in.

Here the trail begins to climb more steeply. A set of stone steps leads out of Arch Rock and the forest changes from hemlock and hardwood to spruce and fir trees. In another half mile you'll reach **Inspiration Point,** where the view opens onto one of the mid-elevation balds.

When you reach **Alum Cave Bluffs,** you're halfway to Mount LeConte. The rock formations aren't caves, but rather deep overhangs that create an impressive shelter from the rain. The Smokies receive more than 85 inches of rain a year, yet the majority of the soil under the bluffs remains dry and dusty, an arid spot in one of the wettest forests in the nation.

Most hikers turn around at Alum Cave Bluffs, but if you're pushing on to Mount LeConte, the path steepens and grows more challenging as you gain elevation. The trail narrows to a set of rock ledges where **steel cables** have been bolted into the mountain for use as a handhold. The drop may be precipitous, but the views are fantastic. Soon, the trail intersects with **Rainbow Falls Trail,** leading you to the summit of **Mount LeConte** in short order.

If you plan on hiking to Mount LeConte and back in a day or spending the night at the lodge, it's in your best interest to arrive early so you can get a parking space.

CHIMNEY TOPS

Distance: 4 miles round-trip
Duration: 3.5 hours
Elevation gain: 1,400 feet
Difficulty: strenuous
Trailhead: Chimney Tops trailhead on Newfound Gap Road

This popular hike leads to an outstanding view from its namesake pinnacles. The trail has suffered some severe storm damage in the past few years, and was closed intermittently until a Trails Forever team completed repairs, fixing drainage issues, installing or refreshing rock steps and staircases, and building elevated turnpikes, as well as other laborious methods to mitigate the impact from hikers and Mother Nature. The 2016 wildfires that ravaged the Smokies and surrounding towns were started on Chimney Tops, so this area will see extensive fire damage for a couple of years to come. At the time of this writing, this trail, along with others, was closed but expected to reopen by early 2017. Trails Forever crews and workers from the National Parks may be on this trail to perform repairs and maintenance in 2017 to make it safe and

five miles to Mount LeConte

ALUM CAVE TRAIL
Arch Rock   1.4
Alum Cave Bluffs 2.3
Mt. LeConte   5.0

enjoyable for visitors. Check with the park for the status of this and other fire-affected trails.

Chimney Tops takes its name from the twin knobs that rise from ridge-like chimneys. These rocky summits are rare in the Smokies, but that's not the draw—what brings people up this steep, challenging trail is the 360-degree view. And it's incredibly steep, gaining nearly 1,000 feet in the last mile. To reach the pinnacles, the actual Chimney Tops, requires a very steep scramble over bare rock, which can be dangerous, and it's easier to climb up than to come back down.

Many people explore the first few hundred yards of this trail because it's right off Newfound Gap Road. The cascades, pools, and boulders found along **Walker Camp Prong** are picturesque and good for wading and sunbathing. As you climb, you'll cross **Road Prong,** another stream, twice. Just after the second crossing the trail splits, with one part following Road Prong and the other heading to Chimney Tops. Stay right and head to the chimneys.

After a brief ascent, the trail steepens significantly. Take a breather here before tackling this long, straight climb. The trail continues and narrows as you walk the ridgeline. Soon, you'll be at the foot of the **Chimney Tops** and you'll see a sign from the National Park Service warning you to proceed at your own risk. Heed this sign, as the last bit of "trail" to the summit is a **scramble** that doesn't require any specialized equipment but is quite risky if you're inexperienced in such terrain.

GATLINBURG TRAIL

Distance: 3.8 miles round-trip
Duration: 2 hours
Elevation gain: 20 feet
Difficulty: easy
Trailhead: Sugarlands Visitor Center

This is one of only two trails in the park to allow **pets** and **bicycles** (the other is the Oconaluftee River Trail in Cherokee). More of a walk than a hike, the Gatlinburg Trail follows the **West Prong Little Pigeon River** and Newfound Gap Road for most of the trip.

It's pretty and not especially challenging, but the optional walk to **Cataract Falls**—a few hundred yards up **Cove Mountain Trail,** which splits off the Gatlinburg Trail near the trailhead—can provide some photo opportunities and a pretty, easy-to-reach waterfall.

SMOKEMONT LOOP

Distance: 6.1 miles loop
Duration: 3-3.5 hours
Elevation gain: 1,400 feet
Difficulty: moderate
Trailhead: Smokemont Campground D section

This horse-friendly trail is an enjoyable hike along forest roads and trails, but the elevation gain pushes it to moderate difficulty.

Starting at the far end of the D Section of **Smokemont Campground,** you'll see a sign marking the **Bradley Fork Trailhead;** follow this trail along Bradley Fork. In the spring, this creekside section is packed with wildflowers and many folks will just hike the first 0.5 mile of the trail. At 1.2 miles, the trail forks, with Chasteen Creek Trail going right and the **Bradley Fork/Smokemont Loop Trail** continuing left.

At 1.6 miles you meet up with **Smokemont Loop Trail** proper. Follow this trail left and cross **Bradley Fork** via a foot log. (Be careful, this one can be a little bouncy.) As soon as you cross, the trail forks again; the left fork follows the creek. Turn right and begin an uphill climb to **Richland Mountain.** This climb will keep going for another 2 miles at a steady incline, so pace yourself.

Once you pass through a small saddle, you'll hear the **Oconaluftee River** and, likely, cars traveling Newfound Gap Road. At the 3.4-mile mark, the trail takes a sharp left turn, marking the place you've been waiting for—the end of the climb and start of the descent. From here you have a 2-mile-long downhill trail. As you get closer to the end, you'll see the **Bradley Cemetery,** with a spur trail leading to it at 5.3 miles. At the Cemetery Trail, **Smokemont Loop** meets a gravel road leading back to the campground in another 0.2 mile.

Fishing

Smallmouth bass and rock bass are fairly abundant in Smoky's waters. Look for smallmouth bass along the **West Prong of the Little Pigeon River,** near Gatlinburg and the park's western entrance, and in the **Little Pigeon River** near Greenbrier. Smallmouth and rock bass are found in the **Little River** on the way to Cades Cove, **Abrams Creek,** and **Fontana Lake,** specifically the feeder creeks like Noland, Hazel, and Eagle Creek.

Horseback Riding

Three commercial stables in the park offer "rental" horses (about $30/hour). **Smokemont** (828/497-2373, www.smokemontridingstable.com) is located in North Carolina near Cherokee. Two are in Tennessee: **Smoky Mountain** (865/436-5634, Gatlinburg, TN, www.smokymountainridingstables.com) and **Cades Cove** (10018 Campground Dr., Townsend, TN, 865/448-9009, http://cadescovestables.com).

ACCOMMODATIONS AND CAMPING

As big as Great Smoky Mountains National Park may be, there are few places to stay within the boundaries—and nearly all them are either campsites or backcountry shelters. The lone exception is LeConte Lodge, a collection of cabins and small lodges with a central dining room/lodge. It's only accessible by hiking in, so you have to be dedicated to stay there.

LeConte Lodge

Just below the 6,593-foot peak of Mount LeConte is the only true lodging in Great Smoky Mountains National Park, the ★ **LeConte Lodge** (865/429-5704, www.lecontelodge.com, Mar. 21-Nov. 22, adults $140, children age 4-12 $85, includes lodging, breakfast, and dinner). Like the mountain's summit, the lodge is accessible only via the network of hiking trails that crisscross the park. And if the accessibility limitation isn't rustic enough for you, this collection of cabins has no running water or electricity. What it does have is views for days and the seclusion of the Smoky Mountains backcountry.

For the most part the environs harken back to the lodge's 1934 opening. LeConte Lodge has no hot showers. In every cabin there is a bucket for a sponge bath—which can be surprisingly refreshing after a hot day on the trail—that you can fill with warm

Reservations are required for the rustic LeConte Lodge.

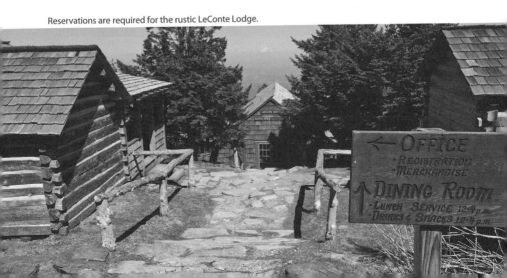

water from the kitchen, though you need to supply your own washcloth and towel. There are a few flush toilets in a separate building, and the only lights, aside from headlamps and flashlights, are kerosene lanterns. Your room does come with two meals: dinner and breakfast. Both are served at the same time every day (6pm for dinner and 8am for breakfast), and feature food hearty enough to fuel another day on the trail.

The lodge doesn't lack for charm, but it does for comfort, so if you're the five-star-hotel, breakfast-in-bed type, this may not be the place for you. Catering to hikers who are happy to have a dry place to sleep and a bed that's comfier than their sleeping bag, it's short on luxury amenities, and rooms are, in truth, bunk beds in small, drafty cabins. But if you're a hiker or if you just love to have a completely different experience when you travel, this is a one-of-a-kind accommodation.

RESERVATIONS

Accommodations for LeConte Lodge are made via **lottery** (www.lecontelodge.com). The lottery is competitive, but it's easy to enter; simply go to their website and fill out the online form, including your desired dates and the number in your party. If your application is chosen in the lottery, you will receive an invoice with your accommodation information. Booking information for the following season becomes available online in midsummer, so keep an eye out and get your application in early.

If you want to stay at LeConte Lodge, but you're late to the lottery party, try to get on the wait list. The process is the same, but the dates are limited—typically weeknights and the larger cabins are all that's available.

You can try one other method: calling (865/429-5704). Cancellations made with less than 30 days' notice skip the wait list and are instead offered to the first inquiry that matches availability. Frequent calls are a good way to snag these last-minute reservations.

GETTING THERE

The **Roaring Fork Motor Nature Trail** (open Mar.-Nov.) at the foot of Mount LeConte is the starting point for a trio of hiking trails that lead to LeConte Lodge. **Bull Head Trail** is a 6.8-mile trip from the trailhead to the lodge, as is **Rainbow Falls Trail.** (Bull Head and Rainbow Falls Trails share a trailhead at the designated parking area on the Motor Nature Trail.) **Trillium Gap Trail,** the trail used by the lodge's pack llamas, passes by the beautiful Grotto Falls on its 6.7-mile route (the trailhead is at the Grotto Falls parking area on the Roaring Fork Motor Nature Trail). Each of these three trails requires a four-hour hike to reach the lodge from the trailhead.

Three other trails lead to Mount LeConte from various points in the park. **Alum Cave Trail** (5 miles one-way) enters from Newfound Gap Road; it's the shortest and easiest to access, but it's also the steepest.

Alternatively, **The Boulevard** connects the Appalachian Trail to LeConte Lodge (13.2 miles from Newfound Gap Overlook). The Boulevard is relatively easy with little elevation change, but there's the issue of exposure on this trail—the rock path has more than a few dizzying drops right beside the trail. These drops, combined with The Boulevard coming in from the Appalachian Trail, deters most day- or overnight-hikers from its use. **Brushy Mountain Trail** (11.8 miles round-trip) leads to the summit from the Porters Creek Trailhead off Greenbrier Road (closed in winter). Despite the significant elevation change, this is a relatively easy trail.

Camping

Smokemont Campground (877/444-6777, www.recreation.gov, year-round, $17-20) is just off Newfound Gap Road, 3.2 miles from the Oconaluftee Visitor Center. There are 142 total sites available between tent campsites and RV sites. It's located on the banks of the Oconaluftee River and thus can get quite buggy, so be prepared.

Eastern Smokies

The eastern side of Great Smoky Mountains National Park was settled before the western side, so there are plenty of coves and hollows with historic structures or the ruins of cabins, barns, and other buildings in the fields and woods and along creek banks and floodplains. There are also many herds of elk here, introduced several years ago in an attempt to revive the species that once roamed these hills.

ROARING FORK
Roaring Fork Motor Nature Trail

One of the most beautiful drives in Great Smoky Mountains National Park is the **Roaring Fork Motor Nature Trail** (open Mar.-Nov.). This one-way loop passes through rhododendron thickets and dense hardwood forests as it follows the old roadbed of the Roaring Fork Community. To get here, turn onto Historic Nature Trail (Old Airport Road) at traffic light #8 in Gatlinburg and follow the signs. Before you reach the trail, you'll drive a short distance on Cherokee Orchard Road, which runs through what was an 800-acre commercial orchard in the 1920s and 1930s; shortly after the orchard, you'll be at the head of the trail and have the chance to purchase an inexpensive tour booklet from a roadside exhibit.

Unfortunately Roaring Fork was one of the areas affected by the 2016 wildfires and, at the time of this writing, trails here were closed. Visitors to the park in 2017 should expect to find a landscape scarred by this fire, it is recovering more quickly than you could imagine possible. The ongoing status of the trails here are unknown, but may experience sporadic closures throughout 2017 as trail maintenance crews perform any work needed to repair fire damage. Fortunately none of the historic structures in this or any part of the park were damaged in the fires.

The roadbed here was built by hand in the 1850s, which explains both its narrowness and serpentine route. Around 25 families lived here, and though it may look quaint and primitive to our eyes, a few of the homes had running water thanks to the system of troughs—some of which are still standing—that carried water right to the houses.

As the road climbs through the forest, roll down your windows and take in a few deep breaths of that fresh, cool mountain air. There is a pair of **overlooks,** though they're overgrown and in poor repair. When you stop, take in the silence. You'll soon find yourself surrounded by the sounds of nature: wind, birds calling, and streams rumbling and echoing through the forest.

Be sure to stop at the cabins still standing here. **Ogle Place,** a two-room cabin surrounded by rhododendrons; **Ephraim Bales Cabin,** which is smack in the middle of a boulder field; and **Alfred Regan Cabin,** which has an amazing trough system still in place, are all worth spending a few minutes exploring and photographing.

Hiking

There are three waterfalls within hiking distance of the Motor Nature Trail: **Rainbow Falls** (the most popular of the hikes), **Grotto Falls,** and **Baskins Creek Falls.** If you're not up for a hike, **Thousand Drips Falls** (sometimes called the Place of a Thousand Drips) is just off the road. In wet times, it's a great cascade plummeting down the mountain; during drier times it's much tamer but still serene.

RAINBOW FALLS TRAIL
Distance: 5.4 miles round-trip
Duration: 3.5-4 hours
Elevation gain: 1,700 feet
Difficulty: strenuous
Trailhead: Roaring Fork Motor Nature Trail, 3.3 miles from Gatlinburg traffic light #8, at the Rainbow Falls and Bull Head Trail parking area

Roaring Fork and Greenbrier Cove

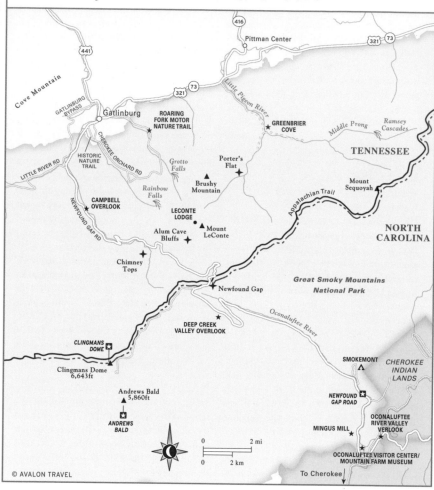

© AVALON TRAVEL

This trail is strenuous due to how steep and rocky it is and how slick it can become in places where the trail nears the water and as you get closer to the falls. Note that Roaring Fork Motor Trail is closed in the winter.

As you leave the parking area, you'll cross **Trillium Gap Trail** and begin to climb alongside LeConte Creek. Follow the trail as it goes through a couple of switchbacks and then crosses the creek on a **log bridge.** Here you'll enter a stretch where some impressive trees

stand. Soon you'll cross LeConte Creek again. At this crossing you can see **Rainbow Falls** above you. Continue up the trail to a spot just below the falls.

Here LeConte Creek plunges 80 feet to the rocks below. During that plunge, the water becomes more of a heavy mist, giving us the name Rainbow Falls. Though you can get some good photography from the trail, there are other interesting shots to be had from different angles around the falls. Be aware that if you scramble around the falls, the rocks are slick and you could slip and hurt yourself, and with a 2.7-mile hike back to the car, who wants to do that? If you decide to explore the area around the falls, use caution and stay safe.

You may notice that the **Rainbow Falls Trail** continues on past the waterfall itself. It is possible to take this trail to the summit of Mount LeConte, but that is a strenuous, steep, full-day hike of close to 14 miles.

GROTTO FALLS TRAIL

Distance: 2.6 miles round-trip
Duration: 2-2.5 hours
Elevation gain: 585 feet
Difficulty: moderate
Trailhead: Roaring Fork Motor Nature Trail, about 2 miles into the trail, Grotto Falls parking area on the left

From the parking area, you'll follow a short, unnamed spur before joining **Trillium Gap Trail,** which leads to **Grotto Falls** before continuing to the top of **Mount LeConte.** As you hike, you'll notice the path is hard packed—that's because this trail is the resupply route for **LeConte Lodge,** so it sees traffic from the llama trains carrying supplies up to the lodge. If you're lucky, you'll see one of these trains.

The forest was once composed mostly of hemlock trees, but thanks to a nasty little bug—the hemlock woolly adelgid—many of these trees are dead or dying. Even though some of the trees are being ravaged, the forest is still thick, and opens dramatically where the stream plunges 25 feet to form Grotto Falls.

The most intriguing part of Grotto Falls is the grotto. Trillium Gap Trail passes behind the falls thanks to a hefty rock overhang. It provides some interesting photographic opportunities that make it is one of the most popular waterfall hikes on this side of the park.

BASKINS FALLS TRAIL

Distance: 3.2 miles round-trip
Duration: 3 hours
Elevation gain: 950 feet
Difficulty: strenuous
Trailhead: Roaring Fork Motor Nature Trail, on the left near the Jim Bales Place

This 30-foot waterfall is like a little secret hidden along the popular **Roaring Fork Motor Nature Trail** (closed in winter). Seldom visited, it's almost a forgotten hike, meaning you can have the falls to yourself.

As soon as you start the hike, you'll pass a cemetery before making a climb up to a ridgeline. A steep descent from the ridge will take you to **Baskins Creek.** Cross the creek (be careful, especially in high water) and make the steep climb over another ridge. From here you can see what's left of an old chimney standing in the woods. Just beyond a tiny, wildflower-filled meadow is the side path leading to the base of the falls. On the right side of this trail is an old **homesite,** followed by a steep descent down to the **falls.**

Many hikers turn around here and return to their car, but it is possible to continue along this trail another 1.5 miles and arrive near the entrance to the Roaring Fork Motor Nature Trail. If you do this, know that you will have a 3-mile walk along the road back to your car.

Backpacking

This backpacking trip will take you from Roaring Fork to the summit of Mount LeConte, the third highest peak in the park (and sixth highest in the Appalachians). Spend the night at either the LeConte Lodge or LeConte Shelter; reservations are required for each.

RESERVATIONS

A backpacking trip to Mount LeConte from Roaring Fork requires some preparation. First, you'll need to register with the **Backcountry Information Office** (Sugarlands Visitor Center, 865/436-1297, https://smokiespermits. nps.gov, 8am-5pm daily, $4/night) for a permit, then make a site reservation.

On Mount LeConte, you'll have only two options: LeConte Lodge, which is a hot ticket and books up early, and the LeConte Shelter, which is much easier to secure. **LeConte Lodge** (865/429-5704,

Mount LeConte Trails

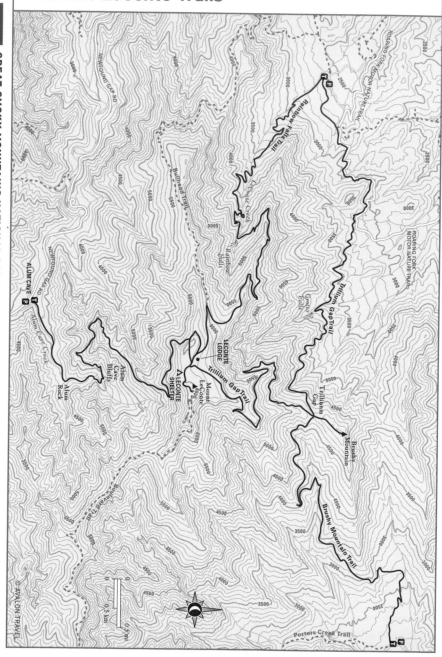

www.lecontelodge.com, Mar. 21-Nov. 22, adults $140, children age 4-12 $85, includes lodging and meals), requires reservations one year in advance. The LeConte Shelter is reserved through the Backcountry Information Office; reservations may be made up to 30 days before your stay. Contact the office as soon as possible to make a reservation; it's one of the most popular shelters in the park.

MOUNT LECONTE VIA GROTTO FALLS

Distance: 13.5 miles round-trip

Duration: Overnight

Elevation gain: 4,000 feet

Difficulty: strenuous

Trailhead: Roaring Fork Motor Nature Trail at the Grotto Falls Trail parking area

From the parking area, the path begins across **Roaring Fork Motor Nature Trail** for 0.1 mile before it meets with **Trillium Gap Trail.** Climb Trillium Gap Trail for 6.6 miles (and some 4,000 vertical feet) to the summit of **Mount LeConte.** Now you're an easy 1.3 miles to **Grotto Falls,** one of the prettiest waterfalls in the park. (Grotto Falls is so named for the grotto behind the veil of water making up the falls.) The hike leads through the remains of a hemlock forest (the trees have been killed by the hemlock woolly adelgid) before it reaches the falls. At the falls you may encounter a strange sight: llamas. LeConte Lodge uses a pack train of llamas for resupply; if you're on the trail early enough, you'll see them at the waterfall.

Passing Grotto Falls the trail will grow steeper. You'll cross a couple of small streams, but the trail is a typical woodland path with the usual rocks and roots underfoot and a decent incline. As you approach Trillium Gap you'll begin to see patches of grass along the trail. At 3.1 miles, you'll reach **Trillium Gap** proper and the intersection with **Brushy Mountain Trail.** Peakbaggers can add another 0.8 mile for the round-trip hike to the summit of Brushy Mountain. Otherwise, continue along Trillium Gap Trail.

From Trillium Gap, the trail grows steeper and rockier, but the forest is quite lush. When the moss, ferns, and smaller vegetation give way to fir trees, you know you're close to LeConte Lodge. After passing a spring, you'll hit **LeConte Lodge.** Just ahead, the trail will intersect with **Bullhead Trail** and **Boulevard Trail;** turn right to approach LeConte Lodge and the spur trail leading to the summit; it's another 0.4 mile to the summit and back.

If you're staying at LeConte Lodge, check in and rest. If you've made a reservation at the **LeConte Shelter,** backtrack to the junction of Bullhead, Trillium Gap, and Boulevard Trails and continue down Boulevard Trail for another 0.2 mile.

GREENBRIER COVE

Greenbrier Cove, like many other coves in the park, was once home to a mountain community. This area was settled in the early 1800s, and families farmed, trapped, and hunted the land until the establishment of the national park. This cove has an interesting footnote: Dolly Parton's ancestors, Benjamin C. and Margaret Parton, moved here in the 1850s and their descendants left when the park was formed.

Greenbrier is stunning, especially in the spring. The cove is known as a wildflower hot spot, but don't underestimate the beauty of this place in any season.

Hiking

RAMSEY CASCADES TRAIL

Distance: 8 miles round-trip

Duration: 5.5 hours

Elevation gain: 2,375 feet

Difficulty: strenuous

Trailhead: Ramsey Cascades Trailhead at the Greenbrier park entrance, 6 miles east of Gatlinburg off US-321

Ramsey Cascades is the tallest waterfall in Great Smoky Mountains National Park, spilling 100 feet in a series of steps before collecting in a pool at the base. As if that wasn't reason enough to undertake this hike, this section of the park is known as a wildflower

Ramsey Cascades Trail

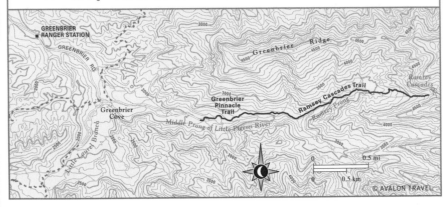

paradise, so a springtime visit is highly recommended.

The first portion of this trail is a continuation of the gravel road you took to the parking area. You'll soon cross **Little Laurel Branch** and almost immediately after, the Middle Prong of Little Pigeon River via a long **footbridge.** If you've timed your hike with the wildflower bloom, the next half mile will be a riot of color.

The hiking here is easy until you reach the 1.5-mile mark, where the Jeep trail you're on ends. To the left (north) is the **Greenbrier Pinnacle Trail,** a trail that's not maintained by the park; **Ramsey Cascades Trail** continues on through a thicket of rhododendron.

Past this point you find yourself on a trail where roots and rocks are more the norm, so watch your footing. Continue along this trail; it will turn steep, you'll cross the **Ramsey Prong** and a side stream, and you'll know you've arrived when you hear the waterfall. The final approach is rocky and slick, with a lot of scrambling, so use caution. When you've taken in all of the **Ramsey Cascades** you can handle, simply reverse your course to the trailhead.

BRUSHY MOUNTAIN TO MOUNT LECONTE

Distance: 11.8 miles round-trip

Duration: 6-7 hours

Elevation gain: 3,000 feet

Difficulty: moderate

Trailhead: Porters Creek Trailhead on Greenbrier Road, 6 miles east of Gatlinburg off US-321

Directions: From traffic light #3 in Gatlinburg (junction of US-441 and US-321), travel east on US-321. Drive 6 miles and then turn right on Greenbrier Road (which becomes a gravel road). At the fork in the road 3.1 miles in, continue straight 1 mile to the Porters Creek Trailhead.

The first mile or so of this trail follows an old gravel road, the **Porters Creek Trail.** In the spring, trillium are profuse here. You'll pass a **cemetery** and several stone walls and then cross a **footbridge** at a fork in the road. Turn left at the fork. You'll meet another fork 100 yards or so down the trail, at which you turn right onto **Brushy Mountain Trail.**

The trail continues for 4.5 miles, climbing some 2,500 feet as it does. At 5.5 miles, you'll meet **Trillium Gap Trail.** Go left on the Trillium Gap Trail and you'll reach **Mount LeConte.** Turn right and you can reach the summit of **Brushy Mountain** in 0.6 mile.

GRAPEYARD RIDGE

Distance: 7.6 miles one-way via shuttle
Duration: 4-5 hours
Elevation gain: 3,250 feet
Difficulty: moderate
Trailhead: Grapeyard Ridge Trailhead in Greenbrier, 6 miles east of Gatlinburg off US-321

This beautiful hike reveals some intriguing sights, such as the remains of a Civilian Conservation Corps (CCC) camp, stone walls, a cemetery, and an old steam engine. This route connects the Greenbrier area of the park with Roaring Fork Motor Nature Trail (closed in winter); it's best to do this as an end-to-end shuttle hike (park a car at one end, drive to the other, and hike back to the car you left). Otherwise, you'll have to arrange transport back to your trailhead or hike back.

Begin the hike along **Greenbrier Road** (closed in winter) and plunge right into a forest thick with galax and mountain laurel. You'll climb quickly, gaining nearly 300 feet in little more than 0.5 mile. At 0.1 mile, pass a spur trail to a **cemetery.** At 0.4 mile, the trail begins to descend, and you'll make the first of many crossings of **Rhododendron Creek** at 0.5 mile. This crossing has no bridge; you'll have to ford the stream without aid, so watch the water levels and only cross if you're confident in your ability and footing. Over the next 1.2 miles, you'll **cross the stream** four more times.

The trail splits from the creek and begins climbing toward James Gap at the 2.1-mile mark, going through a few rhododendron tunnels, which give it an eerie feel. You'll reach **James Gap** at 2.9 miles then quickly descend to **Injun Creek** and the wreck of an old steam engine. The name of the creek comes from the steam engine, (not the native peoples). The engine was part of a logging operation in the 1920s; steam-powered tractor slipped into the creek on the way out and stayed there, too heavy to move.

Turning back here makes this a nice little day hike. If you press on, you'll pass **Backcountry Campsite 32** in 0.3 mile. Here begins another steady uphill climb to

Grapeyard Ridge at the 4-mile mark. Rather than follow the true ridge, the trail traces a path just below it. This path offers better views and a profusion of wildflowers in each little cove you dip into.

The trail descends toward Grapeyard Branch, meeting with **Dudley Creek** at 4.8 miles. Prior to reaching the creek, you'll see fence posts and other signs of habitation; at Dudley Creek there is a low rock wall and evidence of a homestead. The junction with **Big Dudley Trail** at 4.9 miles marks the next point where the trail climbs as it continues on toward Roaring Fork.

A sign for **Roaring Fork** appears at 6.1 miles; at 6.6 miles is the highest point of the trail. Begin your descent into Roaring Fork. At 7.3 miles, a trail leads to Trillium Gap Trail, but continue straight and you'll soon reach the Bales Place and **Roaring Fork.**

PORTERS CREEK TRAIL

Distance: 7.2 miles round-trip
Duration: 3.5-4 hours
Elevation gain: 1,500 feet
Difficulty: moderate
Trailhead: Greenbrier Road 0.9 mile beyond the Ramsey Cascades Trailhead

From the traffic loop 0.9 mile up the road from the **Ramsey Cascades Trailhead,** begin hiking along a gravel road. Rock walls and evidence of homesites are all around; soon you'll cross a small creek and find an old **cemetery.** Cross a larger stream by wading (if the water's not too high) or using the foot log.

In 1 mile an **old traffic turnaround** indicates the start of the trail. **Porters Creek Trail** is the trail to the far left. (Brushy Mountain Trail is the middle trail, and the far right trail leads to a historic farm site that you can explore on the way back.)

Once on begin Porters Creek Trail, you'll cross Porters Creek in 0.5 mile. If you're hiking in the spring, you'll be treated to a carpet of wildflowers. **Fern Branch Falls** awaits 0.4 mile farther, adding to the beauty of this hike. The waterfall is surprisingly high

Hen Wallow Falls Trail

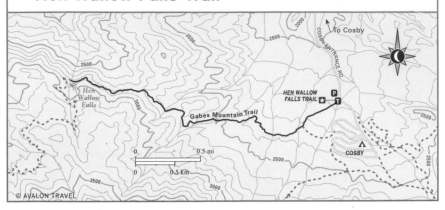

at 35 feet, and the surrounding area is thick with moss and wildflowers in the spring.

Continue past the waterfall to the end of the hike and **Backcountry Campsite 31** at 3.6 miles. Explore the creek for a little while, then when you're ready, head back downhill to the trailhead.

COSBY

For the first half of the 20th century, Cosby was known as the moonshine capital of the world. The national prohibition on liquor turned many locals to making their own. When scientists and workers began to come to Oak Ridge to work on secret military ventures like the Manhattan Project, they weren't accustomed to Tennessee's dry county laws, and the demand for moonshine skyrocketed. Today, there isn't much by way of moonshine production in town, and most of the visitors come here for the national park.

Cosby's present reputation is as a friendly town with one of the lesser-used park entrances. That's good for you, because when autumn leaves begin to change and the crowds pack Gatlinburg and clog the easy-to-access trails along Newfound Gap Road, you can head to Cosby. In town you'll find a few restaurants and a handful of cabin rentals, but the park is the real treasure.

Hiking

★ HEN WALLOW FALLS TRAIL

Distance: 4.4 miles round-trip
Duration: 3.5 hours
Elevation gain: 900 feet
Difficulty: moderate
Trailhead: Gabes Mountain Trailhead, across the road from the Cosby Campground picnic area

From the outset, **Gabes Mountain Trail** is a steady climb on a path that's at times rugged. Follow this trail until you see a sign for the **side trail** leading to the waterfall (2.1 miles into the hike). The 0.1-mile side trail is a little steep, but not problematically so.

Hen Wallow Falls tumbles 90 feet into a small pool below, where there are plenty of salamanders to see. The falls themselves are only 2 feet wide at the top, but fan out to 20 feet at the bottom; during dry months, the falls are still pretty, but less wow-inducing.

To get back to the trailhead, just retrace your steps.

MOUNT CAMMERER TRAIL

Distance: 11.2 miles round-trip
Duration: 7-7.5 hours
Elevation gain: 2,740 feet
Difficulty: strenuous
Trailhead: Low Gap Trailhead, just beyond the Cosby Campground amphitheater area

To start, park in the group parking area and walk along the road to where it curves into the B Section of the campground. Just before **campsite 92** you'll see a trailhead; follow it for a short distance until it crosses Cosby Creek, then turn right on **Low Gap Trail.** From here, the trail climbs a little less than 3 miles up the mountain via a series of winding switchbacks until you reach the Appalachian Trail.

Turn left to join the **Appalachian Trail** for 2.1 miles. The first mile of this trail is more level, so it gives you a chance to catch your breath or make up some time. You'll know when you reach the junction with the **Mount Cammerer Trail** because the Appalachian Trail descends to the right; you want to stay straight. The **summit** is 0.6 mile from where you leave the Appalachian Trail.

At the summit is a **stone fire tower** built in the 1930s and restored by volunteers throughout the years. The view from the deck here is awesome—it's one of the best in the park.

ALBRIGHT GROVE TRAIL

Distance: 6.8 miles round-trip
Duration: 3.5-4 hours
Elevation gain: 1,400 feet
Difficulty: moderate
Trailhead: Maddron Bald Trail
Directions: From Gatlinburg, drive 15.5 miles east on US-321. Turn right onto Baxter Road; at 0.3 mile turn right onto a gravel road. Park near (but don't block) the gate at the dirt road.

Begin hiking on **Maddron Bald Trail,** an old wagon road, which climbs immediately uphill. At 0.7 mile, you'll get your first chance for a breather when you reach a one-room **cabin** on the right. Keep climbing and, at 1.2 miles, you'll meet up with **Old Settlers Trail** (continues right) and **Gabes Mountain Trail** (continues left). Stay straight on Maddron Bald Trail, following the old roadbed for another mile before the wagon road ends at a traffic circle. Here the path begins in earnest.

Cross **Indian Camp Creek** 0.5 mile past the old traffic circle, keeping an eye out for **Albright Grove Loop Trail,** which appears in another 0.1 mile. Since Albright Grove is a loop, you can take this entrance, make the loop, and then descend along Maddron Bald Trail. Or you can climb up another 0.3 mile to the upper junction with Albright and take Maddron Bald Trail back.

Many consider Albright Grove to be a great example of old-growth forest in the national park. Though many of the huge hemlocks trees have died from a pest infestation, they've left gaps in the canopy that allows in sunlight. You'll still see many fine and big trees here, evidence of the forest as it once stood.

After you've explored Albright Grove, head back down Maddron Bald Trail to the trailhead.

Fishing

Anglers can bring their gear to **Cosby Creek,** which has several spots where wild trout are abundant. If you find other anglers along the creek and want some isolation, hike upstream into the headwaters where small brook trout await.

In the spring you'll catch fish along Cosby Creek, but in the summer you'll want to venture into the headwaters. Fall fishing is spectacular (thanks to that distracting and beautiful leaf show), and in the winter you'll catch fish along the stream on all but the coldest days (because you'll be snug and warm somewhere else).

Camping

Cosby Campground (471 Cosby Campground Road A, Cosby, TN, 423/487-2683, www.recreation.gov, Apr.-Oct., $14) has 157 sites for tents and RVs. Despite being home to the park's third-largest campground, Cosby is known as the quietest of the park's gateways. There are a number of trails that originate from the campground.

At the northern end of Great Smoky Mountains National Park, you're close enough to the **Cherokee National Forest** (www.fs.usda.gov/Cherokee, free) to camp in the Pigeon River Recreation Zone. Dispersed camping is allowed provided campers are 100 feet away from water, trails, parking areas, and developed recreation areas.

Accommodations

Cosby has a few accommodations, but selections are limited. Fortunately, a couple of spots stand out.

Creekwalk Inn (166 Middle Creek Rd., 865/453-2000, www.creekwalkinnandcabins. com) is a seven-room bed-and-breakfast with inn rooms ($110-309) and several cabins ($130-259) all set on a 50-acre mountain farm. There are hiking trails and creeks to explore and a killer breakfast is served every morning. Best of all, it's private. The individual cabins are separated, providing privacy for guests and the B&B rooms are so cozy you'll forget anyone else is there. Until breakfast, that is, when everyone shows up for cast-iron skillet cornbread with peach jam, fried potatoes, and sausage, and eggs cooked on a wood stove.

For a sample of mountain life, but with electricity, **Garden of Eden Cabins** (467 Laurel Springs Rd., 423/487-2617, www. gardenofedencabins.com, $75-85) has three cabins in the woods near the national park. The trio of cabins are comfortable and homey, though the decor could use a bit of an update (common in B&Bs and cabins in these parts). Two of the cabins have two bedrooms, making them natural choices for couples traveling together or families or small groups. Each cabin is pet friendly and has a fire ring and a picnic area with outdoor seating; two cabins overlook the creek, which makes quite the lovely lullaby.

At **Cosby Creek Cabins** (4376 Cosby Hwy., 800/508-8844, www.cosbycreekcabins. com, $115-275 plus cleaning fee), you'll find larger and slightly more luxurious cabins scattered around Cosby (with several closer to Pigeon Forge and Gatlinburg). The three-dozen cabins range from one to four bedrooms, and include options like game rooms, fireplaces, and hot tubs. Winter rates ($100-150) making exploring the park in the off-season easy and affordable.

Food

Dining options are few and all of the country cookin' variety. But the food is both filling and tasty, though vegetarians may have a hard time finding a meatless meal.

For an early breakfast at **Janice's Diner** (2765 Cosby Hwy., 423/613-5515, 6:30am-8:30pm daily, $7-20), skip the front room (it's a little dull) and head straight for the dining area in back, where it's homey and welcoming. The diner-style food includes eggs and hash browns, burgers, sandwiches, and a couple of salads. It opens early and everything is affordable, so stop in to fuel up pre-hike or replenish those post-hike calories.

Magnolia Tree Restaurant & Country Market (4925 Hooper Hwy., 423/487-2519, 11:30am-7:30pm daily, $6-19) is one of those dual-purpose places that feels like the inspiration for Cracker Barrel. You know the type: Eat a home-cooked meal in the dining room, then buy some fudge or whimsical country gift in the shop. While that may sound a little corny, you can pick up some road or trail snacks here and get a decent meal. Try the cheesesteak, the BLT, and the chicken pot pie, though not all at once. That's a lot of food and you'll have no room for dessert.

BIG CREEK

Big Creek is the site of a beautiful and seldom-visited front-country campground and has one of the best hikes for beginning day hikers and backpackers. The Big Creek Trail is more of an easy creekside walk than a hike, but it's long enough to make you feel accomplished when you're done.

For more of a challenge, turn Big Creek into a big overnighter by including a summit of Mount Sterling or you can take on Mount Sterling from a couple of different routes, all accessible from this region.

Hiking

BIG CREEK TRAIL

Distance: 10.6 miles round-trip
Duration: 5-6 hours
Elevation gain: 600 feet

Difficulty: easy

Trailhead: Big Creek Campground and Picnic Area off I-40 at Waterville (exit 457)

Big Creek Trail follows an old motor road built by the Civilian Conservation Corps (CCC) in the 1930s, so it's smooth and wide with a very gentle grade for its entire length. The difficult part of this trail is the distance, so be sure to bring plenty of water and something to eat.

Roughly one mile in from the trailhead, you'll see **Rock House,** an impressive rock cliff that has sheltered more than a few loggers, Civilian Conservation Corps workers, hunters, and hikers from a rainstorm. Just beyond Rock House is **Midnight Hole,** where Big Creek flows through a narrow chute in the rock, then drops 6-7 feet into a deep, dark pool before flowing on.

Two miles in, you'll see **Mouse Creek Falls,** a 35-foot cascade that drops right into Big Creek. It's a fantastic spot to sit, relax, take some pictures, and enjoy the woods. It's also a great spot to turn around if you may not be up for the whole 10-mile trip.

Push on past Mouse Creek Falls and you'll come upon **Brakeshoe Spring.** In another 2.5 miles you'll reach **Walnut Bottoms** and **Campsite 37.** This is one of the best campsites in the park if you're going to make this hike an overnighter. From here, it's time to retrace your steps back to the trailhead.

MOUNT STERLING VIA BAXTER CREEK TRAIL

Distance: 12.2 miles round-trip

Duration: 5-6 hours

Elevation gain: 4,200 feet

Difficulty: strenuous

Trailhead: Big Creek Campground and Picnic Area off I-40 at Waterville (exit 457)

You can reach the summit of Mount Sterling from a number of trails—but this one is perhaps the most direct. This hike is strenuous not because of any technical or steep sections of the trail (it's actually well-maintained), but because it's a steady uphill climb with a 4,200-foot elevation gain until you turn around for the return trip. At the

summit, you're rewarded with a fire tower to climb, giving you massive views of this section of the park.

At the trailhead, cross a **footbridge** over Big Creek, which you'll follow for 0.5 mile until the trail begins to climb the lower slopes of Mount Sterling. Before the uphill section, you'll pass an unmarked **spur trail** at 0.3 mile leading to a rock wall and huge stone chimney, the remains of a lodge once owned by a lumber company.

After crossing Baxter Creek (around the 0.7-mile mark), you'll pass through some spectacular forest, including old-growth and one of the largest (if not the largest) tulip trees in the park at more than 175 feet tall. There are several massive trees here including more champion tulip trees, the largest northern red oak, and the Carolina silverbell.

The hike is straightforward for the length of the trail: keep climbing, keep passing amazing trees and lovely spring wildflowers until you reach the summit. At the 5,842-foot summit, you'll notice three things: wind, the temperature, and a **fire tower.** It's cooler, and can be quite windy, which makes the thought of climbing the 60-foot fire tower seem daunting. If you climb, do so carefully and remember the view you'll get at the end. On clear days you can see Balsam Mountain to the west, Mount Guyot to the northwest, Max Patch (along the Appalachian Trail on the TN/NC border) to the east, and Cataloochee Valley just below to the south. When you've had your fill of the views, follow the path back to the trailhead.

BIG CREEK TRAIL AND MOUNT STERLING LOOP

Distance: 17.4 miles round-trip

Duration: 10 hours

Elevation gain: 4,200 feet

Difficulty: strenuous

Trailhead: Big Creek Campground and Picnic Area off I-40 at Waterville (exit 457)

You can make this hike a killer day hike, or break it up into a one- or two-night backpacking experience. All three options follow the same route, with access to backcountry campsites.

Begin by following **Big Creek Trail,** which uses a Civilian Conservation Corps motor road to guide hikers to Rock House (an impressive rock cliff), Mouse Creek Falls, and Brakeshoe Springs. From **Brakeshoe Springs,** hike 2.3 miles to the junction with **Swallow Fork Trail.** If you plan to stay overnight, continue 0.2 mile to **Campsite 37** and Walnut Bottoms. (Campsite 37 is one of the best backcountry sites in the park, so consider a night here if you're backpacking.)

If pressing on, take Swallow Fork Trail and begin a gradual climb, crossing a couple of small streams along the way. You will reach **Swallow Fork** 1 mile in; cross it on a foot log and you'll reach **McGinty Creek** and the remains of what was once a sawmill. This section is lousy with wildflowers in the spring, so take your time and enjoy it when the blooms are out.

From McGinty Creek, hike approximately 1 mile before making one more stream crossing, then start a steep climb to **Pretty Hollow Gap.** At the gap, the **Mount Sterling Ridge Trail** intersects with Pretty Hollow Gap Trail (which reaches Cataloochee in a few miles); turn left (east) for Mount Sterling.

After turning onto Mount Sterling Ridge Trail, you'll find another steep climb, but it's only 0.5 mile and it eases up once you reach the top of the knob. From the top, it's 0.4 mile to the summit and the **fire tower.** Adjacent to the summit, is **Campsite 38,** for a first or second night in the backcountry. (If you're camping, note that it's often windy here and cooler due to the elevation, so pack appropriate sleeping gear.)

At the summit, the trail becomes **Baxter Creek Trail,** which you'll follow back to the Big Creek Trailhead. It's a steady downhill with a couple of notable landmarks. The first is a spring 0.2 mile from the summit, which you'll reach in 150 yards or so off the trail. The second landmark is 2 miles from the summit, where the trail makes a hairpin turn and plunges into another section of old-growth forest. Continue through some impressive and thick woods until arriving back at the trailhead.

MOUNT STERLING

Distance: 5.4 miles round-trip
Duration: 5-6 hours
Elevation gain: 1,900 feet
Difficulty: strenuous
Trailhead: Mount Sterling Trailhead at Mount Sterling Gap
Directions: From I-40, take Waterville (exit 457) and cross the Pigeon River. Stay left and follow the road 2 miles to Mount Sterling. Turn left and drive the curvy 6.7 miles to Mount Sterling Gap. The trailhead is on the west side of the road.

This hike starts off steep and it doesn't relent for a long time. Begin hiking up the trail to a junction with **Long Bunk Trail** in 0.5 mile. Continue climbing until you reach **Mount Sterling Ridge** at 2.3 miles. You have a little climbing left—0.4 mile—before you reach the **summit.** There's an additional 60-foot climb if you visit the fire tower, which has quite a view. On clear days you can see Balsam Mountain to the west, Mount Guyot to the northwest, Max Patch to the east, and Cataloochee Valley just below to the south. When ready, retrace your steps back to the trailhead.

Camping

The **Big Creek Campground** (off Hwy. 284/ Mt. Sterling Rd., 12 sites, first-come first-served, Apr.-Oct., $14) is located off Highway 284. Amenities include a ranger station, pay phone, drinking water, restrooms with flush toilets, a picnic area, and a group camp, as well as equestrian sites (**reservations required** at 877/444-6777 or www.recreation.gov, $25). Trailheads to Baxter Creek Trail, Big Creek Trail, and the Chestnut Branch of the Appalachian Trail lead from the campground.

Big Creek is close enough to the **Cherokee National Forest** (www.fs.usda. gov/Cherokee, free) to camp in the Pigeon River Recreation Zone. Dispersed camping is allowed provided campers are 100 feet

Big Creek Trail and Mount Sterling Loop

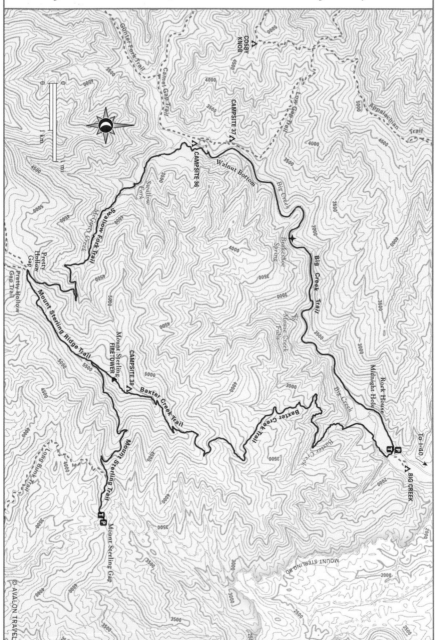

© AVALON TRAVEL

away from water, trails, parking areas, and developed recreation areas. To get there, take I-40 west into Tennessee and the national forest.

It is also possible to drive further north to the French Broad River Recreation Zone for more camping, hiking, and fishing opportunities. To get there within Tennessee, take Highway 701 north to Highway 107, which leads to several trailheads and recreation opportunities.

CATALOOCHEE VALLEY

Nestled in the folds of the mountains and encircled by 6,000-foot peaks, the Cataloochee Valley was settled in the early 1830s. This isolated valley on the northeastern edge of Great Smoky Mountains National Park was home to two communities—Big and Little Cataloochee—and more than 1,200 people in 1910. By the 1940s all but a few were gone, having left the valley for hills and hollows nearby. Today, this is one of the more beautiful spots in the national park, and a few historic structures are all that remain of the communities that thrived here, save a few memories and stories written down.

Cataloochee Valley is not far from I-40, but it can be a little difficult to find because the signage directing you here is poor at best. From I-40, take exit 20 onto US-276. Take an immediate right onto Cove Creek Road. The condition of the road—it's alternately gravel and paved—and the narrow, winding route will make you doubt you made the right turn, but you did. Zigzag up this road for about 12 miles and suddenly it will open up into the wide, grassy expanse that is Cataloochee Valley. Before you begin your descent into the valley, stop at the overlook just past the intersection with Big Creek Road. From here you can marvel at the valley sweeping away before you and the mountains rising up all around.

The valley is open to vehicle traffic from 8am to sunset, so keep that in mind if you're visiting without plans to camp. Though less visited than other areas, like Cades Cove on the western side of the park, Cataloochee sees its fair share of visitors. Most arrive in the evenings shortly before sunset to see the elk grazing in the fields. If you don't plan on camping and you'd rather avoid the crowds, as small as they may be, visit in midday and take a hike and see if you can find the elk in the woods; it's where they go to escape the heat.

★ Cataloochee

There are four prominent structures still standing in Cataloochee Valley: two homes, a school, and a church. A few other structures and ruins, cemeteries, fences, and walls remain throughout the valley as well. The most prominent building is the **Palmer Chapel and Cemetery.** The chapel was built in 1898, and it's been some time since there's been a regular service here. Today the chapel sees sporadic use, the most regular being the annual reunion of the descendants of some of the oldest Cataloochee families. Descendants of the Barnes, Bennett, Caldwell, Noland, and Palmer families gather here to eat, hold a short church service, and maintain the cemetery. Throughout the year there are some great opportunities to capture the chapel in all sorts of lighting, weather, and seasonal conditions.

Across the road is the **Beech Grove School,** the last of three schools to serve the children of the valley. It's empty save for a few artifacts. Beech Grove School operated on a very different school schedule than we're familiar with: The only regular school sessions were held from November to January, sometimes February and rarely into March. This odd schedule was built around the seasons, which freed children for planting and harvesting, as well as hunting and preserving food—staple activities for many living in the mountains.

Just up the road is the **Caldwell House.** We know from records that the owner, Hiram Caldwell, was prosperous, but you could tell that just by comparing this 1906 home with the other historic homes in the park, which

Cataloochee Valley

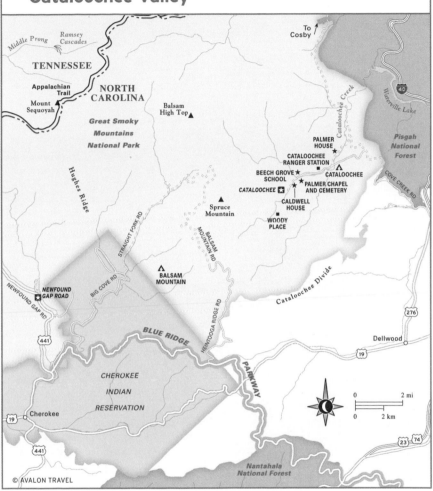

© AVALON TRAVEL

are, by and large, log cabins. The Caldwell House is frame-built (similar to houses now) with paneling on the interior walls.

The final structure is the **Palmer House,** located off Big Creek Road, not far from the Cataloochee Ranger Station. This was once a log home—two, actually, connected by a covered walkway called a dog trot—but as the owners came into money in the early 1900s, they began making improvements and remodeling the home. They covered the exterior and interior with weatherboarding and began using fancy wallpaper in some rooms (scraps of the wallpaper are there today). When the son inherited the property, he remodeled it, adding rooms to the home and operating it as a boardinghouse. Renters were primarily anglers who came to fish in the 3 miles of stocked trout stream the family owned.

Boogerman Trail

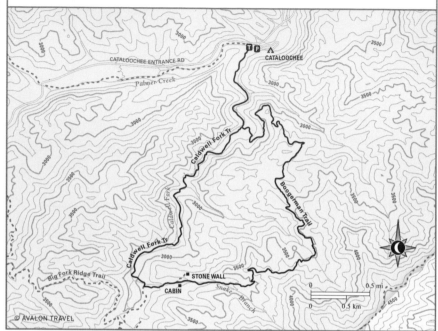

CATALOOCHEE ENTRANCE RD

Palmer Creek

CATALOOCHEE

Caldwell Fork Tr

Caldwell Fork

Boogerman Trail

Big Fork Ridge Trail

Caldwell Fork Tr

STONE WALL

CABIN

Snake Branch

0   0.5 mi

0   0.5 km

© AVALON TRAVEL

Hiking
BOOGERMAN TRAIL
Distance: 7.4-mile loop
Duration: 3.5-4 hours
Elevation gain: 1,050 feet
Difficulty: moderate
Trailhead: just past Cataloochee Campground

This trail isn't named for some fearsome and mythical creature from the woods; it's named for Robert "Boogerman" Palmer, the former owner of much of the land along this hike. Palmer is rumored to have earned his nickname in school, where he told his teacher that he wanted to be "the Boogerman" when he grew up. This trail is anything but fearsome, and in the summer you'll likely see a few other hikers; if it's solitude you're seeking, hit the trail during the shoulder seasons.

Start the hike by crossing **Palmer Creek.** Follow Caldwell Fork upstream for nearly a mile and you'll come to **Boogerman Trail.**

Turn left onto the trail and begin a gentle climb. When you reach a lower ridgeline, the path levels out, then descends through a grove of pine trees before ascending again. Soon, the trail makes a steep ascent to another level ridge. This section features some of the largest trees, mostly poplars, that you'll see on this hike.

As you continue on this short ridgeline section, you'll encounter some signs of human settlement, the first of which is a **stone wall.** Continue your descent and cross the stream you're following a few times, passing more rock walls along the way. If the wildflowers aren't too high, you may spot a large, strange piece of metal just off the trail. It's the remnant of some sort of homesteading equipment, perhaps a sluice gate for a water flume, or maybe a piece from a sawmill. Whatever it is, it's alien here.

When you pass the decayed remains of a **cabin,** you're close to the junction with

Caldwell Fork Trail. At **Caldwell Fork Trail,** turn right and cross Snake Branch (the stream you've been following) and soon thereafter, Caldwell Fork. You'll cross Caldwell Fork several more times before reaching the junction with **Boogerman Trail** and the path back to the trailhead.

ROUGH FORK TRAIL

Distance: 2 miles round-trip
Duration: 1 hour
Elevation gain: 50 feet
Difficulty: easy
Trailhead: Rough Fork Trailhead at the end of Cataloochee Road

One of the easiest hikes in the whole park, the Rough Fork Trail follows a gravel road for nearly the entire length of the trail. Three stream crossings on foot logs are highlights of the hike, which ends at the Steve Woody House.

The trailhead begins on the other side of a gate that marks the end of the paved road and the start of the gravel road. Follow the wide, flat road as it goes through the woods. The path parallels Rough Fork until it crosses on a **foot log.** (Foot logs are long logs that have been flattened on the top to create a walkway; they often have hand rails on one side and can be a little bouncy.) The foot logs across Rough Fork are a bit bouncy, but are fun and safe to cross.

Cross Rough Fork twice more via **footbridges,** then continue following the stream on the right as you make your way to the former home and springhouse (a small wooden shed built over a spring) of **Steve Woody.** Be careful around the springhouse because snakes are frequent visitors.

LITTLE CATALOOCHEE TRAIL

Distance: 6 miles one-way
Duration: 3.5-4 hours
Elevation gain: 2,400 feet
Difficulty: moderate
Trailhead: Pretty Hollow Gap/Cataloochee Horse Trail Trailhead adjacent to Beech Grove School

Little Cataloochee Trail is 6 miles point-to-point, so you'll need to arrange a car shuttle back to the trailhead. Alternatively, take a shorter hike from the other end of the trail.

Begin at the **Cataloochee Horse Camp** (you may have to park 0.2 mile back down by Cataloochee Entrance Rd.) and follow an old road that parallels Palmer Creek. At 0.8 mile, you'll reach the junction with **Little Cataloochee Trail.** Turn right (northeast) and follow Little Cataloochee to the end at Highway 284.

crossing the creek via a foot log on Rough Fork Trail

EASTERN SMOKIES **GREAT SMOKY MOUNTAINS NATIONAL PARK**

The Return of Native Elk

Elk are native to the mountains of North Carolina and Tennessee, but overhunting decimated their population across the region. In North Carolina, the last elk was believed to have been killed in the late 1700s; in Tennessee, the mid-1800s. In 2001, the National Park Service reintroduced elk to the park by bringing 25 elk to Great Smoky Mountains National Park from Land Between the Lakes National Recreation Area in Kentucky. The next year they brought in another 27 animals. Today, they believe somewhere between 150 and 200 elk live in the park.

The majority of the elk can be seen in the **Cataloochee Valley,** though a small herd lives near the **Oconaluftee Visitor Center** and **Smokemont Campground** and can be seen wading across the river and grazing in the fields and forest there.

Adult males, called bulls, weigh 600-700 pounds, while females, referred to as cows, weigh around 500 pounds. Some bulls have antlers that are five feet across. They're territorial, and bulls sometimes see humans as a threat and may charge. It's best to watch the elk from a safe distance. In Great Smoky Mountains National Park it is illegal to approach elk within 50 yards (150 feet) or any distance that disturbs or displaces the animals.

At certain times of the year, you may see calves walking close by their mothers. Never approach or touch a calf. If an elk calf feels threatened and its mother is not nearby, its natural defense is to lie down and be still. It may look orphaned, but mom's within earshot, so back away slowly.

Elk are most active in the early morning and evening, much like deer. Also like deer, their diet is primarily grass, bark, leaves, and acorns. There are no natural predators of elk in the Smokies today, though sick, injured, and young elk are sometimes targets of opportunity for black bears, coyotes, or even the boldest of bobcats.

As you hike, you can look for signs of former homesteads in the form of cultivated flowers like daffodils, yucca plants, and fruit trees. There are many **homestead sites** along the trail, but most are grown over, though you can spot them.

For a while the trail will be steep; at approximately 3 miles, you'll meet up with an old roadbed that makes the hike easier. At 3.3 miles, you'll reach **Dan Cook Place,** a cabin that was reconstructed after the original was destroyed by vandals in the mid-1970s. Continue along the trail to the **Little Cataloochee Baptist Church** and **cemetery.** The original church has been maintained and is the site of occasional services.

From the church, the road descends rather steeply, passing the former community of **Ola.** Follow the road to a short side trail leading to **John Hackson Hannah Cabin,** then a junction with **Long Bunk Trail.** It's another 1.1 miles to the end of the trail at Highway 284. Use a car shuttle, or hike back along the road (adds another 3 miles or so), or backtrack to make this a big 12-mile day.

For a shorter hike that sees a few historic structures, drive to the end of the trail on Highway 284 (the trailhead is marked) and hike to the Little Cataloochee Baptist Church and Dan Cook Place (6 miles round-trip).

Fishing

Fishing is plentiful off **Cataloochee Creek** and its tributaries, with the main quarry being wild trout.

Camping

The ★ **Cataloochee Campground** (Cataloochee Entrance Rd., 877/444-6777, www.recreation.gov, Mar.-Oct., $20, reservations required) has 27 tent and RV sites. There is also a horse camp with seven sites not far up the valley; down the valley there's a group campground with three sites and room for much larger parties. This highly recommended campsite is one of the most secluded you'll find in the front country. The campground is located 3.1 miles along the entrance road.

BALSAM MOUNTAIN ROAD

Since most of the crowds who visit Great Smoky Mountains National Park use Newfound Gap Road exclusively, it's nice to find a route that's less traveled and possibly more beautiful. One such route is **Balsam Mountain Road** (open May-Nov.), a lovely drive where you may be lucky to see 10 other cars.

Accessible only from the Blue Ridge Parkway near Soco Gap, the road traverses 14 miles of ridgeline. To reach Balsam Mountain Road, turn off the Parkway at Milepost 458 and follow Heintooga Ridge Road to the Heintooga Overlook and Picnic Area; here the road changes names to Balsam Mountain Road, and turns to gravel.

As soon as it turns into Balsam Mountain Road, it becomes one-way, so you're committed to follow it to its end. This will take about 1.5 hours (if you don't stop to hike or take in the scenery), primarily because the gravel road forces you to slow down. It's narrow but well maintained, so you can drive most cars along the route. If you're in doubt of the road's condition or are concerned about your vehicle's clearance, check online (www.nps.gov/grsm) for road closures and advisories.

Balsam Mountain Road is an excellent place to see spring wildflowers, summer rhododendron, and fall leaves. At these times, traffic may pick up, but the idea of a gravel road discourages enough visitors to keep this road the one less traveled.

When you've driven about 13 miles along Balsam Mountain Road, it becomes two-way again. Here, it begins to follow Straight Fork, which will lead you right onto Straight Fork Road (closed in winter), which cuts through the Cherokee Indian Reservation to US-441.

Hiking
FLAT CREEK TRAIL
Distance: 5.2 miles round-trip
Duration: 3.5-4 hours
Elevation gain: 900 feet
Difficulty: moderate
Trailhead: Heintooga Overlook and Picnic Area

You can hike Flat Creek Trail as a 5.2-mile out-and-back trail or do it as a 6.2-mile loop. If following the loop, note that the last 3.6 miles are along Heintooga Ridge Road (closed May-Nov.).

From the picnic area, walk out to **Heintooga Overlook** for a great view. Just past the overlook the trail forks; go right and follow **Flat Creek Trail** as it descends, crossing the creek and entering a rhododendron thicket. Soon the forest opens up and becomes grassy, a sign of previous logging activity.

At 1.9 miles, you'll reach a path (right) that leads to Flat Creek Falls, but don't bother—the views aren't good and it's difficult (and dangerous) to try. Stay on Flat Creek Trail as the trail enters a thick forest, descends, and then crosses a fork of **Bunches Creek.** Shortly after Bunches Creek, you'll climb up to **Heintooga Ridge Road.** Turn around and head back, or continue hiking up the road for a 6-mile hike.

BALSAM MOUNTAIN TRAIL
Distance: 8.2 miles round-trip
Duration: 6 hours
Elevation gain: 3,000 feet
Difficulty: strenuous
Trailhead: Balsam Mountain Road, 8.2 miles from the end of Heintooga Ridge Road at Pin Oak Gap

You have two choices for this hike: a long day hike or an overnighter with a stay at Laurel Gap Shelter. The route is the same no matter which you hike. Laurel Gap Shelter is only 4.1 miles from the trailhead, so if you chose to stay, you'll either have two easy days or one long day if you decide to hike to the summit of Balsam High Top then on to the shelter for water and rest.

The straightforward trail climbs

aggressively uphill for 1.9 miles, where you'll reach the now-overgrown **Ledge Bald** and begin to ascend. In 0.4 mile is the junction with **Beech Gap Trail,** which comes in from the left (west) and leads back to Balsam Mountain Road after a 2.5-mile hike. Ignore the trail and press on, ascending again until you reach the ridge. Follow the ridge through a hardwood forest to a grove of fir trees, the mountain's namesake balsam trees. These trees mark **Balsam High Top,** the 3.5-mile mark on the trail. To visit the summit (no views, just do it if you're a peakbagger), you'll have to go off-trail. Otherwise, keep hiking another 0.6 mile to **Laurel Gap Shelter** and the spring there. Make camp or get a little water, have a snack, and rest up. When you're ready, hike out by backtracking the trail.

Camping

The frontcountry campground at **Balsam Mountain** (46 sites, first-come first-served, May-Oct., $14) is located off Balsam Mountain Road at Heintooga Ridge Road. Amenities include an amphitheater, a small section for tents-only, restrooms, and a ranger station with nearby access to Round Bottom Picnic Area and the Flat Creek trailhead.

An equestrian-friendly campground at **Round Bottom Horse Camp** (Round Bottom-Straight Fork Rd., 865/436-1261 or 877/444-6777, www.recreation.gov, Apr.-Oct., $20) has five campsites, pit toilets, stalls, and bedding for horses. Its location north of Cherokee, just inside the park and far up narrow Big Cove Road, makes it perfect for long rides with larger groups.

Western Smokies

The western Smokies are a bit wilder than the eastern Smokies. As pioneers moved in from the east, they first settled the coves and hollows there, then found passes through the Smokies and settled there. The mountains are tall and steep, and the valleys deep, and where there are coves and meadows, they're broad, rich-soiled places that, before the national park, were home to several small communities.

LITTLE RIVER ROAD
Elkmont

At the **Elkmont Campground,** only 8 miles from Gatlinburg, drifts of male fireflies rise up from the grass to flash their mating signal, but they don't do so as individuals—they blink in coordinated ways that still baffle researchers. For a two-week window every summer (often **early to mid-July,** but it depends on a variety of factors), their nightly light show delights crowds. It starts slowly, with only a few of these insects showing off. Then more join in, and more until they reach a crescendo.

Slowly, they begin to synchronize until, at the peak, whole fields may flash all at once, giving you a sudden and startling blink of light and just as sudden darkness. Or they may flash in waves moving around the fields and hillsides. Or large groups may appear to flash their lights at one another and wait in the darkness for a response. Whatever the reason for their display, the synchronous fireflies are amazing little creatures. Nineteen species of fireflies live in Great Smoky Mountains National Park, but these are the only fireflies in the park to synchronize their flashing.

The synchronous fireflies may have been one of the reasons the Wonderland Park Hotel was built here in Elkmont. In 1908, the little logging town of Elkmont was born, and in 1912, the Wonderland Park Hotel was built. Cottages dotted the hillsides and bottoms. Once the park was established, cottage owners were granted lifetime leases on their property, and family members continued to renew the leases at 20-year intervals until the early 1990s. The Wonderland Park Hotel and the

The Firefly Lottery

Viewing the synchronous fireflies at Elkmont is deservedly popular—so much so, that in 2016, the park instituted a lottery system to control access and limit traffic congestion. The new lottery assigns parking passes and provides shuttle transportation during the eight days of the event (late-May to early June). Hopeful visitors can apply online during the three days the lottery (877/444-6777, www.recreation.gov, limit one pass per household, passes are free, $1.50 application fee) is open; applicants will have two dates to choose from. Once the lottery closes, results become available about a week later. Up to 1,800 parking passes will be made available (about 225 cars per day). The lucky winners will receive a parking pass for Sugarlands Visitor Center; after parking at your assigned arrival time, you'll board the shuttle to Elkmont and back.

In 2016, the lottery opened on April 29 and closed May 2. Successful applicants received notices of their passes by May 10. At time of publication, it remains to be seen whether the lottery system was successful, or the resulting impact on attendance. While there are other places within the park to see fireflies—pretty much any meadow or grassy area—only Elkmont has the synchronous fireflies.

cottages were at one time slated for demolition, but the **Elkmont Historic District** is now listed in the National Register of Historic Places. The hotel collapsed in the early 2000s, and the Park Service has visions of restoring a few of the remaining cottages, but work has yet to begin in earnest.

Other properties include the **Appalachian Clubhouse** (500 Elkmont Rd., 877/444-6777, www.recreation.gov, Apr.-mid-Nov., $250-400 daily venue rental), which has been restored to its 1930s glory. The clubhouse hosts a number of special events every year. The enormous meeting space is anchored by a stone fireplace at one end; doors along the east side open to a large covered porch. A sizable caterer's kitchen (it's bare bones: outlets and counters only, no appliances or refrigerators) means the building can easily house a large meeting, wedding reception, or get together of any kind.

The **Spence Cabin** (500 Elkmont Rd., 877/444-6777, www.recreation.gov, Apr.-Oct., $150-200 daily venue rental), also called River Lodge, is a restored historic Elkmont building that serves as a base for special events and gatherings. Smaller than the Appalachian Clubhouse, this restored cabin shows off what it was like to vacation here in the 1920s and '30s; meeting rooms are smaller with no large central gathering place.

Neither the Appalachian Clubhouse nor Spence Cabin lack for charm, but these are not overnight accommodations; rather, they are event spaces ideal for day-long events like family reunions, Scout Troop meetings, and corporate retreats.

Hiking

LAUREL FALLS TRAIL

Distance: 2.5 miles round-trip
Duration: 1.5-2 hours
Elevation gain: 400 feet
Difficulty: easy to moderate
Trailhead: parking area 3.9 miles west of Sugarlands Visitor Center on Little River Road

As the shortest and possibly easiest waterfall hike in Great Smoky Mountains National Park, Laurel Falls is the most popular of such hikes. The trail is paved and the grade is gentle (after you get past a short, steep section at the start of the trail), and the falls are a little over 1.3 miles from the trailhead.

Prepare to be dazzled when you reach the falls. Laurel Falls drops 75 feet in a wide, picture-perfect cascade. It's a gorgeous spot to photograph, but you have to be there early in the day to get a shot of the falls without people in it.

SUGARLAND MOUNTAIN

Distance: 12.3 miles one-way
Duration: 6 hours
Elevation gain: 5,308 feet
Difficulty: easy
Trailhead: Fork Ridge Trailhead 3.5 miles west on Clingmans Dome Road

This is a long hike at 12.3 miles, so you'll need to arrange for a car shuttle system at one end of the trail. Fortunately, the hiking is all downhill—which can be just as taxing as uphill, so watch your footing and hike at a sustainable pace. There have been numerous bear sightings around this trail, so keep your eyes and ears open.

From the Fighting Creek Gap Trailhead, drive up to Clingmans Dome Road (closed in winter) and begin the hike downhill. The trail begins by taking a short access trail to the **Appalachian Trail.** Turn left on the **Appalachian Trail** and hike 0.3 mile to a junction with Sugarland Mountain Trail. Turn right and take **Sugarland Mountain Trail,** your path for the next 12 miles.

The first mile is a rocky trail through a spruce-fir forest that is somewhat reminiscent of The Forest Moon of Endor from *Return of the Jedi*. About 0.3 mile after start is the **Mount Collins backcountry shelter**—other than that, it's just wildflowers and songbirds. After one mile, you'll begin to climb. Views open up here and there, giving you a glimpse of Mount LeConte and the Chimneys, and, in the distance, Pigeon Forge and Gatlinburg.

The trail passes below the summit of **Sugarland Mountain** (5,494 feet) at 2.3 miles. It's an off-trail scramble to reach the true top, so it's best to stick to the trail.

From here the trail descends, then, at the 3.5-mile point, begins to climb slightly and makes a sharp western turn. At this point, you should have a good view of Gatlinburg and the Chimneys (if the weather's clear). Continue downhill; the trail becomes easier as the woods change from fir-dominant to a hardwood forest. At 8.3 miles is what was once **Campground 21.** You'll reach **Huskey**

Gap Trail in 9.3 miles and a view of Mount LeConte that may be overgrown.

At 11 miles is **Mids Gap** and an 0.5-mile-long uphill stretch. After a downhill day, it will feel big. Once you top out, begin a steep descent down to the trailhead and your shuttle car.

LITTLE RIVER TRAIL

Distance: 12.3 miles round-trip
Duration: 4.5 hours
Elevation gain: 1,100 feet
Difficulty: easy
Trailhead: Elkmont Campground

This hike looks long, and it can be if you hike the whole length. Or you can follow as much of it as you want for a hike of 1, 2, or 10 miles. In the spring, the trail is filled with wildflowers; in October, it's a fall-color extravaganza; and year-round you'll see anglers fly-fishing in the water by the path. But in **late spring,** this is the place to be to see the **synchronous fireflies.** The path here was once used for logging and you'll see evidence of this all along the route—look around and you'll notice there's no old growth as in some sections of the park.

The first mile passes through the homeland of the synchronous fireflies, those curious fireflies that blink in unison during their spring mating season; the rest of the hike is a trek alongside the **Little River.** At times the path is a bit more like a trail than a road, but it always follows the logging roadbed.

Most hikers turn around at the 3.7-mile mark, the point where Little River Trail meets **Goshen Prong Trail.** I recommend pressing on a little farther, only 0.2 mile or so to a **bridge** over the river, which is quite scenic.

CUCUMBER GAP AND LITTLE RIVER LOOP

Distance: 5.5 miles round-trip
Duration: 2.5-3 hours
Elevation gain: 800 feet
Difficulty: easy to moderate
Trailhead: Elkmont Campground

This hike makes a loop using Cucumber Gap

Trail and a portion of Little River Trail. It's a lovely hike for wildflowers in spring and fall color in October. The trails are easy; the railroad bed of Little River Trail and the typical forest trail of Cucumber Gap make a good combination and the length is just about perfect for a day hike.

Just past the **Little River Trailhead** is a second parking area to the right of the gate; park here to start the trail on the gravel road past the gate on **Jakes Creek Trail.** There's a steep, but short climb to the junction with Cucumber Gap. **Cucumber Gap** will give you a break from climbing—it's a long, gentle ascent through the tulip tree-dominated forest. Cross **Huskey Branch** just a little ways above the waterfall, which you'll see in a few moments. After reaching the junction with Little River Trail, turn left and cross Huskey Branch again, this time right at **Huskey Branch Falls.** From here it is 2 easy miles back to the Little River trailhead and parking area.

Backpacking

The **Great Smoky Mountains Institute at Tremont** (9275 Tremont Rd., Townsend, TN, 865/448-6709, www.gsmit.org) offers a range of outdoor and Smoky-centric educational opportunities. Classrooms and offices are located just off TN-73/Little River Road (0.2 mile beyond the intersection to Townsend). At the end of this road is a long, but excellent, hike that will get you on the Appalachian Trail and provide some of the best photo opportunities the park has to offer.

LYNN CAMP PRONG

Distance: 21 miles round-trip
Duration: 12 hours or 1-2 days
Elevation gain: 3,650 feet
Difficulty: strenuous
Trailhead: Road near the Great Smoky Mountains Institute at Tremont

This hike is picture-postcard perfect (seriously, you'll see shots from this trail on park postcards and calendars)—and brutal. If you want to get deep in the Smokies and experience the rugged, wild nature of this place, this hike is for you. If you'd rather get some trail miles in and see some beautiful scenery, you can do that too, but the hike will be considerably shorter and take much less time.

At first, this trail seems easy as it follows a gravel road and old railroad grade for the first 0.5 mile. At 0.5 mile, you'll see a photographer's dream: **Lynn Camp Prong,**

sunrise over the Little River

a large set of cascades on the stream. For the next 0.2 mile or so, you'll have plenty of chances for some great photos—don't be surprised if you see a number of other photo hounds out here.

After passing the cascades, the trail continues to follow the creek for 3 more miles, where a bridge crosses **Indian Flats Prong.** Now the trail begins to grow steep. If you're thinking of cutting the hike short, push on through this steep section to **Indian Flats Falls** (4 miles), then turn around.

Continue on and turn left (north) on **Lynn Camp Prong Trail.** Campsite 28 is located another 1.5 miles up the trail. To stay the night, reserve a campsite in advance through the **Backcountry Information Office** (Sugarlands Visitor Center, 865/436-1297, 8am-5pm daily, https://smokiespermits. nps.gov, $4/night). You can also push on to Derrick Knob Shelter along the Appalachian Trail, another 6 miles or so up the trail.

From Campsite 28, it's a nonstop 2.2-mile climb to the ridgeline and the junction with **Miry Ridge Trail.** Turn right at the junction and continue 2.5 miles to a junction with the **Appalachian Trail.** Turn right and face the steepest climb of the hike as you ascend **Cold Spring Knob.** Finally, descend to a junction with **Greenbrier Ridge Trail.** (If you're staying at Derrick Knob Shelter, it's another 0.3 mile down the trail.) To continue, turn right and hike northeast down Greenbrier Ridge Trail.

As you descend, you'll encounter a pair of lovely stream crossings that may distract you with their beauty, but pay attention (especially in high water) as the footing can be tricky and the water strong. After passing the second creek crossing, you're now within 0.5 mile of **Indian Flats Falls** and the easy hike alongside Lynn Camp Prong back to the trailhead.

Fishing

Anglers take note: this area of the park offers some fantastic fishing. Along the east prong of **Little River** and all along Little River proper you can reel in trout, smallmouth bass, and rock bass. The formation of the bottom along the East Prong and along Little River is right for smallmouth and rock bass: rocky, heavy with roots and some debris, filled with plenty of nooks and crannies to hide, but with plenty of deep pools and slow currents where the feeding is good. In the headwaters you can find places that trout love.

Camping

The **Elkmont Campground** (434 Elkmont Rd., Gatlinburg, TN, 865/430-5560, www. recreation.gov, $17-23) has 220 campsites, 55 of them along the Little River, with front-row seats to the firefly light show for those here at the right time. This is the largest of the campgrounds in Great Smoky Mountains National Park, and one of the most visited. In addition to the firefly show and the attraction of Little River, this site also serves as a good base for exploring the area.

Elkmont Campground Concessions (www.elkmontcampgroundconcession.net, 4pm-8pm daily Mar. 8-May, 9am-9pm daily June-Aug. 15, 4pm-8pm daily Aug. 16-Oct., 4pm-6pm daily Nov.) has a handful of snack foods and beverages as well as firewood, ice, and a few camping items.

CADES COVE

Easily the most popular auto tour loop in Great Smoky Mountains National Park, Cades Cove receives around two million visitors a year. They come for the scenery—a long, wide, grassy-bottomed valley surrounded by undulating mountains—to see the handful of preserved homesteads and historic structures, and because it's one of the park's best, and most reliable, spots to see wildlife.

★ Cades Cove Loop

The **Cades Cove Loop** is approximately 11 miles long, but in the summer and especially in the fall when the leaves are at their best, expect to spend two hours or more on this one-way road through the valley floor—and that's if you don't stop to photograph the wildlife

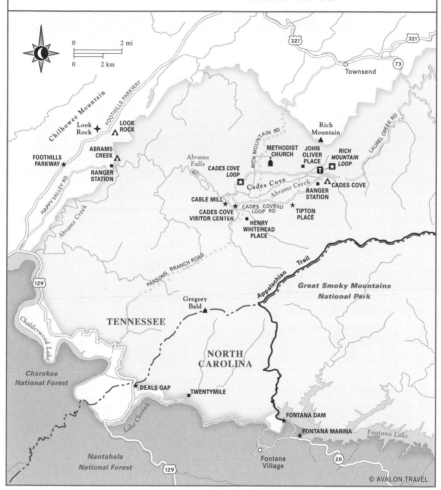

Cades Cove and Fontana Lake Area

© AVALON TRAVEL

or explore the historic structures. If you're the curious type or find the light is perfect for taking pictures, you can easily double the amount of time you spend here. When you do stop, be sure to pull off the road and leave enough room for traffic to pass. One source of traffic jams in Cades Cove is visitors who stop in the middle of the road to ooh and aah at the wildlife and scenery.

The popularity of this drive is well deserved. In the hours around dawn and dusk,

wildlife is especially active. Vast herds of white-tailed deer are the most common sight (I once tallied 50 in a field before I quit counting), but black bears are also frequently spotted. The bears like to cozy up to the apple trees that dot the cove, and you'll occasionally spot them and their cubs napping or eating in the branches.

You may notice that the fields look especially manicured. They are, to an extent. Far from being mown and maintained like a golf

Black Bears

Biologists estimate there are more than 1,500 black bears living in Great Smoky Mountains National Park, and if you know where and when to look, your chances of seeing one in the wild are quite good.

Though I've seen bears in a number of spots throughout the park, one of the most reliable places to see them is **Cades Cove.** Here, in the early morning and as dusk settles, the bears are more active, prowling the forest's edge and even eating apples that have fallen from the trees.

As awesome as it is to see a bear, they can present a problem to park visitors, and we can present a problem to them. With the great number of visitors to Great Smoky Mountains National Park, many bears have grown accustomed to seeing people and have therefore lost their natural fear of humans, automobiles, and horses. As they grow more used to people, we decide to give them "treats" and lure them closer to our cars and our campsites with food. Bears that are too accustomed to people, especially bears that have been fed a few times, can grow bold, even borderline aggressive, searching campsites and open cars for food or even approaching open car windows or picnic tables.

Fortunately, serious incidents with black bears are rare, but they do occur. In 2000, a mother bear and her cub attacked and killed a camper near the Elkmont Campground. Every year, campsites and trails are closed due to bear activity and the potential for interaction between bears and visitors.

Park staff and volunteers do their best to educate visitors on proper human-bear interaction. Throughout the park you'll see signs and placards advising you on how to properly store and dispose of food and reminding you not to approach bears. Remember that bears are wild animals and unpredictable, and keep these tips in mind:

- **Do not approach** within 50 yards or any distance that disturbs a bear, and do not allow a bear to approach you. For a good view, invest in a pair of binoculars.

- **Never feed bears.** It only gets them used to humans and causes them to think of us as a source of food.

- **Store food** in appropriate containers and in the proper places when camping. If you're not sure of the proper procedure, ask a ranger.

- **Dispose of garbage** in bear-proof receptacles.

- **Report** nuisance bear behavior or visitors breaking these rules to park officials.

In the unlikely event that **a bear approaches you,** stand tall, wave your arms, and make as much noise as possible. If you need to, throw sticks or rocks at the bear. In most cases, this will intimidate the bear and deter it from coming any closer. If the bear charges, don't run—they can sprint 30 miles per hour, so you don't stand a chance. Instead, keep making noise and back away slowly, never turning your back to the bear. Often, bears will make bluff charges, so this is likely what you're seeing. If a black bear actually makes contact, fight back with anything and everything available to you; with a loud-enough and fierce-enough fight, the bear may see you as too much to deal with and leave you alone.

course, the fields in Cades Cove are allowed to run wild, but only so wild. The National Park Service maintains the fields and fences, mowing, repairing, and reseeding as necessary to keep the valley looking much like it did when settlers lived here.

To take this lovely-in-any-season drive, follow Little River Road west from the Sugarlands Visitor Center for 17.2 miles; there it will turn into Laurel Creek Road and lead you into Cades Cove in another 7.4 miles. You can also access Cades Cove by entering the park at Townsend on TN-73, then turning right on Laurel Creek Road, following it for 16 miles to the entrance to the cove. Cades Cove is closed to vehicle traffic every Saturday and Wednesday morning from May until late September. On those days, the loop is open exclusively to bicycle and foot traffic until 10am. The rest of the year the road is open to motor vehicles from sunrise to sunset daily, weather permitting.

Sights

According to some historians, long before European settlers pushed west through the Smokies, the Cherokee Indians had hunting camps and possibly even a small settlement established in Cades Cove. In fact, the name Cades Cove is believed to have come from Chief Kade, a little-known Cherokee leader. By the early 1820s, the first Europeans were here, building cabins and barns and carving homesteads out of the forest. More settlers arrived having heard of the rich, fertile bottomland in Cades Cove, and by 1850 nearly 700 people called the valley home. As the collection of cabins and homesteads grew into a community, buildings like churches and schools were constructed. Families lived here even after the National Park Service began purchasing land. The last remaining school in Cades Cove closed in 1944 and the post office in 1947.

Today, a number of historic structures remain standing along the valley floor. Among them is the most photographed structure in the park, the **Methodist Church.** From time to time a wedding is held here, though it's more common for visitors to leave handwritten prayers on scraps of paper at the altar.

The **Cable Mill Area** is the busiest section of the loop. Here you can see an actual mill in operation, and can even buy cornmeal or flour ground on-site. In addition to the mill and Methodist Church, the area contains two other churches, a few barns, and log houses, and a number of smaller structures.

Halfway around the loop, you'll find the **Cades Cove Visitor Center** (Cades Cove Loop Rd., Townsend, TN, 865/448-2472, 9am-4:30pm daily Dec.-Jan., except Christmas Day, 9am-5:30pm daily Feb. and Nov., 9am-6:30pm daily Mar. and Sept.-Oct., 9am-7pm daily Apr. and Aug., 9am-7:30pm daily May-June), which has a good bookstore and gift shop, and, most important, the only public restroom you'll find on the tour.

taking a break at Cable Mill in Cades Cove

Hiking

ABRAMS FALLS TRAIL

Distance: 5 miles round-trip
Duration: 3 hours
Elevation gain: 350 feet
Difficulty: moderate
Trailhead: Turn right onto a gravel road 4.9 miles from the start of the Cades Cove Loop; at 0.4 mile in is a parking area and the trailhead.

Several trails lead off into the woods from this parking area, but it's obvious which route to take—the most well-worn trail you see. If you're in doubt, follow the group in front of you, as Abrams Falls is the destination for most hikers who set off from this lot. Only a few steps from the trailhead is a **kiosk** that will set you on the right path.

The trail is pretty straightforward—it follows **Abrams Creek** all the way to the waterfall. The only real elevation gains come when you thrice leave the creek to climb up and around a ridge, crossing a feeder stream in the process. The first stream is Arbutus Branch, then Stony Branch, then Wilson Branch, which is very close to the falls.

After you cross Wilson Branch on a **log bridge,** you'll follow the trail downstream, cross Wilson Branch once again, and arrive at the falls.

Abrams Falls is pretty, and in wet weather can be downright thunderous. Slick, mossy rocks make up the wall where the 20-foot waterfall, which has the largest volume of water of any waterfall in the park, tumbles into the pool below. Tempted as you may be to take a dip after a sweaty hike, don't do it; the currents are strong and a few folks have drowned here.

ROCKY TOP AND THUNDERHEAD MOUNTAINS TRAIL

Distance: 13.9 miles round-trip
Duration: 7-8 hours
Elevation gain: 3,665 feet
Difficulty: strenuous
Trailhead: Anthony Creek Trailhead at the Cades Cove picnic area

Hiking to the famed Rocky Top is borderline brutal—you gain more than 3,500 feet in elevation, and on the trail's first few miles you share the path with horses, so it can get quite muddy and slippery. However, this exceptional hike is worth it. Time your hike for mid-June to see the rhododendron and mountain laurel in full bloom.

Shortly after starting the **Anthony Creek Trail,** you'll reach Crib Trail Junction, then **Anthony Creek Horse Camp** (reservations required, 877/444-6777, www.recreation.gov, $20). Follow Anthony Creek Trail 3.5 miles to the **Bote Mountain Trail,** where hikers will turn right.

Climbing Bote Mountain Trail, you'll enter a long series of rhododendron "tunnels" and at 5.1 miles in, you'll reach **Spence Field** and the **Appalachian Trail.** Turn left and you'll get some stunning views of North Carolina and equally stunning views of hillsides and meadows covered in mountain laurel. Continue east along the Appalachian Trail to reach Rocky Top and Thunderhead Mountain.

Thunderhead Mountain is made up of three distinct summits. The first summit is **Rocky Top,** 1.2 miles from the Bote Mountain/Appalachian Trail junction and arguably the best view in the park. Next is the middle peak, sometimes called **Rocky Top Two,** just 0.3 mile beyond Rocky Top. Finally, another 0.3 mile on, is the unremarkable summit of **Thunderhead.** Many hikers turn around at Rocky Top, never summiting Thunderhead.

★ RICH MOUNTAIN LOOP

Distance: 8.5-mile loop
Duration: 4-4.5 hours
Elevation gain: 1,740 feet
Difficulty: moderate
Trailhead: Park at the entrance gate to Cades Cove; the trail begins in the opposite parking lot.

The first part of this hike passes one of the meadows that makes Cades Cove such a fabulous place. For 1.4 miles you'll walk through the woods and along the edge of the meadow until you reach the **John Oliver Cabin.**

Rich Mountain Loop

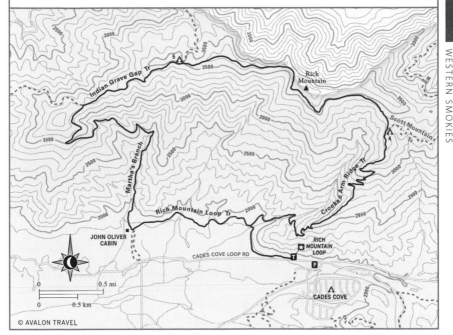

The trail continues behind the cabin and soon meets up with **Martha's Branch** and begins to climb. As you climb, you'll cross the branch a number of times. At mile 3, you'll find a place where you have a tight view of Cades Cove; don't sweat it, better views are coming.

Continue 0.3 mile to **Indian Grave Gap Trail** and turn right. In 0.8 mile is **Campsite 5** (for backpackers) and the junction with Rich Mountain Trail. The saddle here has nice views.

Avoid the junction and follow Indian Grave Gap Trail 0.3 mile to a side trail. This path is only about 100 yards long and takes you to the highest point on Rich Mountain, **Cerulean Knob,** and the foundation of the former fire tower. Views are okay, but not fantastic. Get back to the main trail and continue east where you'll find a much better view than on the top.

When you reach a power-line clearance, you're almost at **Scott Mountain Trail** and

Campsite 4. From the junction of these trails, continue straight ahead on **Crooked Arm Ridge Trail** (it's what Indian Grave Gap Trail turns into). This trail is steep and rutted and littered with the evidence of horses, so watch your step—that horse evidence can be slippery.

This trail leads back to **Rich Mountain Loop Trail** 0.5 mile from the parking area.

CHESTNUT TOP TRAIL

Distance: 5.4 miles one-way

Duration: 4 hours

Elevation gain: 1,950 feet

Difficulty: strenuous

Trailhead: Chestnut Top trailhead, 100 yards north of the Townsend "Y" where Little River Road meets TN Route 73

Chestnut Top Trail can be tackled two ways: As an end-to-end hike with a shuttle vehicle at either end, or as an out-and-back, which makes for a longer hike. Either way, this hike is filled with wildflowers in the spring and is quite lovely.

After parking across TN-73 from the **trailhead,** lace up and get ready to go. The first 0.6 mile is a steady climb. In the spring, the forest is carpeted with wildflowers; the first flowers appear in early March and flowers will continue to bloom for the next two months.

As soon as you wrap up this killer climb, the trail levels out a little. That soon ends as you begin climbing again toward **Schoolhouse Gap** along **Chestnut Top Lead. Tuckaleechee Cove** is to the right of the trail; you'll catch glimpses of it through summer foliage and have good views of it the rest of the year.

At 4.3 miles you'll reach a junction with **Schoolhouse Gap Trail.** Turn around here for an out-and-back hike of 8.6 miles (which is almost all downhill), or turn left on Schoolhouse Gap Trail and continue hiking 1.1 miles to the **Schoolhouse Gap Trailhead** on Little River Road (requires a shuttle car).

Biking

The **Cades Cove Store** (near Cades Cove Campground, 865/448-9034) rents bicycles in summer and fall (adult bikes $7.50/hour, kids' bikes $4.50/hour). Plan to get there early—well before the campground store opens. (I showed up 30 minutes before the store opened and took my place 40 deep in line. I did not rent a bike that day.)

The park closes off the loop road through Caves Cove on Wednesday and Saturday mornings (sunrise-10am) from the second week in May until the second-to-last Saturday in September, so that cyclists and hikers can enjoy the cove without having to worry about automobile traffic.

Camping

The **Cades Cove Campground** (10042 Campground Dr., Townsend, TN, 877/444-6777, www.recreation.gov, $17-20) is a popular

spot where you'll definitely want to reserve a campsite. This campground is open year-round, and though the occupancy is a little lower in the dead of winter, you'll still find a few intrepid visitors taking refuge from the cold in one of the 159 campsites here. Hikers, take note: There are several backcountry campsites off the trails in Cades Cove, making it a good base for overnight trips.

At the **Cades Cove Campground Store** (865/448-9034, www.cadescovetrading.com, 9am-5pm daily Mar.-May, 9am-9pm daily June-Aug. 15, 9am-5pm daily Aug. 16-Nov.) you can grab breakfast, a sandwich or wrap, pizza, and other snack bar items as well as a very limited selection of groceries and camping supplies.

Parsons Branch Road

Parsons Branch Road (closed in winter) is a great drive. Take a right turn just beyond the Cades Cove Visitor Center parking area and you'll find yourself on a 10-mile long, one-way gravel road leading to US-129 and Deals Gap on the extreme southwestern edge of the park. At times pothole riddled and crossing 18 or so small streams along the way, the road is a slow one, taking around an hour to drive. If you're careful, the drive is doable in a sedan, but you may feel more comfortable in a vehicle with a little more clearance.

The road passes **Henry Whitehead Place,** an odd-looking pair of conjoined cabins with an interesting backstory. Henry Whitehead, a widower with three daughters, remarried Matilda Shields Gregory after she and her small child had been abandoned by her husband. During the crisis, the community rallied and built her the small cabin, which is in back of the main structure that Whitehead built after they married.

You'll cross the same stream several times before climbing to the crest of the drive. Here you'll find the trailhead for **Gregory Bald Trail.** This is the halfway mark of the road and it is, as they say, all downhill from here.

GREGORY BALD TRAIL

Distance: 11.4 miles round-trip
Duration: 6-7 hours
Elevation gain: 3,370 feet
Difficulty: strenuous
Trailhead: Cades Cove, 2 miles down Parsons Branch Road

The hike to Gregory Bald is a tough one. The trail is steep, you gain more than 3,000 feet, and to finish in a reasonable amount of time your pace has to be quick and constant. Tackle this trail if you're confident in your endurance or if you have a little extra time to spare in case it takes longer to complete. Note that Parsons Branch Road may close seasonally.

Start off with an easy uphill—think of it as a warm-up—to the top of a short knob before the trail levels off. Cross **Forge Creek,** then enter an old-growth forest thick with rhododendron. How thick? So thick that even though you'll be close to the creek for a little ways, you won't often see or hear it. Follow this trail and cross the creek twice more.

Soon you'll pass **Campsite 12** and begin to climb a steep ridge via a set of switchbacks. The rhododendron gives way to galax and mountain laurel, even blueberry bushes, as you climb. Moderate your pace because it's all uphill until you're within 0.2 mile of **Rich Gap.**

At Rich Gap you'll find a four-way intersection. Straight ahead leads to Moore Spring; left leads to the Appalachian Trail at Doe Knob (2.1 miles). Turn west (right) on **Gregory Bald Trail** and follow the ridgeline to Gregory Bald.

From Gregory Bald you'll have some great views—provided it's not too foggy in the valley. To the northeast you can see Cades Cove; to the southwest are the Unicoi Mountains and Joyce Kilmer-Slickrock Wilderness; and to the south is Fontana Lake and Shuckstack Tower. Unfortunately you can't see anything to the west because of the trees. Turn back and retrace your steps to return to the trailhead.

ABRAMS CREEK

Abrams Creek is located in the southwestern corner of the park, 20 miles west of Townsend via the Foothills Parkway and 33 miles north of Fontana Dam (via Hwy. 28 and Happy Valley Rd.). Getting here is easy considering the remoteness of the area and the infrequent visitors.

Look Rock is a concrete observation tower that offers a good look at the Smokies. A short hike (just under one mile) leads to the tower and if you're in this part of the park, it's worth the trip.

Hiking

RABBIT AND ABRAMS CREEKS LOOP TRAIL

Distance: 15.2 miles round-trip
Duration: 7-8 hours
Elevation gain: 4,000 feet
Difficulty: strenuous
Trailhead: Abrams Creek Campground near the ranger station
Directions: From the Abrams Creek Campground, turn right on Happy Valley Road and drive 2.3 miles; turn right onto Flats Road and continue for 0.6 mile. Turn left at the Foothills Parkway sign and follow the signs to the parking area.

Though the mountains are rugged and this hike gains 4,000 feet in elevation, it's a gentle if long hike that's earned a strenuous reputation due its length. Begin the hike by following Rabbit Creek, where wildflowers are plentiful in spring. After 2.5 miles you meet Hannah Mountain Trail; ignore it and keep straight on **Rabbit Creek Trail,** which leads to Cades Cove and the Abrams Falls Trailhead.

At the **Abrams Falls Trailhead,** follow this path to the popular waterfall. You'll reach **Abrams Falls** in 2.5 miles and will have some great photo opportunities. After you've had your fill of waterfalls, continue along the trail as it ascends to **Hannah Mountain Trail.** Turn left to cross the creek and follow Hannah Mountain Trail 1.8 miles to an intersection with Rabbit Creek Trail. Turn right onto **Rabbit Creek Trail** to return to where you started.

LITTLE BOTTOMS TRAIL

Distance: 6.2 miles round-trip
Duration: 3 hours
Elevation gain: 930 feet
Difficulty: moderate
Trailhead: Cooper Road Trail Trailhead at Abrams Creek Campground

Little Bottoms Trail follows Abrams Creek then descends into Cades Cove near Abrams Falls. As with many trails in the Abrams Creek Campground area, you can use this hike to access Cades Cove, or you can hike it as an out-and-back hike of easy length. This creekside hike is amazing during the spring wildflower bloom and offers several great opportunities for leaf-peeping and fall photography.

Start off on **Cooper Road Trail,** another trail that leads into Cades Cove. Follow the trail 0.9 mile to where **Little Bottoms Trail** branches off to the right. Turn right and follow Little Bottoms up a moderate ascent as you crest a ridge, then begin a steep descent down into the valley to follow the course of Abrams Creek. There are **five crossings** of feeder streams along this hike; shortly after the fifth crossing, you'll reach a junction with **Hatcher Mountain Trail.** Turn around and return to the campground.

Camping

Abrams Creek Campground (Abrams Creek Campground Rd., Tallassee, TN, 865/436-1200, May-Oct., $14) sits in the southwestern corner of the park just off the Foothills Parkway. Though this campground is at a pretty low elevation of only 1,125 feet, the mountains here are quite rugged and the woods thick. Not many people visit this section of the park, so if you want a little solitude and a sound night's sleep, put this campground on your to-do list.

There are 16 primitive sites that are first-come, first-served. The only real amenity is a restroom. Backpackers and backcountry campers take note: The trail system branching out from Abrams Creek Campground offers access to several **backcountry campsites** including Campsite 1, 17, 15, and 16.

DEEP CREEK

Just south of Cherokee and just north of Bryson City, Deep Creek is a spot more popular with locals than tourists, but it's worth a stop. Deep Creek is relatively placid, aside from a couple of waterfalls a ways upstream. If you're not into wading or tubing, don't worry—this is a lovely place to picnic

Mountain laurel blooms along Abrams Creek.

and hike or even camp away from the crowds found in some of the more popular spots in the park.

Hiking

There are two nice waterfalls to see here. Juney Whank Falls (what a name, right?) is less than a half-mile from the Deep Creek Campground and cuts an impressive figure as it drops a total of 90 feet in two stages. Indian Creek Falls is a stunning, 60-foot-high set of falls and cascades located a mile from the campground.

JUNEY WHANK FALLS TRAIL

Distance: 0.6-mile loop
Duration: 30 minutes
Elevation gain: 120 feet
Difficulty: moderate
Trailhead: parking area at the end of Deep Creek Road across from the campground

Juney Whank Falls supposedly got its name from Junaluska "Juney" Whank, a Cherokee Indian said to have been buried near the falls. The path here is pretty straightforward: it's short, at times steep, and at the end, a little slick. You'll walk across a log bridge to get a look at the tall, skinny falls, which actually descend in two stages. The first stage drops 40 feet to a stone outcropping, then flows beneath the log bridge to fall and cascade another 50 feet.

INDIAN CREEK FALLS TRAIL

Distance: 2 miles round-trip
Duration: 1 hour
Elevation gain: 160 feet
Difficulty: easy to moderate
Trailhead: parking area at the end of Deep Creek Road across from the campground

This easier but longer hike takes you past a smaller waterfall, Tom's Branch Falls, on your way to Indian Creek Falls. For about a mile, you'll follow a gently graded roadbed, and soon you'll arrive at the falls. Really, Indian Creek Falls is more of a steep, long, slick cascade of water than an actual waterfall, but it's quite serene.

DEEP CREEK LOOP TRAIL

Distance: 4.9 miles round-trip
Duration: 2.5-3 hours
Elevation gain: 900 feet
Difficulty: easy
Trailhead: Deep Creek Campground

This short hike is excellent for new hikers; the trail is easy and in good shape, plus you'll hike past Tom Branch Falls and Indian Creek Falls. The trail starts on a gravel road. Almost immediately, you'll pass **Tom Branch Falls** (which you can see well in autumn and winter). After crossing a **bridge** at the junction with **Indian Creek Trail** (to the right), pass **Indian Creek Falls,** which is more of a long cascade but no less attractive. Continue hiking along Indian Creek Trail, then pass **Stone Pile Gap Trail.** Staying on Indian Creek Trail, you'll pass a junction with **Sunkota Ridge Trail** and begin to descend to **Deep Creek Trail.** Turn left on Deep Creek Trail and follow it back to the start of the trail.

Fishing

Along **Deep Creek** you'll find some primo trout fishing. Bring a fly rod and get ready to reel in a few brown, rainbow, and brook trout. Anywhere along the creek is fine to cast a line, but some of the best spots are in the places where people aren't. This means hiking up **Deep Creek Trail,** a 15.9-mile trail that follows the creek back to Newfound Gap Road. The trail is straightforward as it follows an old roadbed that turns into a true trail, but it is beside the creek for nearly the entire length.

Camping

At the end of Deep Creek Road are the trailheads leading to the waterfalls. You'll also find the **Deep Creek Campground** (877/444-6777, www.recreation.gov, Apr.-Oct., $17). There are nearly 100 campsites here, many of which fill up with locals. If you want to camp here, arrive early or reserve well in advance.

Outside the park, there's also the **Deep Creek Tube Center and Campground** (1090 W. Deep Creek Rd., Bryson City, NC,

828/488-6055, www.deepcreekcamping.com, camping $23-50, cabins $69-195), a charming collection of tent and RV campsites and cabins for rent. As the name implies, they rent tubes for use on Deep Creek. Rentals ($5 for all-day use of your tube) are cheap, so you can play in the water as long as you like.

Road to Nowhere

An odd place to visit is the so-called **Road to Nowhere.** Just south of the Deep Creek entrance outside Bryson City is a short stretch of highway leading north into Great Smoky Mountains National Park. Lonely, even spooky, the road is all that remains of a parkway planned to trace a path through the Smokies along Fontana Lake. Construction was started on the parkway before being abandoned. Today, the road stops quite abruptly about 6 miles inside the park, at a stone tunnel. Though hard feelings over the failed parkway have softened, many families still hold a grudge against government officials who vowed to build a road along the lake to provide access to old family cemeteries there.

Cars are prohibited from using the tunnel at the end of the Road to Nowhere, but visitors on foot are welcome to stroll right through. After passing through the tunnel, there a hike waiting for you that clocks in at 36.5 miles. Fortunately, it follows the northern bank of Fontana Lake, giving you a little reward for the effort.

The Road to Nowhere is accessible from Bryson City. To get there, drive north on Everett Street, which becomes Fontana Road, then Lakeview Drive, before arriving at a parking area in about nine miles. A tunnel marks the end of the road.

GOLDMINE LOOP TRAIL

Distance: 4.9 miles round-trip
Duration: 2.5-3 hours
Elevation gain: 400 feet
Difficulty: easy
Trailhead: Lakeview Drive Tunnel at the end of The Road to Nowhere

Though this hike actually begins on the far

side of the tunnel, it really begins when you walk through the tunnel and emerge on the other side to find the two-lane road just ends. As you step off the road, walk a short way on a roadbed to follow the proper trail. In a little less than 0.2 mile you'll meet **Tunnel Bypass Trail**, and soon after that you'll reach **Goldmine Loop Trail.** To follow the trail, turn left and begin a steep descent as it traces a path along a ridge, then heads down to a miniscule stream.

Cross the stream and take a look around—you'll see a chimney in a field, evidence of the homes that once stood here. There are many such signs along the trail, so keep a keen eye on the woods for other signs of the former homes.

Drawing closer to the lakeshore, pass a short trail to **Campsite 67** (on the left); pass this and continue along Goldmine Loop. After a short hike you'll reach the shores of **Fontana Lake** deep in a little cove, which makes for some excellent fall photos. The trail climbs back up alongside **Tunnel Branch,** a small creek that feeds the lake. The ascent grows steep until you meet the other end of **Tunnel Bypass Trail.** Continue along the trail and in 0.4 mile you'll be back at the tunnel.

LAKESHORE TRAIL

Distance: 35.6 miles one-way
Duration: 2.5-3 hours or multiple days
Elevation change: 1,100 feet
Difficulty: easy
Trailhead: Lakeview Drive Tunnel at the end of The Road to Nowhere

The Lakeshore Trail runs along the northern shoreline of Fontana Lake. The 36.5-mile route is doable as a day-hike in sections, but it best done as a multi-night backpacking trip.

The total elevation gain for this hike is nearly 11,000 feet as you climb up and down, up and down as you crest 10 ridges and knobs in excess of 2,250 feet, with lots of elevation variance along the way. Whether you take this on as a legendary day-hike or an overnight backpacking trip, arrange for transportation before you set out. This means a car shuttle at the end of the trail or parking your own shuttle cars at opposite ends.

The trail begins at the tunnel at the end of The Road to Nowhere. After passing through the tunnel, follow a short bit of road to the point where it turns into a trail. You'll reach your first potential campsite, **Campsite 74,** in just over 2 miles at **Forney Creek Trail.** (Skip it unless you plan on making this a weeklong backpacking trip.)

In 6.6 miles, you'll reach Anthony Branch and Chambers Creek; just after crossing Chamber Creek, approach the lakeshore to find a 0.1-mile trail to **Campsite 98.** This can be a good stopping point if this is a two-night trip. **Campsite 77** is just over 15 miles in, making it a good stopping point if you're aiming for a one-night trip. Or you can press on to **Campsite 76,** at the 11-mile mark.

From Campsite 77, it is 4.2 miles to **Campsite 81** on the south side of the trail. (The trail is lakeside, but the campsite is still 0.2 mile from the water; don't expect a lake view.) Continue on 3.6 more miles to the junction with Hazel Creek Trail and **Campsite 86; Campsite 85** is 2 miles up Hazel Creek Trail, **Campsites 84 and 83** are 4.5 and 5.3 miles up the trail respectively. This is a good place to stop for a two-night trip, but the Campsite 86 can see a good bit of traffic. You may want to press on another 1.4 miles to **Campsite 88.**

All along the trail, spur trails lead to the coves and shoreline. These vary in length, but feel free to follow them at your leisure. **Hazel Creek Trail** is one of the larger trails in this region of the park; it forms part of a larger network of trails on which you could have a 100-mile, 10-night campout if you wanted. There's plenty to see and do if you're a hardcore hiker and one trip here will certainly lead to another—this is a beautiful part of the park.

From Campsite 88, it is 3 miles to Flint Gap and Eagle Creek Trail (**Campsites 89 and 96** are a couple of miles up the trail). Another 0.5 mile leads to **Campsite 90** on the banks of Eagle Creek. A small spur trail leads down to the cove, if you want to see the water. In another 0.4 mile, you'll reach the intersection with Lost Cove Trail (**Campsite 91** is one mile down the trail). Lost Cove leads 2.7 miles to the Appalachian Trail at Sassafras Gap, just north of Shuckstack; from there it's 3.7 miles south to the trailhead at Lakeview Drive West.

Continue along **Lakeshore Trail** and you'll be on the final leg of the hike, a windy 5.2-mile trek that crosses more than a dozen creeks and streams before it reaches Lakeview Drive West and the parking area. On the off chance Fontana Dam is closed (for repairs or security reasons), you may have to hike down Lakeview Drive and cross the dam to get to your car on the other side, adding almost 2 miles to the hike.

BACKCOUNTRY PERMITS

Because so many trails branch off Lakeshore Trail, this region is a hotbed of backcountry campsites. There are eight backcountry campsites—72, 73, 76, 77, 78, 81, 87, and 98—on or near Lakeshore Trail; four of those (72, 73, 78, and 87) are boat-access only. There are another eight campsites within a day hike of Lakeshore.

In 2015, there was increased bear activity in this section of the park. One camper was injured when a bear pulled him from his hammock, leading to the closure of several backcountry campsites and a shelter along the Appalachian Trail.

Before you hike or backpack anywhere in the park, check with rangers for bear activity and trail closures. Review proper etiquette regarding bears and proper handling of food in and around your campsite.

To camp backcountry, you'll need a permit from the **Backcountry Information Office** (Sugarlands Visitor Center, 865/436-1297, https://smokiespermits.nps.gov, 8am-5pm daily, $4/night). They can also answer any questions you have about the campsites (and they're quite helpful, don't be shy).

FONTANA LAKE AREA

At the southern edge of Great Smoky Mountains National Park lies Fontana Lake, a 10,230-acre reservoir created in the 1940s as part of the Tennessee Valley Authority's (TVA) efforts to supply electricity to the various communities and government and industrial facilities in the region.

Fontana Dam

The 480-foot-tall, 2,365-foot-wide **Fontana Dam,** complete with three hydroelectric generators, was completed in 1944. It provided much-needed electricity to the factories churning out materials for World War II, including Oak Ridge, Tennessee, where research leading to the atomic bomb was conducted.

To build Fontana Dam, the Tennessee Valley Authority (TVA) purchased more than 1,000 tracts of land and relocated roughly 600 families comprising five communities. Those folks left behind homes, schools, churches, and barns, all of which were covered by the lake. This displacement of so many families and elimination of these small communities was part of the tradeoff that resulted in the modernization of the region via cheap, readily available electric power, and the great number of jobs required to complete the project. The dam also provides much-needed flood control to a region that receives between 55 and 82 inches of rainfall each year. The TVA can regulate the depth of the lake by releasing water in anticipation of flood events, and the water level of Fontana Lake can vary by as much as 50 feet.

Fontana Dam is the highest concrete dam east of the Mississippi, and its impoundment provides great recreational opportunities. The Appalachian Trail crosses the dam itself, and thousands of boaters and anglers take to the lake each year. There are more than 238 miles of shoreline along Fontana Lake, and over 10,000 acres of water surface.

The exhibits at the **Fontana Dam Visitor Center** (Fontana Dam Rd., off NC-28 near the state line, www.tva.com/sites/fontana. htm, 9am-6pm daily May-Oct., free) tell the story of the region and the construction of the dam. There's also a small gift shop, and a viewing platform overlooking the dam. Hikers take note: They also sell backcountry camping permits (perfect for those long overnight trips along Lakeshore Trail) and have showers in the back.

Fishing and Boating

Fishing is big on Fontana Lake. Trout love the feeder streams and headwaters that flow into the lake, and largemouth, smallmouth, and rock bass are all throughout. You'll even find walleye and muskies in the deep water (and it gets deeper than 400 feet deep in some points). On any given day, you'll spot anglers on boats and kayaks and more than a few fly rods strapped to the backpacks of hikers headed out to try the streams along the north banks of the lake.

If you have your own boat, you can launch it from the **Fontana Marina** (40 Fontana Dam Rd., 828/498-2129, www.fontanavillage.com), or you can rent a kayak, canoe, or paddleboard (from $20/hour to $100/day) or a pontoon or fishing pontoon boat (from $50/hour to $330/day). Fishing guide services and seasonal tours of the lake are also available.

Fontana Lake is partially in the national park, and partially outside of it—which makes fishing here a little more complicated. If you plan on fishing in the lake, you have two options: Get a **North Carolina fishing license** (www.ncwildlife.org) and review the guidelines (to be on the safe side), or rely on a fishing guide to supply a license and understand the rules (most do).

GUIDES

Fontana Guide Service (3336 Balltown Rd., Bryson City, 828/736-2318, www.fontanaguides.com, $200-500 full day trips, price depends on group size) has a number of options depending on season, interest, and skill level, including options to fish in the national park.

In addition to fly-fishing excursions, they also offer kayak fishing, bass and lake fishing, as well as night fishing in select spots.

Fly Fishing the Smokies (Bryson City, 828/488-7665, www.flyfishingthesmokies. net) has a number of guides and options for a day or more of fly-fishing the streams on the north shore of the lake and other trout waters. Wade the streams with them for a half-day (1 person $150, 2 people $175) or full-day (1 person $200, 2 people $250) outing; try a float trip (half-day $225 per boat, full-day $300 per boat); or go backcountry camping and fly-fishing in the Great Smoky Mountains National Park ($500-850 per person). They also offer bass fishing on nearby Fontana Lake (half day $225, full-day $300).

A top fishing guide in the area, **Steve Claxton's Smoky Mountain Adventures** (828/736-7501, http://steveclaxton.com) specializes in leaving civilization behind in favor of camping, catching wild mountain trout, and getting a true taste of the wilderness. Three-day, two-night camping trips for 5-7 people run around $400 per person; four-day, three-night trips are $450-500 per person. He also offers daylong fishing trips (1 person $225, 2 people $250, 3 people $300).

Root Hog Fishing Guide Service (828/862-7958, www.fontanafishingguide. com) runs fishing charters ($180 for one person 4-hour trip, $55 additional person; $240 for one person 6-hour trip, $55 additional person; $275 for one person 8-hour trip; $75 additional person) on Lake Fontana and fly-fishing trips ($160 for one person 4-hour trip, $65 per additional person; $225 for one person 8-hour trip, $75 per additional person). Owner and guide Dwight Pigman has been fishing here for decades, so he knows where to find the fish.

Accommodations and Food

Just outside the park, **Fontana Village** (300 Woods Rd., Fontana Dam, 828/498-2211 or 800/849-2258, www.fontanavillage.com, lodge $109-219, cabins $109-459, camping $15-40) offers a place to lay your head in your choice of accommodations: tent or RV camping, one- to three-bedroom cabins, and lodge rooms. There are 100 lodge rooms, 110 cabins, and 20 campsites. At the lodge you'll find complimentary wireless Internet in the public areas; other amenities include an outdoor pool and lazy river, as well as a fitness center and small day spa.

The complex contains two restaurants, a snack bar, an ice cream shop, and a general

Lake Fontana

store. **Mountainview Restaurant** (828/498-2211, 7:30am-2:30pm and 5:30pm-8pm daily, breakfast $4-9, lunch $8-14, dinner $14-28) serves steaks, chicken, and a nice selection of seafood that includes several preparations of trout. Reservations are recommended during weekends and in peak season. **Wildwood Grill** (828/498-2211, 11:30am-9pm daily Apr.-Oct., $8-19) serves pizza, burgers, and an array of fried appetizers. In the summer, concerts on the deck give visitors a little listening enjoyment to go with dinner.

TWENTYMILE

One of the most remote sections of the park, Twentymile is on the southern end, just past Fontana Lake and Dam and alongside the smaller Cheoah Lake. Despite the name, Twentymile Trail only goes 5 miles into Great Smoky Mountains National Park, but you can make it into a 20-mile journey by combining it with other trails, or you can keep it to a manageable day hike of around 8 miles by doing a smaller loop. Though this part of the park is out of the way, Twentymile is a popular hike, so expect to see some fellow hikers, especially on weekends and through the week on beautiful days in summer and autumn. There is a trio of **backcountry campsites** (reserve at www.smokiespermits.nps.gov) at Twentymile Trail: campsites 13, 92, and 93.

Hiking
TWENTYMILE LOOP TRAIL
Distance: 7.6-mile loop
Duration: 3.5-4 hours
Elevation gain: 1,200 feet
Difficulty: easy
Trailhead: Twentymile Ranger Station
Directions: Twentymile Ranger Station is 6 miles west from Fontana Dam on NC-28. Turn at the sign for Twentymile.
This hike is very easy, following a roadbed and a well-maintained trail along Twentymile Trail, Twentymile Loop Trail, and Wolf Ridge Trail. There are a number of stream crossings along this route, and though there are log bridges spanning Moore Springs Branch and

Twentymile Creek, floods may wash them away, and if you're there before repair crews can fix the bridges, you may have to wade across.

From the trailhead, go 05. mile to where **Wolf Ridge Trail** branches off to the left. Follow Wolf Ridge Trail for 1.1 miles to **Twentymile Loop Trail.** Along Wolf Ridge, you'll cross Moore Springs Branch five times as you climb. Along the way, there are abundant wildflowers, including bloodroot, fire pink, and trilliums, and the opportunity to see bears, deer, and other wildlife.

After following Wolf Ridge just over a mile, you'll see Twentymile Loop Trail branching off to the right. Cross Moore Springs Branch and follow the trail 2.9 miles along an easy grade before descending to a crossing of Twentymile Creek and the junction with **Twentymile Trail.**

Turn right on Twentymile Trail to descend back along the creek and to the trailhead. From here, it's just over 3 miles back to your car.

GREGORY BALD VIA TWENTYMILE TRAIL
Distance: 15.7-mile loop
Duration: 9 hours—strenuous day hike or overnighter
Elevation gain: 3,650 feet
Difficulty: strenuous
Trailhead: Twentymile Ranger Station
Directions: Twentymile Ranger Station is 6 miles west from Fontana Dam on NC-28. Turn at the sign for Twentymile.
This hike makes Twentymile live up to its name, even though it's a mere 15.7 miles. It's doable in a day, but it's a long, hard day, so camping for a night in the backcountry is recommended.

From the trailhead, follow **Twentymile Trail** for 0.5 mile until it intersects with **Wolf Ridge Trail.** Turn here and follow Wolf Ridge Trail 6.3 miles to **Gregory Bald Trail.** The grade of Wolf Ridge Trail is somewhat steep, but more than that, it's a relentless uphill climb all the way to where you crest the ridge before reaching **Parson Bald.** As you approach the ridge and Parson Bald, you'll find copious amounts of blueberry bushes, and, if they're in season, a fair number of bears enjoying blueberries. The same holds true at Parson Bald, just over the ridge. If you're on the trail in August, when the blueberries tend to ripen, be cautious.

When you reach Parson Bald, it's a short, easy walk to Sheep Pen Gap, where you'll find **Campsite 13** (reservations and information 865/436-1297, www.smokiespermits.nps.gov) and the end of Wolf Ridge Trail. Turn right on Gregory Bald Trail and climb just under a half mile to **Gregory Bald.** There are azaleas in great abundance and during midsummer the bald is a riot of blooms. But even if you come when there's not a bloom to be found, the views make the hike worth it.

From here, keep heading east to **Rich Gap,** where you'll come upon a four-way trail junction. Follow **Long Hungry Ridge Trail** to the right, heading south. This trail is pretty flat for the first mile, then it begins to descend, and the descent becomes increasingly noticeable as you move down the trail. You'll find **Campsite 92** 3.4 miles from Rich Gap. Once you've reached the campsite, you've left the steepest part of the hike behind you.

Continue down Long Hungry Ridge Trail to the place where it meets Twentymile Trail, following Twentymile Creek 2.6 miles back to the junction with Wolf Ridge Trail. At this point, you're only 0.5 mile from the trailhead.

Transportation and Services

CAR

The 33-mile-long Newfound Gap Road (US-441) bisects the park from north to south. It's the most heavily traveled route in the park and provides a good introduction for first-time visitors. Newfound Gap Road starts at the southern terminus of the Blue Ridge Parkway, just outside Cherokee, North Carolina, and ends in Knoxville, Tennessee, 70 miles to the northwest through Great Smoky Mountains National Park.

From Cherokee, you can head straight to the eastern entrance of Great Smoky Mountains National Park via Newfound Gap Road. Take US-441/TN-71 north through Great Smoky Mountains National Park and into Gatlinburg, Tennessee. It's easy to make the trip from one end to the other in an afternoon, though it may take a little longer in peak seasons. Knoxville, Tennessee, is 36 miles to the northwest of Great Smoky Mountains National Park along US-441 and TN-71.

There are **no gas stations** along Newfound Gap Road. You'll need to fuel up and buy snacks in Cherokee.

AIR

Asheville Regional Airport (61 Terminal Dr., Asheville, NC, 828/684-2226, www.fly-avl.com) is about one hour east of Cherokee. **McGhee Tyson Airport** (2055 Alcoa Hwy., Alcoa, TN, 865/342-3000, www.tys.org) is about one hour west of Gatlinburg.

SERVICES

Groceries and camping supplies are limited in Great Smoky Mountains National Park. Food is virtually nonexistent, so bring snacks. The Sugarlands and Oconaluftee Visitor Centers have a small selection of vending machine beverages and a few convenience items (batteries, memory cards), but little else.

Medical

If you find yourself in an emergency situation in the park, dial 911 if you have cell access. When speaking with the 911 operator, inform the operator that you are in Great Smoky Mountains National Park and give your location as best you can (if you're in the backcountry, that means the trail name and nearest campsite or shelter to you). The

Calendar of Events

- **Wildflower Pilgrimage** (Apr.): Hikes, talks, and photography sessions explore the park's abundant and diverse wildflowers (www.springwildflowerpilgrimage.org).

- **Music of the Mountains** (mid-Apr.): This three-day festival celebrates the musical traditions of the Appalachians with demonstrations and concerts at the Sugarlands Visitor Center, as well as locations in Cosby and Townsend.

- **Junior Ranger Day** (late Apr.): Get the kids started on their Junior Ranger Badge with this park-wide celebration of youthful discovery—then keep it going with the weekly Junior Ranger programs throughout the year.

- **Cosby in the Park** (mid-May): Hikes, music, and demonstrations of domestic life create a deeper connection with the park during this one-day event.

- **Women's Work Festival** (mid-June): At Mountain Farm Museum, learn about the role women played in the making and maintaining of a mountain home and farm.

- **Mountain Life Festival:** (mid-Sept.): Mountain Farm Museum comes alive with demonstrations of domestic and cultural life—from music to demonstrations of domestic chores such as soap making and cooking.

- **Festival of Christmas Past** (mid-Dec.): Get a taste of the holidays in the Smokies with demonstrations of arts and crafts (spinning, weaving, and quilting); music, singing, and storytelling; and children's activities like games and toy-making.

operator will send rangers and emergency responders. If you don't have cell service, send another hiker or driver for help.

The nearest hospitals are **LeConte Medical Center** (742 Middle Creek Rd., Sevierville, TN, 865/446-7000, www.lecontemedicalcenter.com), about 25 minutes from the west park entrance; **Blount Memorial Hospital** (907 E. Lamar Alexander Pkwy., Maryville, TN, 865/983-7211, www.blountmemorial.org), an hour away from the west park entrance; and **Swain County Hospital** (45 Plateau St., Bryson City, NC, 828/488-2155, www.westcarehealth.org), a little less than 30 minutes from the eastern park entrance in Cherokee.

RANGER PROGRAMS

Few of us will ever have the opportunity to get to know a park as well as a park ranger. Every day they're immersed in the landscape, the culture, the history, and the beauty of their respective park and they work with a legion of volunteers to create enrichment programs that will expand the use and appreciation of parks (and the outdoors as a whole) in the public. Great Smoky Mountains National Park has some mighty fine park rangers and they work hard to introduce every visitor to the beauty, the stories, and the flora and fauna of the park. Through the **Junior Ranger Program,** they get kids (age 5-15) excited about the Smokies; through their Not-So-Junior Ranger Program they get everyone age 13-130 involved too.

Rangers lead daily hikes along nature trails and creekside paths, they take visitors on nighttime hikes of Cades Cove, host campfires and storytelling sessions, lead hayrides and history lessons, introduce us to the animals—from furry to slimy—of the park, and celebrate the history and culture here. A full schedule of seasonal programs is available online (www.nps.gov/grsm).

Guided Hikes

Hiking in the Smokies is as simple as picking up a map, choosing a trail, and heading into the woods; however, some people prefer to hike with a group and a guide. Fortunately the park trail system accommodates both styles. Several organizations lead outings and excursions—from day hikes to trip planning assistance to overnight backpacking trips.

FRIENDS OF THE SMOKIES

Friends of the Smokies (828/452-0720, www.friendsofthesmokies.com, Mar.-Dec., $20/members, $35/nonmembers) is one of my favorite groups; they provide support to the Trails Forever program and help with trail repairs and maintenance. Friends leads hikes along some of the classic trails in the park. Hikes include spots like Little Cataloochee Trail and Grotto Falls, overnighters to places like Mount LeConte, and trips to Mount Sterling. Each hike highlights one of the programs supported by Friends of the Smokies. Look at their schedule for upcoming trips and registration information.

SMOKY MOUNTAINS HIKING CLUB

Smoky Mountains Hiking Club (www.smhclub.org) runs weekly outings in the Smokies and in east Tennessee, though their primary mission is to assist with the maintenance of the Appalachian Trail within the park. They've been around since 1924 and currently have more than 600 members, so these hikes are always with a group of experienced and knowledgeable outdoors enthusiasts. The weekly outings are free and open to anyone who wants to participate; trips include on- and off-trail hikes as well as workdays. Check the website for the schedule and to register.

A WALK IN THE WOODS

Several commercial outfitters lead walks, hikes, and overnight trips in the park in addition to providing trip planning assistance and hiker shuttles. **A Walk In The Woods** (865/436-8283, www.awalkinthewoods.com) is a guide company offering nature walks ($20-160), hikes ($95-260/first hiker, $20-47/additional hiker), backpacking trips ($254-1,600, discounts if supplying your own equipment), hiker shuttles (cost varies depending on trailhead and time of day), and trip planning ($50 plus $7 pp/night, including your Backcountry Permit Fee).

WILDLAND TREKKING

Wildland Trekking (800/715-4453, www.wildlandtrekking.com) offers trips include multiday backpacking trips ($440-1,225), inn-based hikes that include overnight accommodations ($1,225-1,995), day hikes ($115-355), a Fontana Lake Paddle and Hiking expedition ($795), and backpacking and inn-based trips around the region ($825-2,130).

Appalachian Trail

From Georgia to Maine, the Appalachian Trail's nearly 2,200 miles traverse some rugged, lonesome, and picturesque landscapes, cresting ridges and summiting peaks, crossing streams and rivers, passing through bogs and marshes, climbing near-vertical peaks, and even following city streets.

Cutting through the heart of Great Smoky Mountains National Park, the **Appalachian Trail** runs along the high ridgeline that forms the border between North Carolina and Tennessee. There are 71.6 miles of the **Appalachian Trail** in Great Smoky Mountains National Park, and it's a highlight for thru-hikers (those taking the **Appalachian Trail** north to Maine or south to Georgia, all in one enormous hike), segment hikers (those hiking the whole thing one piece at a time), and day hikers (the rest of us).

This guide to the **Appalachian Trail** within Great Smoky Mountains National Park doesn't cover the trail mile by mile but includes enough to get you out for a multiday backpacking trip. For the lowdown on the

Appalachian Trail, contact the **Appalachian Trail Conservancy** (www.appalachiantrail.org) or visit the **National Park Service** (www.nps.gov/appa), where you'll find trip planning information, maps, trail reports, and more.

Most people hike the Great Smoky Mountains National Park section as a seven-day trek, though you can tailor this trek to suit your hiking style and the time you have—stretching it out to 10 or 12 days with a little planning, or pushing the pace to complete it in three brutal days.

Permits

Though there are no fees required to hike the Appalachian Trail, there are requirements when hiking the **Appalachian Trail** in Great Smoky Mountains National Park. Thru-hikers are eligible for a **thru-hiker permit** (www.smokiespermits.nps.gov, $20); thru-hikers must begin and end their hike at least 50 miles from the border of the park and only travel on the **Appalachian Trail** while in the park.

Segment hikers and backpackers need a permit from the **Backcountry Information Office** (Sugarlands Visitor Center, 865/436-1297, https://smokiespermits.nps.gov, 8am-5pm daily, $4 pp/night). A permit is not required for day hikers.

Trail Shelters

For AT thru-hikers there's only one choice for where to stay in Great Smoky Mountains National Park: **Appalachian Trail shelters.** Of the 12 sites at each shelter, four spots are reserved for thru-hikers only and they're first-come, first-served. If you're thru-hiking and find a shelter full, you are permitted to pitch your tent next to the shelters.

Segment hikers and backpackers can reserve spots in these **Appalachian Trail** shelters, or at any of the numerous backcountry campsites along and near the Appalachian Trail.

There are too many backcountry campsites near the **Appalachian Trail,** as well as other backcountry shelters, to list here. For a complete list, consult a park trail map (www.nps.gov/grsm).

There are a dozen shelters located south to north along the **Appalachian Trail** in the park:

- Mollies Ridge at 4,570 feet
- Russell Field at 4,360 feet
- Spence Field at 4,900 feet (has a privy nearby)
- Derrick Knob at 4,890 feet
- Silers Bald at 5,460 feet
- Double Spring Gap at 5,507 feet (has a privy nearby)
- Mount Collins at 5,870 feet (has a privy nearby)
- Icewater Spring at 5,920 feet (has a privy nearby)
- Pecks Corner at 5,280 feet
- Tricorner at 5,920 feet (has a privy nearby)
- Cosby Knob at 4,700 feet (has a privy nearby)
- Davenport Gap at 2,600 feet

DAY HIKING

Day hikers are drawn to the Appalachian Trail's fantastic balds (high natural and agricultural meadows), like Andrews Bald and Silers Bald; peaks like Mount Cammerer and Rocky Top (yes, the one from the song); and just to say they've hiked part of the Appalachian Trail. The route through the park is always high and at times rocky, at other times steep (at other times both), but the views are worth it.

Day hikers who want to log a few miles of the Appalachian Trail will find a few opportunities to get their boots muddy. Notable day hikes include:

- **Charlies Bunyon** (8.1 miles round-trip): Access the Appalachian Trail north from the trailhead at the Newfound Gap Road Overlook.
- **Mount Cammerer** (11.2 miles round-trip): Take the Low Gap Trail at the Cosby

Campground to the Appalachian Trail, then proceed to the summit and a stone fire tower. Note: Only 4.2 miles are on the Appalachian Trail.

- **Rocky Top** (13.9 miles round-trip): Follow the Anthony Creek Trailhead from the Cades Cove picnic area to Bote Mountain Trail. At Spence Field, you'll meet up with the Appalachian Trail; follow it to Rocky Top and spectacular views. Note: Only the last portion is on the Appalachian Trail.

THRU-HIKING

From Fontana Dam to Davenport Gap, the **Appalachian Trail** brushes past peaks of 5,000 feet (or even 6,000 feet) in elevation, including the highest point along the entire trail, the 6,643-foot Clingmans Dome. Gaps (low points in the mountains) along this stretch top out at nearly 4,000 feet.

Most thru-hikers begin in Georgia in the spring and hike north to Maine. These hike descriptions follow that northbound flow of foot traffic. The **Appalachian Trail** is broken down into two hikes: one from Fontana Dam to Newfound Gap, the other from Newfound Gap to Davenport Gap. Notations and mileage markers are given for the **Appalachian Trail** shelters, as well as points where other trails connect with or cross the **Appalachian Trail**.

Western Smokies
FONTANA DAM TO NEWFOUND GAP
Distance: 40.3 miles one-way
Duration: Multiple days
Elevation gain: 4,900 feet
Difficulty: strenuous
Trailhead: Fontana Dam

This section of the **Appalachian Trail** hits the highest peak in the Smokies, Clingmans Dome, which is also the highest point along the entire length of the trail. There are **seven shelters** along this route: Mollies Ridge (mile 10.3), Russell Field (mile 13.1), Spence Field (mile 16), Derrick Knob (mile 22.3), Silers Bald (mile 27.8), Double Spring Gap (mile 29.5), and Mount Collins (mile 35.8).

Begin the hike at **Fontana Dam** and get ready for a big uphill push; you'll gain 3,035 feet in the first 11 miles. After crossing Fontana Dam, you'll leave the paved road at 0.6 mile and begin to climb **Shuckstack Mountain.** At 3.2 miles, you'll reach the gap between Shuckstack and Little Shuckstack, then at 3.8 miles you'll hit a viewpoint that offers a great look at Fontana Lake.

When you reach 4 miles, there is a road

The Appalachian Trail cuts through the center of the park.

Fontana Dam to Newfound Gap

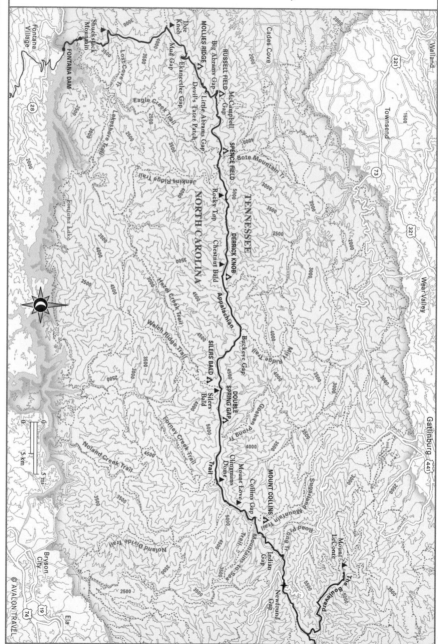

on the east side of the trail that leads to a fire tower at the top of Shuckstack Mountain. Make the side trip if you want, otherwise keep hiking and descend to Sassafras Gap and the intersection with Lost Cove Trail to the east and Twentymile Trail to the west.

You'll continue up and down as you follow the terrain, and at 7.5 miles reach the summit of Doe Knob (4,520 feet), then descend some steep 300 feet to Mud Gap at 7.9 miles, only to climb again to Ekaneetlee Gap (3,842 feet) at 8.9 miles. Keep climbing and you'll reach **Mollies Ridge Shelter** at 10.3 miles. Depending on your pace, the time allotted for your hike, and your reservations (if necessary) make camp here.

At 10.9 miles you'll reach Devil's Tater Patch (4,775 feet) and begin a long section of what's often referred to as a "roller-coaster" section, meaning it's up and down as the trail follows the undulating ridgeline. You'll have frequent and steep ascents and descents, but little overall change in elevation between here and the 25-mile mark at Buckeye Gap.

From Devil's Tater Patch, descend to Little Abrams Gap (4,120 feet) then to Big Abrams Gap (4,080 feet) at 12.7 miles. At 13.1 miles you'll reach **Russell Field Shelter** and a spring. At 13.8 miles you'll reach McCampbell Gap (4,328 feet).

When you hit the 15.9 mile mark you've reached the south end of **Spence Field;** the shelter is 0.1 mile on, then 250 yards down Eagle Creek Trail on the east side of the **Appalachian Trail.** Bote Mountain Trail intersects with the **Appalachian Trail** at 16.4 miles, you meet Jenkins Ridge Trail, marking the north end of Spence Field.

As the trail begins to climb from Spence Field, you might as well start humming *Rocky Top* as you're approaching the summit of the mountain made famous in song. Rocky Top's 5,441-foot peak awaits at 17.2 miles, then the summit of Thunderhead (5,527 feet) 0.6 mile further. The views from Rocky Top are great but absolutely nonexistent from Thunderhead.

From here to Derrick Knob you'll pass through five additional gaps, then, at 22 miles,

reach Chestnut Bald; **Derrick Knob Shelter** is 0.3 mile ahead on the west side of the trail.

At 25.1 miles you'll find yourself at the 4,817-foot Buckeye Gap and begin a 7.3-mile, 1800-foot ascent to Clingmans Dome. Along the way you'll hit **Silers Bald** (5,607 feet) at 28 miles, where the views are quite good; Jenkins Knob at 29 miles; **Double Spring Gap** shelter (5,570 feet) at 29.5 miles. Begin a steep ascent, pass Goshen Prong Trail to the west at 30.1 miles, summit Mount Buckley (6,582 feet) at 31.9 miles, then reach Clingmans Dome Bypass Trail at 32 miles.

If you want to top out on the 6,643 foot Clingmans Dome and hike to the top of the observation platform (recommended, especially if the weather is good), take a detour on a side trail to the east; head to the top, then back to the trail. You're now at 32.4 miles and are less than 8 miles from Newfound Gap, the end of this section of the **Appalachian Trail.**

Continue descending to the summit of Mount Love (6,446 feet) and Collins Gap (5,886 feet). At 35.8 miles you'll reach Sugarland Mountain Trail and **Mount Collins Shelter** (0.5 mile west). The **Appalachian Trail** joins North Carolina's Mountains-to-Sea Trail at the 36.2 mile mark.

Indian Gap (5,317 feet) and the intersection of Road Prong Trail await at 38.6 miles. At 39.4 miles, a few openings in the trees provide views of Mount LeConte to the west. Ascend a graded trail to **Newfound Gap** (5,045 feet) and the overlook there.

Eastern Smokies
NEWFOUND GAP TO DAVENPORT GAP

Distance: 31.3 miles one-way
Duration: Multiple days
Elevation gain: 4,380 feet
Difficulty: strenuous
Trailhead: Newfound Gap

Along this section you'll have 11 major climbs and descents like Mount Cammerer, Cosby Knob, Mount Guyot, Charlies Bunion, and Mount Kephart. There are **five shelters** here: Icewater Spring (mile 3), Pecks Corner (mile

Newfound Gap to Davenport Gap

© AVALON TRAVEL

10.4), TriCorner Knob (mile 15.6), Cosby Knob (mile 23.3), and Davenport Gap (mile 30.4).

Begin at **Newfound Gap,** taking a wide trail past the rock overlook and into the woods. You'll reach a viewpoint at 1.9 miles, then reach a junction with Boulevard Trail at 2.7 miles. The Boulevard leads to Mount LeConte, and from LeConte a day hiker can descend to Roaring Fork Motor Nature Trail via Trillium Gap Trail or descend to Newfound Gap Road via Alum Cave Bluffs Trail. **Appalachian Trail** hikers should proceed past the junction and reach **Icewater Spring Shelter** at the 3-mile mark.

The trail passes east around Charlies Bunion at 3.9 miles and then Dry Sluice Gap (5,375 feet) at 4.1 miles. Pass Dry Sluice Gap Trail (leading to Smokemont Campground) at 4.2 miles. Porters Gap (5,500 feet) is the next landmark at 5.8 miles, then False Gap (5,400 feet) at 6.5 miles. At the 9.1-mile mark you'll be at Bradleys View where you'll have some of the best views of North Carolina that you'll find.

At 10.4 miles you'll reach a junction with Hughes Ridge Trail, which will take you to **Pecks Corner Shelter** to the east. There is another outstanding view at 11.3 miles where you'll be looking down into the headwaters of Eagle Rocks Creek. Begin climbing at Copper Gap (5,478 feet), 12.1 miles in, and head on to the summit of Mount Sequoyah (6,003 feet) at 13.1 miles.

Descend to Chapman Gap (5,801 feet) at 13.8 miles, then climb again to Mount Chapman (6,218 feet) at 14.6 miles. You'll cross Big Cove Gap (5,825 feet) at 15.5 miles and 0.1 mile further on, the trail to **TriCorner Knob Shelter.**

The junction with Balsam Mountain Trail

lies at the 15.8-mile mark, and a sharp ridge at 16.2 miles. The next landmarks are Guyot Spur (6,360 feet) at 16.8 miles, Guyot Spring at 17.4 miles, and the so-called "Hell Ridge" section at 17.9 miles. The four-mile Hell Ridge earned its name not from the tough trail but from a forest fire that raged here after pre-park logging left it particularly vulnerable; you'll notice the absence of the larger and old-growth trees you've seen elsewhere along the trail.

Deer Creek Gap (6,020 feet) at 18.5 miles and Yellow Creek Gap at 19.1 miles are the next two landmarks before you reach Camel Hump Knob (5,250 feet) at 20.8 miles. At 22.7 miles you'll be at the north end of Hell Ridge and pass back into a lovely deciduous forest. **Cosby Knob Shelter** awaits at 23.3 miles, then Low Gap (4,242 feet) and the interaction with Low Gap Trail at 24 miles. The **Appalachian Trail** brushes past Sunup Knob at 25 miles, then crests the ridge and the North Carolina-Tennessee border on the slopes of Mount Cammerer at 25.9 miles. If you want to summit Cammerer and the stone fire tower there, you'll find the 0.6-mile spur trail at 26.1 miles.

There's a great view at 26.9 miles, and a spring east of the **Appalachian Trail** at 28.2 miles. Lower Mount Cammerer Trail comes in at 28.5 miles, then Chestnut Branch Trail at 29.4 miles. Davenport Gap Trail waits at the 30.4-mile mark; it's 200 yards or so off the west side of the trail. From here it's 0.9 mile to the **Davenport Gap Shelter.** Here you'll find State Route 1397, the Pigeon River, and I-40...

And, of course, the end of the Appalachian Trail as it passes out of Great Smoky Mountains National Park and turns northwest into North Carolina and toward Maine.

Tennessee Gateways

There was a time when this was the frontier, when the Smoky Mountains stood too high and too rough to pass.

But settlers made their way across this a huge green wall with what few supplies they could carry to carve out an existence in the virgin wilderness, not to mention the threat—or perceived threat—of hostile natives. They found coves of rich bottomland around which to settle outposts. Eventually these outposts turned into communities, which turned into towns and cities, and something like what we see today was carved out of the wild—Gatlinburg at the foot of the Smokies, Pigeon Forge on the river just a few miles distant, and Knoxville growing large on the bluffs of the deep, wide Tennessee River.

Today the setup is the same, but the inherent risks of frontier life are gone. In their place, Gatlinburg and Pigeon Forge are tourist hot spots, or even tourist traps. (I mean that in the most flattering, fun, kitsch-filled sense of the term.) Gatlinburg is, proudly, the gateway to the Smokies, and Great Smoky Mountains National Park rubs shoulders with the town limits. Not to be outdone, Pigeon Forge is the home of Dollywood—an amusement park that's part rides, part Appalachian culture, and part homage to Dolly Parton's childhood.

The two towns are bright dots of light connected by a glittering ribbon—a sharp contrast to their next-door neighbor, the most-visited national park in the United States. Some 30 miles west of the park, Knoxville is the nearest city of any size, and it's as pretty and proper a Southern city as there ever has been. It offers a cosmopolitan respite from the wildness of the Smokies and the country kitsch of Gatlinburg and Pigeon Forge, all while maintaining its own identity as an intellectual and creative urban center that's grown up but has never forgotten its roots.

PLANNING YOUR TIME

To get a true sense of this complex place and a real taste of the cultures at work here, plan to spend at least **four days.** Split your time evenly between Gatlinburg and Pigeon Forge, with two days in each. (The in-your-face faux-hillbilly attractions are so silly you

---

Previous: Tennessee Theatre; downtown Knoxville. **Above:** sampling craft beer in downtown Knoxville.

Look for ★ to find recommended
sights, activities, dining, and lodging.

Highlights

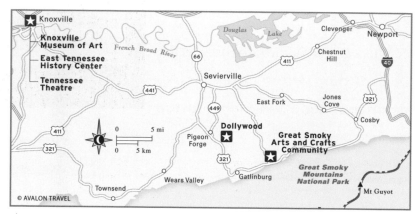

★ **Great Smoky Arts and Crafts Community:** Interact with more than 120 traditional Appalachian artists, artisans, and craftspeople (page 101).

★ **Dollywood:** At this theme park owned by the country music legend roller coasters go hand in hand with Appalachian music, culture, and history (page 106).

★ **East Tennessee History Center:** This landmark tells the story of the Tennessee foothills through surprising exhibits (page 115).

★ **Knoxville Museum of Art:** Enjoy an impressive collection of contemporary pieces, including works by artists native to the city and region (page 116).

★ **Tennessee Theatre:** The official state theater of Tennessee is an architectural marvel offering a glimpse of Gilded Age opulence (page 116).

Tennessee Gateways

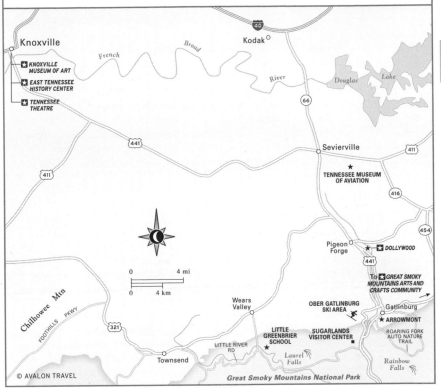

Knoxville

KNOXVILLE MUSEUM OF ART

EAST TENNESSEE HISTORY CENTER

TENNESSEE THEATRE

Kodak

French Broad River

Douglas Lake

441

411

Sevierville

411

★ TENNESSEE MUSEUM OF AVIATION

416

454

Pigeon Forge ★ DOLLYWOOD

441

To GREAT SMOKY MOUNTAINS ARTS AND CRAFTS COMMUNITY

0   4 mi

0   4 km

Chilhowee Mtn

FOOTHILLS PKWY

321

Wears Valley

OBER GATLINBURG SKI AREA

Gatlinburg

★ ARROWMONT

LITTLE GREENBRIER SCHOOL

SUGARLANDS VISITOR CENTER

ROARING FORK AUTO NATURE TRAIL

LITTLE RIVER RD

Townsend

Laurel Falls

Rainbow Falls

© AVALON TRAVEL

Great Smoky Mountains National Park

can't help but embrace them.) Pay a visit to the Great Smoky Arts and Crafts Community, where more than 120 artists, artisans, and craftspeople practice traditional Appalachian arts. Head to Dollywood for a sense of the area's history while waiting in line for a roller coaster. Taste some traditional food—from barbecue to country-kitchen standards—and clear the slate for an evening of moonshine tasting, as most distilleries use versions of old family recipes likely made in the nearby hills.

After that, head to Knoxville for **two days** and soak in the contemporary, creative vibe of the city. You'll likely hear some traditional or bluegrass musicians, but listen close and you'll find the ways they're making these old styles current. At the Knoxville Museum of Art, and throughout downtown, the art here is

certainly of the place, and seeing how it blends old with new gives you an idea of how these worlds come together. Visit the Ijams Nature Center, one of the premier urban wilderness areas in the nation, and see why several magazines have called this city one of the top outdoor towns in the South. If you're here on a weekend, Market Square is a happening spot with outdoor concerts, plenty of al fresco dining options, and a lovely farmers market.

When to Go

Winter is the slowest time here. Great Smoky Mountains National Park, a major draw for Gatlinburg, sees fewer visitors; Dollywood, the major draw for Pigeon Forge, shuts down for the season. Knoxville is also slower, but it's still a city, so there's plenty to do.

Spring gets busy; it also gets rainy. Those rains bring out wildflowers and gardens in full, glorious bloom, and visitors flock in earnest as soon as the first buds show themselves.

Summer can get warm and a little humid, but brings loads of visitors. Dollywood opens, and the number of visitors grows as the temperatures climb. The cool hollows of the Smokies offer a respite from the heat, while Dollywood's Splash Country waterpark lets you cool off in a different way.

Autumn is prime time in this region. Visitors come to Knoxville to watch autumn leaves turn...and to watch University of Tennessee football. On game weekends, you may have a hard time finding parking, a hotel, a dinner reservation, or a Knoxville resident not wearing a bright Tennessee-orange shirt. Gatlinburg and Pigeon Forge are packed as well, with visitors driving through Great Smoky Mountains National Park to take thousands of photos of the awesome autumnal color. Traffic is heavy and rooms should be booked well ahead of time. It's worth the minor hassle of the crowds, though. The Smokies are stunning when the leaves change, and Knoxville on game day—especially if you score a ticket—is absolutely boiling with energy.

Gatlinburg

On a typical Saturday night, when 40,000 people pack the restaurants and sidewalks of Gatlinburg, you would never know that only about 4,000 people live here. As the unofficial capital of the Smokies and gateway to the national park, Gatlinburg benefits greatly from the 10 million visitors drawn here for the views, the wildlife, the hikes, and the kitsch. And if there's anything Gatlinburg has in abundance, it's kitsch.

Gatlinburg is unabashedly a tourist town, and owning up to that fact makes it all the more charming. On Parkway, the cheekily named main drag, there are T-shirt shops, candy stores and fudgeries, taffy pullers, more than one Ripley's attraction, novelties both racy (in that family-friendly, double-entendre way) and tame, knife shops, mini golf, ice cream parlors, restaurants, and more odd little art, craft, and gift shops than you can count. Don't let that deter you from staying (and even enjoying yourself) here. The Ripley's Aquarium is quite nice, and at Great Smoky Arts and Crafts Community and the Arrowcraft Shop, you'll find modern interpretations of traditional mountain arts that were handmade nearby.

The 2016 wildfires that started in GSNMP spread quickly and reached Gatlinburg and Pigeon Forge. The results were disastrous: 14 lives lost; 2,400 homes, businesses, and structures destroyed; more than $500 million in damages. After evacuating the town, fire crews and public safety officers stepped in to battle the blaze and evacuate those who needed it. As of the end of 2016, cleanup and rebuilding efforts are underway and expected to continue through 2017. We have noted businesses impacted by the wildfires as well as their expected open dates.

SIGHTS
Space Needle

All of downtown Gatlinburg is a sight to behold. The mountains surround you, that namesake Smoky mist rising from them, and the street glitters and twinkles like a sort of vacationland Milky Way. One of the best ways to take it all in is from the **Space Needle** (115 Historic Nature Trail, 865/436-4629, www. gatlinburgspaceneedle.com, 9am-midnight Sun.-Thurs., 9am-1am Fri.-Sat., adults $9.50, seniors and military $6, children 4-11 $5, free under 3). I know what you're thinking, "But the Space Needle is in Seattle." Yeah, it is; this is the other one. From the observation deck

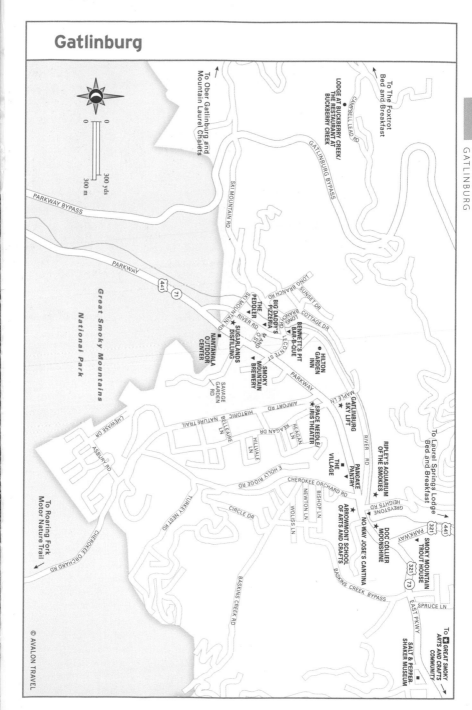

Gatlinburg

407 feet above Gatlinburg, you have truly stellar views. For the best views, get to the top shortly before sundown and watch as the mountains darken and the strip of downtown comes alive with lights. At the foot of the tower, there's a two-level, 25,000-square-foot arcade with games galore, laser tag, a gift shop, snack bar, and restrooms.

Gatlinburg Sky Lift

The **Gatlinburg Sky Lift** (765 Parkway, 865/436-4307, www.gatlinburgskylift.com, 9am-9pm daily Apr.-May, 9am-11pm daily June-Aug., 9am-10pm daily Sept.-Oct., as posted Nov.-Mar., adults $15.50, children 3-11 $12) is a ski lift that carries you 1,800 feet up the side of Crockett Mountain to a gift shop and snack bar. You have pretty views of Gatlinburg on the way up and back down, and even better views from the top; nighttime tends to be the best time to ride the Sky Lift. The Sky Lift was built in the early 1950s and was the first chair lift in the region, seeing more than 100,000 visitors by its third season in operation. You'll find it in the heart of downtown; it's impossible to miss.

During the 2016 wildfires that hit the region, the Sky Lift suffered some damage to their mountaintop structures but are rebuilding and expected to be open for the 2017 season.

Moonshine Distilleries

Moonshine is a high-octane corn liquor made in the hills, hollows, and coves all throughout and around GSMNP, especially in Gatlinburg. Today, moonshine is brewed legally and there are a few distilleries right in Gatlinburg, the best of which is **Sugarlands Distilling Company** (805 Parkway, 865/325-1355, www.sugarlands-distilling.com, 10am-11pm Mon.-Sat., noon-7pm Sun., tours free). Sugarlands' distillery puts their whole distilling process on display. Watch from screened windows open to the distilling floor or show up for a free tour. There's a gift shop where you can buy all sorts of logo-emblazoned clothing and

Sugarlands Distilling Company

drinking gear and, of course, moonshine. Before you buy a quart or two (or a case—it's that good and it makes a fun gift), stop by the Sippin' Posts where, with valid ID, you can sample all of the moonshine flavors Sugarlands sells. Sugarlands also has a great performance space called The Back Porch where all sorts of musicians and storytellers come to play songs and spin yarns.

At the other end of downtown from Sugarlands is **Doc Collier Moonshine** (519 Parkway, 800/398-5132, www.doccollier.co, 10am-7pm Mon.-Thurs., 10am-7pm Fri.-Sat., noon-7pm Sun.). Using the recipe of famed (he was famous locally anyway) Doc Collier, his ancestors continue the tradition of making some of the finest 'shine in Tennessee and selling it to the thirsty public at their Gatlinburg storefront. According to the family, Doc's moonshine was in such high demand that he needed a better way to distribute it, so he bought a mercantile, selling provisions to some customers and jars of white lightning to those in the know. In the store, you can see some great photos and even pieces of Doc's equipment while you sample some moonshine before grabbing a bottle and going on your way.

Ripley's Aquarium of the Smokies

Ripley's Aquarium of the Smokies (traffic light #5, 88 River Rd., 865/430-8808, www. ripleyaquariums.com/gatlinburg, 9am-8pm Mon.-Thurs., 9am-10pm Fri.-Sun. Jan.-Feb.; 9am-9pm Mon.-Thurs., 9am-10pm Fri.-Sun. Mar.-Memorial Day; 9am-10pm Mon.-Thurs., 9am-11pm Fri.-Sun. Memorial Day-Labor Day; 9am-9pm Mon.-Thurs., 9am-10pm Fri.-Sun. Labor Day-New Year's Day; adults $28, children 6-11 $16, children 2-5 $8) is one of countless Ripley's attractions in Gatlinburg and Pigeon Forge. The other attractions are skippable unless you have kids in tow, but the aquarium is another story. Ripley's Aquarium is the largest aquarium in the state, with more than 1.4 million gallons of water. Exhibits include the Touch a Ray Bay, where you can touch a stingray; the Penguin Playhouse, where tunnels lead you through the exhibit, putting you eye to eye with penguins as they do their thing; and Shark Lagoon, where a 340-foot-long glide path takes you under the lagoon where sand tiger and nurse sharks swim with sea turtles and moray eels. There are two on-site restaurants and a monstrous gift shop.

Arrowmont School of Arts and Crafts

Gatlinburg has a surprising artistic side, and the artists and craftspeople here take their work very seriously. Many of them are carrying on mountain traditions, while others are finding new modes and mediums to express the inspiration they draw from the landscape. Artists go to the **Arrowmont School of Arts and Crafts** (556 Parkway, 865/436-5860, www.arrowmont.org, 8:30am-5pm Mon.-Fri., 8:30am-4pm Sat., workshops $325-1,100) to hone their techniques. Founded in 1912 as a philanthropic project

by the Pi Beta Phi women's fraternity, the Phi Beta Phi Settlement School sought to deliver basic education and health services to the children of the area. The schoolchildren brought the school staff homemade gifts—baskets, weavings, woodcarvings—made by their parents. Recognizing the talent here, the school brought in a weaving teacher and began some vocational education. Then in 1926, the school opened the Arrowcraft Shop, a market selling crafts and wares made by the people of the region. As this gained popularity, the idea of summer craft workshops came about. In 1945, 50 students attended the first of many summer workshops. Today the school holds weekend and one- and two-week workshops for adults every spring, summer, and fall. Classes include traditional and contemporary takes on weaving and fiber arts, pottery, metal and jewelry, painting, and drawing. Three galleries in the school include rotating and permanent exhibitions and are open year-round.

Arrowmont sufferd some losses during the wildfires that hit Gatlinburg in 2016, but the damages were not severe and workshops are expected to continue unhindered, though rebuilding efforts will be underway during part or all of 2017 to replace the lost and damaged structures.

ENTERTAINMENT AND EVENTS
Nightlife
One spot to grab a drink other than moonshine is **Smoky Mountain Brewery** (1004 Parkway, 865/436-4200, www.smoky-mtn-brewery.com, 11:30am-1am daily, food $5-25, drinks $3-12), a microbrewery with close to a dozen handcrafted beers brewed here or at one of the three nearby sister breweries. Mainstay beers include a light beer, red ale, pilsner, porter, and pale ale; they also brew seasonal and specialty beers, like the creamy Winter Warmer Ale and the Brown Trout Stout. Stop in and grab a hot pretzel (or some wings or a pizza) and a sampler flight of beers.

Wedding Fever

To say that Gatlinburg is a popular place to get married is a gross understatement. This tiny town is second in the nation only to Las Vegas in the number of weddings held each year. On average, around 20,000 couples tie the knot here (that's 55 ceremonies a day) and the number of witnesses and guests they bring push the number of people in town for weddings north of 600,000. Guess that explains why Gatlinburg is called the "wedding capital of the South."

What makes Gatlinburg such a hot spot for weddings, even celebrity weddings (Billy Ray Cyrus, Patty Loveless, and a few other names of note were married here)? It could be that Tennessee makes it easy. No blood tests or waiting periods are required before getting married. It could be the abundance of wedding venues both natural and man-made. It could be the fact that there are plenty of romantic spots where one can retreat with their betrothed.

If being here has you in the mood for marriage, it's easy to find a place. In Gatlinburg alone there are more than a dozen chapels and more officiants than you can count. You can find all the information you'll ever need for planning a Smoky Mountain wedding at the website of the **Smoky Mountain Wedding Association** (www.somkymountainweddingassociation.com).

Performing Arts

There are a number of stage shows going on nightly throughout Gatlinburg. The **Iris Theater** (115 Historic Nature Trail, 888/482-3330, www.iristheater.com, showtimes vary, tickets adults $25, military and seniors $18, children 5-12 $8) is the home stage to several performers. **Head Case Starring Mentalist Bill Gladwell** (7pm Tues. and Fri.-Sat.) uses Bill's mastery of suggestion, skills as a hypnotist, and untold mental powers to create a thought-provoking, family-friendly show where he'll demonstrate everything from mindreading to psychokinesis. **A Brit of Magic!** (check schedule and buy tickets well in advance, they sell out) is a comedy and magic show with Keith Fields, a Briton living here in the Smokies. **Comedy Hypnosis with Guy Michaels** (usually 7pm Wed. and 9pm Thurs.-Sat.) is just that, family-friendly hypnosis where the hypnotist Guy Michaels gets willing audience members to become the stars of the show.

Then there's the **Sweet Fanny Adams Theatre** (461 Parkway, 877/388-5784, www.sweetfannyadams.com, box office open 10am-10pm on show days, shows vary, tickets adults $25, seniors, military, and AAA $23, children under 12 $9), home to a musical comedy revue

and "outrageous humor and hilarious fun" since 1977. Shows vary by the theater season, but typically include an improv showcase, a vaudeville-type revue, a holiday show, and other original musical comedies.

Festivals and Events

Throughout the year there are several events that draw attention to the things that make Gatlinburg the place it is. The **Spring Wildflower Pilgrimage** (865/974-0280, www.springwildflowerpilgrimage.org, adults $25-75, students $15, children under 12 free), usually during mid-April, is a five-day event with around 150 guided walks and presentations that celebrate the spring blooms, a photography contest, and more. From the end of September to early November, celebrate **Oktoberfest at Ober Gatlinburg** (865/436-5423, www.obergatlinburg.com) with a beer hall, sing-alongs, yodeling, and authentic German food. **Gatlinburg Winter Magic** (800/588-1817) is a 120-day celebration of all things winter and holiday. From early November through February, the city is a riot of millions of LED bulbs strung up in trees and forming elaborate displays. There's a chili cook-off, carolers, a Christmas parade, and more.

SHOPPING

Gatlinburg's touristy side has a big personality, and there are plenty of shops selling T-shirts and the expected souvenirs, but for something that truly speaks to the heritage of this place, you'll need to do a little looking around.

For a unique shop/museum (there is only one other place in the world like this and it's in Spain), stop in at **The Salt and Pepper Shaker Museum** (461 Brookside Village Way, 865/430-5515, www.thesaltandpeppershakermuseum.com, 10am-4pm daily in summer; 10am-2pm Mon.-Sat., noon-4pm Sun. in winter; $3 adults, ages 12 and under free). The name tells you what you'll find here, but it doesn't prepare you for the more than 20,000 salt and pepper shakers from around the world and the growing collection of pepper mills. The collection began on a lark, growing from one pepper mill into this massive assembly of the most banal of kitchen accessories. It's weird, so it's worth the cost of admission, especially when you can apply your admission fee to any gift shop purchase—and who doesn't want a salt and pepper set shaped like outhouses?

★ Great Smoky Arts and Crafts Community

Your first stop should be the **Great Smoky Arts and Crafts Community** (turn right at traffic light #3 and go three miles to Glades Rd., www.gatlinburgcrafts.com). Founded in 1937, it is among the largest (if not *the* largest) group of independent artisans in the United States. There are more than 120 artisans and craftspeople running shops, studios, and galleries along this eight-mile loop consisting of Glades Road, Buckhorn Road, and US-321. Look for the logo denoting membership in the community so you know that the goods you're seeing and buying are from genuine local and regional artisans. One thing that sets this community apart is the fact that you can interact with the artists in their studios and galleries. You can watch them work, ask questions, maybe even lend a hand (if asked). With so many galleries and studios to visit,

you can easily spend a day or two if you want to take a peek into each and every gallery, shop, and studio.

The shop artisans range from candlemakers to watercolor artists to photographers to leatherworkers to the creators of traditional mountain crafts. **Ogle's Broom Shop** (670 Glades Rd., 865/430-4402, 10am-5pm Mon.-Sat.) is one such traditional crafts shop, with third-generation broom makers. The shop was opened by the grandfather of current owner David Ogle. He carries on the tradition today, making brooms from broomstraw and hand carving canes and walking sticks.

Otto Preske, Artist in Wood (535 Buckhorn Rd., 865/436-5339, www.ottopreskeartistinwood.com) is a superb woodcarver. He carves and turns Christmas ornaments, hiking staffs, fireplace mantels, religious carvings, and highly detailed figures and relief carvings. The work is stunning, and to watch him carve is simply amazing.

Throughout the community there are several basket weavers, but none like those you'll find at **Licklog Hollow Baskets** (1360 E. Parkway, 865/436-3823). Not only do they have the strangest name, the work here is superb. Whether you're buying for form or function, you'll find a basket that fits your style and probably your budget.

One of my favorite stops is **Woodland Tiles** (220 Buckhorn Rd., 865/640-0989, www.woodlandtilesbymarie.com). Here they make tiles and functional pottery pieces inspired by the leaves on the trees surrounding Gatlinburg. Custom glazes capture the jewel green of summer and the blazing colors of fall, and the sizes and shapes are spot-on—the tiles mirror the leaves that inspired them.

The Village

In downtown Gatlinburg you'll find **The Village** (634 Parkway, 865/436-3995, www.thevillageshops.com, 10am-5pm daily Jan.-Feb., 10am-6pm daily Mar., 10am-8pm Sun.-Fri. and 10am-10pm Sat. Apr.-May and Nov., 10am-10pm June-Oct., hours vary Dec.), a collection of 27 shops centered on a courtyard and housed in a Bavarian-style structure. Among the shops here are **The Sock Shop** (865/325-6000, www.sockshoptn.com), where you'll find comfy, crazy, cool, and quirky socks. They also sell wool socks, dress socks, and more, as long as it goes on your feet. **The Day Hiker** (865/430-0970, www.thedayhiker.com) provides the basic gear you need to take day and short overnight hikes in GSMNP. **The Silver Tree** (865/430-3573) is a silver lover's paradise with plenty of silver jewelry and accessories to peruse. Last but not least is **The Donut Friar** (865/436-7306, www.the-donut-friar.com, from 5am daily), an amazing bakery making donuts, cinnamon bread, and other pastries. They sell coffee to go with your morning donut.

RECREATION

There is no end to the outdoor recreation opportunities near Gatlinburg. At **Nantahala Outdoor Center Gatlinburg** (1138 Parkway, 865/277-8209, www.noc.com, 10am-9pm daily), you'll find a huge retail store selling everything you'd ever need to gear up for an outdoor adventure. NOC is the region's leader in outdoor guide services, providing white-water rafting, float trips, and kayaking on several rivers across the region; guided hikes and fly-fishing trips; and more. Their trips vary by season, so check the website or ask someone at the store about current trips and activities.

Rafting in the Smokies (813 E. Parkway, 800/776-7238, www.raftinginthesmokies.com, Tues.-Thurs. and Sat. Memorial Day-Labor Day, $42, but they often run specials) is another white-water rafting outfitter. Trips depend on the weather and water levels, so it's a good idea to call ahead or check online for current trips and reservations. Once you've gotten it nailed down, check in at the rafting outpost in Hartford and I-40 Exit 447. Rafting in the Smokies has a number of other outdoor offerings on deck, such as a zip line canopy tour ($39), ropes course ($33), and

family adventure packages that roll all this (and geocaching, horseback riding, and more) into one day ($65-116).

Zip Gatlinburg (125 Historic Nature Trail, 865/430-9475, www.thegatlinburg-zipline.com, zip line $59, ropes course $50, trapeze net $10) has a 9-element zip course, a 27-element ropes course, and a trapeze net on the hillside overlooking town. Between the zips, the swinging platforms, and a pair of sky bridges, you'll get your fill of high-flying thrills. The trapeze net was originally intended for aerial adrenaline enthusiasts too young or light for the zip line (read: the kids), but it's plenty of fun for anyone with the gumption to jump on.

Ober Gatlinburg

Ober Gatlinburg (1001 Parkway, 865/436-5423, www.obergatlinburg.com, hours vary by activity, but generally 9:30am-9pm daily in spring, summer, and fall, 10am-7pm in winter, individual activities $4-12, activity passes $22-33 adults, $19-28 children 5-11), the mountaintop resort that looks out over Gatlinburg, is a ski resort in the winter and a mountain playground the rest of the year. There are eight ski and snowboard trails and Ober Gatlinburg is equipped with plenty of snowmaking equipment to make up for what Mother Nature doesn't supply. Warm-weather activities include the awesome Alpine Slide, a sort of luge that follows one of the ski slopes down the hill; a pair of raft-based waterslides; a maze; and year-round indoor ice skating. There's also the Wildlife Encounter, where you can see many of the native species found in the area. If you're hungry, there are several places to grab a bite ranging from a slice of pizza to a steak.

The resort is a little dated and leans toward the cheesy end of the spectrum, and many people skip it if it's not ski season. Others think it's worth the little bit of time and money to take the tram to the top of the hill and ride the Alpine Slide.

FOOD

Dining in Gatlinburg, especially for foodies, can be tricky. In a town where literally millions of people pass through, you get a lot of restaurants that have stopped caring about repeat customers and seek only to provide a heaping plate of food and mediocre service at premium prices, knowing their diners will be in for one, maybe two meals during their visit. And there are plenty of major chains ready to take your dining dollars. That said, it is possible to find a good, even great, meal here.

The **Smoky Mountain Trout House** (410 Parkway, 865/436-5416, from 5pm nightly, around $20) has a mesmerizing aquarium window teeming with rainbow trout. (It mesmerized me as a kid when, after walking past it a dozen times, I finally convinced my parents to eat there.) The menu is trout-heavy: rainbow trout grilled, broiled, pan fried, or seasoned with dill or parmesan; trout almandine; and smoked trout. There are a few menu items—prime rib, a rib eye steak, country ham, chicken, catfish, and shrimp—that aren't trout. The food tastes better than the dining room would have you believe, and this is a pretty good meal, especially if you like trout.

A longtime Gatlinburg eatery, **The Peddler** (820 River Rd., 865/436-5794, www.peddlergatlinburg.com, from 5pm Sun.-Fri., from 4:30pm Sat., $23-37) is still a solid choice for a steak. The dining room overlooks the river, making it a nice spot to eat. The menu is steak-heavy, but they also have shrimp, chicken, and trout, and every entrée comes with a pretty robust salad bar.

Bennett's Pit Bar-B-Que (714 River Rd., 865/436-2400, www.bennetts-bbq.com, breakfast from 8am daily, lunch from 11am daily, dinner from 3pm daily, breakfast buffet $9.99 adults, $4.99 kids, lunch $9-15, dinner $10-36) serves hickory-smoked barbecue in many forms: pork ribs, pulled pork, chicken, beef brisket, hot smoked sausage, and burnt ends (a brisket treat that's not to be missed). The platters of food are, as they are in most barbecue joints, obscenely big, so don't feel bad if you can't finish your meal.

For the last several years, **Alamo Steakhouse and Saloon** (705 E. Parkway, 865/436-9998, www.alamosteakhouse.com, lunch 11am-3pm daily, dinner from 3pm daily, $14-31) has been widely lauded as having the best steak, so sit down and order one—they have plenty of options to choose from. If you're not in the mood for steak, there are a number of pork, chicken, and seafood dishes. The service is generally very good, but, like all restaurants in a busy vacation town, can get bogged down in the high season.

★ **Big Daddy's Pizzeria** (714 River Rd., 865/436-5455, www.bigdaddyspizzeria. net, from 11am daily, $9-23) has locations in Gatlinburg, Pigeon Forge, and Sevierville. Their claim to fame is a wood-fired brick oven and a creative flair in the creation of their pies. Get the tried-and-true pepperoni and cheese, or go wild with the Smoky Mounty Cheese Steak (with shaved prime rib, caramelized onions, gorgonzola cheese, and potato slices), the Herbivore (a veggie packed delight), or one of their other signature pizzas. They also have sandwiches prepared on house-made focaccia, fresh salads, and meatballs.

Across the street from the aquarium is **No Way Jose's Cantina** (555 Parkway, 865/436-5673, www.nowayjosescantina.com, 11:30am-10pm daily, $5-15). Grab a riverside seat and order a basket of chips and killer homemade salsa before you even glance at the menu. The rest of the menu is pretty standard Tex-Mex fare, but tastes fresh.

Gatlinburg has pancake houses in spades. The oldest pancake house in town opened in 1960 and it also happens to be the first of its kind in Tennessee. **Pancake Pantry** (628 Parkway, 865/436-4724, 7am-4pm daily June-Oct., 7am-3pm daily Nov.-May, $6-10) still puts out a great spread of flapjacks. There are 24 varieties of pancakes and crepes, as well as a half-dozen waffles and omelets and French toast. Breakfast is served all day, but if you feel like a burger or sandwich for lunch, they have a few of those too.

Wild Plum (555 Buckhorn Rd., 865/436-3808, www.wildplumtearoom.com, 11am-3pm

Mon.-Sat., closed mid-Dec.-Mar. 1, $10-16) is a lunch-only restaurant inspired by Austrian teahouses. They serve the Southern classic, tomato pie, but the real stars of the menu are the chef's specials. The specials vary daily, but in the past have included lobster pie, a salmon burger, smoked salmon sandwiches, and yellowfin tuna.

Hands down the best fine-dining experience in Gatlinburg, ★ **The Restaurant at Buckberry Creek** (961 Campbell Lead Rd., 865/430-8030, www.buckberrylodge.com, breakfast from 8am daily, dinner 5:30pm-9pm Thurs.-Sat. Jan.-Feb., Tues.-Sat. Mar.-Sept. and Nov.-Dec., daily in Oct., $20-45) serves a small, ever-changing menu. During tomato season, expect to see fried green tomatoes as a first bite and tomatoes on and in most of the salads and entrées; wild mushrooms and ramps may appear in spring, and other ingredients will take the stage as they ripen throughout the season. Entrées commonly include pan-seared duck, beef tenderloin, and tuna, sea bass, or another flavorful fish. Don't skip dessert: The crème brûlée and the fresh sorbet are quite nice. Unfortunately, diners won't be able to enjoy a meal here for some time as the Restaurant (and Lodge) suffered a total loss in the 2016 wildfires. The owners are planning to rebuild, so keep an eye on them toward the end of 2017 for re-opening dates.

ACCOMMODATIONS

Something about being in Gatlinburg makes me want to stay in a cabin. Fortunately, there are plenty of options whether you're traveling solo, as a pair, or with even the largest of groups. ★ **Mountain Laurel Chalets** (440 Ski Mountain Rd., 800/626-3431, www.mtnlaurelchalets.com, $99-899/night) has several lodges and large houses sleeping anywhere from 10-20 people if you're traveling with your extended family, or smaller cabins that sleep a couple or small group on a getaway. The cabins are spread out over a huge property, so they're private in addition to being cozy. Some of the cabins, the last ones

in line for a refresh, are dated, but others are quite nice inside, so it's worth checking cabin descriptions online.

Located between Gatlinburg and Pigeon Forge, **Autumn Ridge** (505 Crest Rd., 865/436-4111 or 800/397-4343, www.autumnridgerentals.com, Jan.-Mar. from $105, Apr.-Dec. from $115, Oct. and holidays from $125) has five cabins, each with a two-night minimum and a view you'll come back for. King-size beds are the norm here, as are whirlpool tubs or hot tubs and wood-burning fireplaces (firewood provided). This is a romantic spot and a popular one for honeymooners, so make your reservation sooner rather than later.

Laurel Springs Lodge Bed and Breakfast (204 Hill St., 865/430-9211 or 888/430-9211, www.laurelspringslodge.com, $135-169) is lovely, comfortable, and highly regarded. There are five rooms, all well decorated and comfortable, and a gourmet breakfast is served every morning. Downtown is a short walk away, but even though you're close, you're away from the buzz of Gatlinburg's main drag and can relax when you come back to your room.

The Foxtrot Bed and Breakfast (1520 Garrett Lane, 865/436-3033, www.thefoxtrot.com, $190-230) is a little different than most B&Bs in that an actual chef prepares breakfast. That's just one thing that sets it apart. The Foxtrot is high on a hill well above the noise, traffic, and bustle of downtown Gatlinburg, making it a true retreat. There are several packages you can add to your room, like spa packages, honeymoon and anniversary packages, cooking schools, and more.

One of the finest places to stay in Gatlinburg is ★ **The Lodge at Buckberry Creek** (961 Campbell Lead Rd., 865/430-8030, www.buckberrylodge.com, $205-460). Though it calls itself "The Great Camp of the Smokies," the rooms here are anything but camp-like. Sure, the walls are wood paneled and elements of the decor say rustic, but the finishes speak to luxury. Situated on 26 acres, The Lodge is surrounded by hiking trails, a trout stream, and romantic pavilions along the banks of Buckberry Creek. With the best fine-dining restaurant in Gatlinburg located in the complex, this is the kind of place you could come for the weekend and never leave the property. Unfortunately, the Lodge was a total loss in the 2016 wildfires. Rebuilding efforts are ongoing. Look for reopening dates in late 2017 and early 2018.

Throughout Gatlinburg there are a number of chain hotels with prices ranging from budget to mid-range. Three of the more reliable hotels are The Park Vista, Hampton Inn Gatlinburg, and Hilton Garden Inn. **The Park Vista** (705 Cherokee Orchard Rd., 865/436-9211, www.parkvista.com, $135-190), a Doubletree by Hilton hotel, has excellent views from each room's private balcony. The rooms are spacious and comfortable, and the hotel is adjacent to the Roaring Fork Motor Nature Trail. Unfortunately, the Park Vista suffered some damage in the wildfires. Repairs are expected to be completed in 2017 and service should be uninterrupted for most visitors.

The **Hampton Inn Gatlinburg** (967 Parkway, 865/436-4878, www.hamptoninn3. hilton.com, $150-199) has private balconies and is within walking distance of most of Gatlinburg's attractions. Finally, the **Hilton Garden Inn** (635 River Rd., 865/436-0048, www.hiltongardeninn3.hilton.com, $140-249) is also walkable to downtown and has free parking.

Several smaller hotels, cabins, and condominium resorts were damaged or lost in the wildfires that ravaged the Smoky Mountains in late 2016, making accommodations all the more precious in Gatlinburg and Pigeon Forge. With that in mind, make travel plans early and make your reservations sooner rather than later.

TRANSPORTATION AND SERVICES

Car

Most visitors arrive in Gatlinburg via Newfound Gap Road (US-441) heading west from Cherokee, North Carolina, through Great Smoky Mountains National Park. From Cherokee it's an approximately 45-minute drive through the park. Gatlinburg is easy to find: one minute you're in the park, the next minute you're in Gatlinburg.

For those driving from the north or west, I-40 is the most convenient road into town. From I-40, take Exit 407 and hop on US-66 south; this road feeds into US-441 and leads past Sevierville and Pigeon Forge to Gatlinburg. This is the easiest and most heavily traveled route into town from I-40. You can avoid the peak-season crowds by taking Exit 435 near Knoxville (an hour away) and following US-321 south into Gatlinburg.

Coming in from the east on I-40, the best bet is to take Exit 443 and drive along the beautiful Foothills Parkway to US-321 south, from which you cruise right into town.

PARKING

Finding parking in Gatlinburg can be quite tough. There are a number of public and private parking lots and garages where you can park your car if you're not staying at a hotel nearby. Parking rates vary depending on public or private ownership, so for affordability, it's often best to stick to the public parking garages at **Ripley's Aquarium of the Smokies** (88 River Rd., $1.75 first hour, $1 each hour after, or $6/day) and the **McMahan Parking Garage** (520 Parkway, at traffic light #3, $1.75 first hour, $1 each hour after, or $6/day).

Air

The **McGhee-Tyson Airport** outside of Knoxville is 42 miles from Gatlinburg. Head south to Maryville on US-129. Once you're in Maryville, take US-321 north to Pigeon Forge, then turn right and take US-441 into Gatlinburg.

Public Transit

Gatlinburg has a great trolley system that can get you to and from every attraction in Gatlinburg and nearby Pigeon Forge, including Dollywood. The **Gatlinburg Trolley** (88 River Rd., Suite 101, 865/436-3897, www.gatlinburgtrolley.org, 10am-10pm daily Mar.-Apr., 8am-midnight daily May-Oct., 10am-6pm Sun.-Thurs and 10am-10pm Fri.-Sat. Nov.-Feb., extended hours on select holiday and event dates) has more than 100 stops in Gatlinburg alone. It's cheap, with most rides only $0.50, but your best bet is to pick up an All Day Trolley Pass ($2) from the **Gatlinburg Welcome Center** (1011 Banner Rd., 865/277-8957, www.gatlinburg.com, 8:30am-7pm daily), the **Parkway Visitor Center** (520 Parkway, 10am-6pm daily) at traffic light #3, or the **Aquarium Welcome Center** (88 River Rd., 9am-9pm daily).

Services

There are three visitors centers in Gatlinburg: the **Gatlinburg Welcome Center** (1011 Banner Rd., 865/277-8957, www.gatlinburg.com, 8:30am-7pm daily), the **Parkway Visitor Center** (520 Parkway, 10am-6pm daily) at traffic light #3, and the **Aquarium Welcome Center** (88 River Rd., 9am-9pm daily).

On the radio, **WWST** (93.7 FM) plays the Top 40. **WSEV** (105.5 FM) is an adult contemporary station.

LeConte Medical Center (742 Middle Creek Rd., Sevierville, 865/446-7000, www.lecontemedicalcenter.com) is the nearest hospital, just over 20 minutes away. The **Gatlinburg Police** (1230 E. Parkway, 865/436-5181) are available if the need arises.

Pigeon Forge and Sevierville

The dominating presence in Pigeon Forge and Sevierville is that of Dolly Parton. Her namesake amusement park is in Pigeon Forge and she was born and raised in Sevierville, where a statue of Dolly stands in front of the courthouse. You'll see her face, hear her music, and maybe even meet one of her many cousins everywhere across these two towns.

These towns have grown a lot since Dolly was born, thanks largely to the popularity of Great Smoky Mountains National Park. More growth came when the amusement park that would become Dollywood opened its doors, and again when nearby Knoxville hosted the World's Fair. But to keep more than 10 million annual visitors coming back year after year, Pigeon Forge and Sevierville had to become destinations unto themselves, and, for the most part, they've succeeded. Pigeon Forge has become one of the biggest "tourist traps" (which I say not with disdain, but astonishment—the place is a wonderland of vacation delights) on the East Coast. Want to ride go-karts and go bungee jumping at 9pm on a Wednesday? No problem. Midnight mini golf? Got it. Roller coasters, neon signs, and

fudge shops? Pigeon Forge has got you covered. But don't be fooled by all the neon, hotels, and attractions: Pigeon Forge remains a small town, with fewer than 7,000 year-round residents.

In the midst of this swirl of touristy flotsam is a surprising center for engaging with the community's culture: Dollywood. This amusement park has been around in some form or another since the 1960s, though in the early days it was kitsch over culture. As the park matured and expanded, so did its attention to the culture of mountain living. Today the park is home to some great bluegrass and country shows and a good deal of shops and exhibits where Appalachian crafters showcase their skills and their wares.

SIGHTS
★ Dollywood
At **Dollywood** (2700 Dollywood Parks Blvd., Pigeon Forge, 800/365-5996, www.dollywood.com, Apr.-Dec., $52-65, parking $11), you might just catch a glimpse of Dolly Parton walking through the park or performing for the crowds at the park's opening day. Even if

you don't see the country music icon, the park has plenty of rides, cultural stops, shows, and nature experiences to keep you busy.

Dollywood started in 1961, when Rebel Railroad, a small attraction with a steam train, general store, blacksmith shop, and saloon, opened. By 1977, the park had grown and changed hands more than once. Renamed Silver Dollar City, the park eventually caught the attention of Dolly Parton. In 1986, Dolly became a partner and lent the park her name. Since then it's become Tennessee's most-visited tourist attraction (outside GSMNP) and is consistently named among the top theme parks in the world.

Dollywood has a great look: one-part Appalachian village, one-part small Southern town. There arc tree-lined streets and paths, and several streams follow their courses through the park. You don't see the rides until you're right up on them because they're tucked away in the woods.

One of the best-known spots in the park is **Showstreet,** where stages and theaters are always busy with musicians, square dances, and storytellers. There's also a bevy of master craftspeople practicing their Appalachian arts for all to see: blacksmiths, basket-makers, candlemakers, and woodworkers. On Showstreet, you may see some of Dolly's relatives playing and singing in shows throughout the year. Seasonal shows include a half-dozen Christmas concerts, Harvest Celebration Southern Gospel, and more.

Also on Showstreet is a carriage, sled, and wagon shop called **Valley Carriage Works.** The Carriage Works takes orders from clients from around the world and builds beautiful, fully functional, historically accurate carriages. At the Museum of the Cherokee Indian in Cherokee, North Carolina, you can see a replica Cherokee wagon that they built to commemorate the 165th anniversary of the Trail of Tears.

It's easy to find a souvenir in the park, whether you want a Dollywood keepsake or a handcrafted gift from one of the shops in Craftsman's Valley, where you'll find handcrafted goods like leather belts, blown glass, and baskets.

Given that the park allows nature to be such a prominent feature in its design, it's no surprise to learn that Dollywood has partnered with the American Eagle Foundation and is authorized by U.S. Fish and Wildlife Services and thc Tennessee Wildlife Resources Agency to possess eagles and other birds for education, exhibition, rehabilitation,

TENNESSEE GATEWAYS
PIGEON FORGE AND SEVIERVILLE

amusement park ride at Dollywood in Pigeon Forge

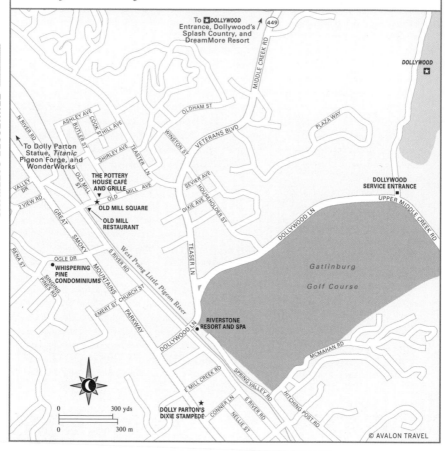

Pigeon Forge

and breeding. The 30,000-square-foot **aviary** is home to the nation's largest group of non-releasable bald eagles (many of these birds have been injured and wouldn't survive if released into nature). Daily shows put visitors in proximity to these incredible birds.

Dollywood has more than 40 **rides and attractions** that range from kid-friendly to thrilling. My favorites were the Blazing Fury, an indoor roller coaster where you're trying to outrun an out-of-control fire; Thunderhead, a great wooden coaster; and Daredevil Falls, an updated version of the log-flume ride.

Plenty of snack stands and restaurants are located throughout the park. I remember loving the berries and cream and having my first plate of whole-hog barbecue here. The memories are good, but those meals aren't cheap. But, it's an amusement park and you'll be there all day, so what are you going to do?

Dollywood's Splash Country

Waterparks abound in Pigeon Forge and Sevierville, but the best is **Dollywood's Splash Country** (2700 Dollywood Parks Blvd., Pigeon Forge, 800/365-5996, www. dollywood.com, May-Sept., $43-48, parking $11). This water park has 29 waterslides, a lazy river, three water-play areas for kids, a 7,500-square-foot leisure pool, and 25,000-square-foot wave pool. There are also concessions and a gift shop, stroller rentals, and lockers to rent.

Dolly Parton Statue

Local artist Jim Gray sculpted a **statue** (125 Court Ave.) that shows Dolly with a wide smile and her guitar, as if she's ready to write a song at any moment. Stop by downtown Sevierville to take a picture with the statue, located on the courthouse lawn.

Tennessee Museum of Aviation

Head to the Gatlinburg-Pigeon Forge Airport in Sevierville to brush up on your aviation history at the **Tennessee Museum of Aviation** (135 Air Museum Way, Sevierville, 866/286-8738, www.tnairmuseum.com, 10am-6pm Mon.-Sat. and 1pm-6pm Sun. Mar.-Dec., 10am-5pm Mon.-Sat. and 1pm-5pm Sun. Jan.-Feb., adults $12.75, seniors $9.75, children 6-12 $6.75). Housed in a 35,000-square-foot hangar, the museum has a number of exhibits and a dozen historic aircraft, including two airworthy P-47 Thunderbolts (that sometimes take to the air),

a MiG-21, and F-86 Saberjet. But the best treat is when you visit the museum and one of the historic World War II aircraft is taking flight.

Titanic Pigeon Forge

One somewhat odd attraction is the *Titanic* **Pigeon Forge** (2134 Parkway, Pigeon Forge, 800/381-7670, www.titanicpigeonforge. com, 9am-close daily, closed Jan. 12-15 and Christmas Day, adults $27, children 5-12 $11.25). This massive museum includes three decks and 20 galleries spread over 30,000 square feet. The galleries feature artifacts salvaged from the sunken luxury ship. There's a reproduction of the Marconi wireless room, a first-class suite and third-class cabin, as well as a full-scale reproduction of the grand staircase. Touring the ship takes about two hours.

WonderWorks

From the outside, the building that houses **WonderWorks** (100 Music Rd., Pigeon Forge, 865/868-1800, www.wonderworksonline.com, 9am-10pm daily, adults $25, seniors and children 4-12 $17) appears to be upside down. Inside this science-inspired amusement center are more than 100 interactive exhibits; some, like the Tesla Coil and

WonderWorks

the Earthquake Café, are strange and seem dangerous, while others challenge you to use your imagination to solve puzzles or test your willpower. While it's definitely geared toward kids in the tween range, adults will find plenty to marvel at.

ENTERTAINMENT

If you want to wet your whistle in Pigeon Forge, your options are exclusively bars in restaurants. The two best of these are at the Island in Pigeon Forge. **Smoky Mountain Brewery** (2530 Parkway, Suite 15, Pigeon Forge, 865/868-1400, www.smoky-mtn-brewery.com, 11am-midnight daily, food $5-25, drinks $3-12) brews every drop of their draft beer in-house or at one of their three sister restaurants, and they serve up some good grub if you want something to munch on or are hungry enough for a full meal. **Mellow Mushroom** (131 Island Dr., #3101, Pigeon Forge, www.mellowmushroom.com, 10am-midnight daily, $9-20) specializes in the best national and regional craft beer and some very tasty pizza, subs, and salads.

Dolly Parton's Dixie Stampede (3849 Parkway, Pigeon Forge, 865/453-9473, www.dixiestampede.com, daily, call for showtimes, adults from $50, children from $25) is one-part dinner, one-part show. The dinner's a four-course country feast and the show is jam-packed with horseback stunts, comedy, pyrotechnics, and some genuinely surreal sights to take in while you're eating in what is essentially a small arena.

The Smoky Mountain Opry (2046 Parkway, Pigeon Forge, 865/428-7469, www.smokymtnopry.com, daily, showtimes vary, adults $50, children $20) is a variety show filled with singers and dancers, jugglers and aerial acrobats, magicians, comedians, and musicians; they even have a white lion for some reason. They also have a Christmas show that draws quite the crowd.

SHOPPING

There's no shortage of touristy shopping around here, but you can find specialty shops, galleries, and decent shopping if you know where to look.

Pigeon Forge earned part of its name from a forge set up in 1820 by Isaac Love. (The other part of its name came from the incredible number of passenger pigeons the early settlers found living along the banks of the Little Pigeon River.) A decade later Love's son established a mill, which is now on the National Register of Historic Places. **The Old Mill Square** (175 Old Mill Ave., Pigeon Forge, 865/428-0771, www.old-mill.com, hours vary by store) is a collection of shops and restaurants in a cute restored and re-created historic area. **The Old Mill General Store** (865/453-4628, 8:30am-9pm Mon.-Sat., 9am-8pm Sun., hours vary off-season) has all sorts of country provisions, including fresh-ground grains milled next door at the Old Mill. **The Old Mill Farmhouse Kitchen** (865/428-2044, 9:30am-8pm Sun.-Thurs., 9am-9pm Fri.-Sat., hours vary off-season) also sells a variety of provisions and ingredients that you need to cook your own country meal at home. They also have a nice pottery shop and gift baskets.

You can get your fill of candy at **The Old Mill Candy Kitchen** (865/453-7516, 9am-8:30pm Mon.-Thurs., 9am-9pm Fri.-Sat., 9am-8pm Sun., hours vary off-season), and kids will love visiting **The Old Mill Toy Bin** (865/774-2258, 9:30am-8pm Sun.-Thurs., 9am-9pm Fri.-Sat., hours vary off-season), where they'll find all sorts of wooden toys and old-fashioned playthings.

The **Incredible Christmas Place** (2470 Parkway, Pigeon Forge, 865/453-0145, 9am-9pm daily Memorial Day-July 4, 9am-10pm daily July 4-Dec., call for hours Jan.-May) is just that, an incredible store that's all Christmas, all the time. Get bows, ornaments, decorations, trees, lights, and any number of collectibles from Boyds Bears, Department 56, and Snow Buddies.

At **The Apple Barn Cider Mill and General Store** (230 Apple Valley Rd., Sevierville, 865/453-9319, www.applebarncidermill.com, 9am-7pm Mon.-Thurs., 9am-9pm Fri.-Sat., 9am-5:30pm Sun.), you can buy fresh cider, a bushel of just-picked apples, a pie hot from the oven, and more. At this great stop, you'll be in a working orchard with more than 4,000 trees, and you can watch the cider presses at work while you munch on an apple donut.

Tanger Outlets (1645 Parkway, Sevierville, 865/453-1053, www.tangeroutlet. com, 9am-9pm Mon.-Sat., 10am-7pm Sun.) in Sevierville has dozens of shops including brand-name outlets like Coach, Levi's, Michael Kors, Polo Ralph Lauren, Samsonite, Vera Bradley, and Banana Republic.

If you're looking for a home decor souvenir, look no further than **Aunt Debbie's Country Store** (1753 Wears Valley Rd., Sevierville, 865/366-7359, www. auntdebbiescountrystore.com, 8am-5pm Mon.-Sat.). Barnwood signs, cedar swings, primitive decor, and rustic elements that would bring a touch of the Smokies into your home are on display here. There's a lot to see, so when you stop by, be sure you budget a bit of time to this store.

RECREATION

There is plenty to get into when you're in Pigeon Forge and Sevierville. Of course you can hike in the national park, but you can also go white-water rafting, ride a crazy alpine coaster, or even skydive—with a twist.

You can try indoor skydiving at **Flyaway Indoor Skydiving** (3106 Parkway, Pigeon Forge, 877/293-0639, www.flyawayindoorskydiving.com, 10am-8pm daily, $34 first flight, $22 additional flight). Indoor skydiving is done in a vertical wind tunnel—think a silo with some giant fans in the base—with an experienced skydiving instructor. After a brief ground school where you'll familiarize yourself with the proper body positions, basics of maneuvering yourself, and hand signals used to communicate with your instructor, you'll get dressed and be ready to fly. In the wind tunnel, it's disorienting the first time you leave your feet and assume the skydiving position because you're floating a few feet off the net

where you were just standing. Relax, follow your instructor's directions, and enjoy the experience. If you're lucky, before or after your session, you'll get to see some experienced indoor skydivers perform amazing acrobatic tricks that look like something out of *The Matrix* as they whirl around the tunnel with precise control.

One of the newest, and most interesting, outdoor activities is the **Smoky Mountain Alpine Coaster** (867 Wears Valley Rd., Pigeon Forge, 865/365-5000, www. smokymountainalpinecoaster.com, 9am-9pm daily weather permitting, adults $15, children 7-12 $12, children 3-6 $5). This odd little quasi-roller coaster puts you in a track-mounted sled complete with an automatic speed control and manual brakes and sends you down a one-mile track, spiraling through tight turns and down a few steep(ish) drops.

Get a view of the Smokies that few others see with **Scenic Helicopter Tours** (tickets at 1965 Parkway, Sevierville, heliport at 1949 Winfield Dunn Parkway, Sevierville, 865/453-6342, www.scenichelicoptertours.com, flight times vary, $28-1,230). Choose from a dozen tours flying over different parts of the region. Short tours like the 8-mile flight along the French Broad River are fun and affordable, while the huge, 100-mile Smoky Mountains Spectacular will set you back more than a thousand bucks, but it's worth it because this tour circles much of the national park.

Smoky Mountain Ziplines (509 Mill Creek Rd., Pigeon Forge, 865/429-9004, www.smokymountainziplines.com, daily, times vary, call for availability, $70-125) has a 9-line and 14-line canopy tour as well as two super zip lines that are 800 feet long and 100 feet high. This is fun and family-friendly. Note that for kids to zip solo, they must be at least 8 years old and 60 pounds; children 5-7 or under 60 pounds may be able to ride tandem with the guide.

Though most of the golf you've seen has been of the mini variety, the **Gatlinburg Golf Course** (520 Dollywood Lane, Pigeon Forge, 800/231-4128, www.golf.gatlinburg.com, daily, call for hours and tee times, $30-60) offers you a full-sized round on a beautiful course. Designed by William Langford and renovated twice by Bob Cupp & Associates, this 18-hole course has some dramatic holes. The signature 12th hole, nicknamed "Sky Hi," is 194 yards long and has a 200-foot drop from the tee to the green, making it a puzzling hole for many golfers and a fun one for all. The pro shop here has everything you'll need to play a round, including a full-service restaurant so you can grab a bite and a beer after you're finished.

The Island In Pigeon Forge (131 Island Dr., 865/286-0119, www.islandpigeonforge. com, 10am-11pm Mon.-Thurs., 10am-midnight Fri.-Sat., 10am-10pm Sun.) is a tourist extravaganza. You'll find a half-dozen restaurants and as many snack shops, 20 or so stores selling everything from jerky to puzzles to gems, and rides galore. Rides and entertainment options include the 200-foot-tall Great Smoky Mountain Wheel, a mirror maze, and a huge arcade.

FOOD

At the Old Mill there's a quaint collection of shops and a pair of restaurants. **The Old Mill Restaurant** (160 Old Mill Ave., Pigeon Forge, 865/429-3463, www.old-mill.com, 8am-8pm daily, off-season hours vary, breakfast $7-11, lunch $9-11, dinner $13-28, kids $6-9 at each meal) is family-friendly and has a small selection for kids. The Pigeon River flows by right outside the dining room, and this is a bigger draw than the food, which is traditional country fare (though breakfast is pretty good).

The Pottery House Café and Grill (175 Old Mill Ave., Pigeon Forge, 865/453-6002, www.old-mill.com, lunch 11am-4pm daily, dinner 4pm-late Sun.-Thurs., 4pm-8pm Fri.-Sat., lunch $8.50-12, dinner $8-19) is known for its delicious quiche and outstanding dessert. They serve everything from steaks to fried chicken livers (served with buffalo sauce and blue cheese dressing) and sandwiches. Rather than trout, which is served by many area eateries, they serve catfish here, which is

just as good. If you like what you get for dessert, it's likely you can get a whole cake or pie to take home with you.

★ **Poynor's Pommes Frites** (131 The Island Dr., Suite 3107, Pigeon Forge, 865/774-7744, 11am-10pm daily, $5-10) may not look like much from the outside, but the food is great. The specialty is the pommes frites (french fries). Done in a Belgian style (fried, cooled, then fried again), they're crispy on the outside and fluffy inside, and served either plain, with your choice of sauce, or even topped with cheese, bacon, onions, and jalapenos. You can't make a meal of french fries, so Poynor's serves a short menu of bratwurst served on a German hard roll.

★ **Mel's Diner** (119 Wears Valley Rd., Pigeon Forge, 865/429-2184, www.melsdinerpf.com, 7am-1am daily, breakfast $3-10, lunch and dinner $6-10) serves up classic diner food with a side of 1950s flair. With tasty, relatively inexpensive dishes served at breakfast, lunch, and dinner (and even rare late-night dining), you can't go wrong here. The breakfast plates are quite hearty, and the burgers and sandwiches piled high with toppings, but save room for dessert and order a whopping six-scoop banana split or a more reasonable shake or malt.

If you're prepared for a feast, head to **Huck Finn's Catfish** (3330 Parkway, Pigeon Forge, 865/429-3353, www.huckfinnsrestaurant.com, from 11:30am daily, lunch $8, dinner $12-19). Their all-you-can-eat catfish and chicken dinners are their claim to fame. They serve a limited lunch menu of catfish and chicken done up several ways and "all 'u' can eat vittles"; vittles include hush puppies, mashed potatoes, fries, coleslaw, pickles, and baked beans. If you like your meal, buy a T-shirt to commemorate it, because if you buy a shirt, your next meal is free.

All throughout the Smokies, pancake houses rule the breakfast world. Though it looks nothing like a log cabin, one of the best in Pigeon Forge is **Log Cabin Pancake House** (4235 Parkway, Pigeon Forge, 865/453-5748, www.logcabinpancakehouse.com,

7am-2pm daily). The silver-dollar pancakes are good, and there are 20 pancake choices plus waffles and the expected breakfast dishes. They have a lunch buffet if you're starving when it's time for your midday meal, otherwise, it's hard to beat their patty melt.

The wings at **Blue Moose Burgers and Wings** (2430 Teaster Lane #108, Pigeon Forge, 865/286-0364, wwwbluemooseburgersand-wings.com, 11am-midnight daily, $8-24) are the best in town. There are around two dozen wing sauces, plus a menu that includes wraps, sandwiches, burgers, salads, and a couple of platters. If you're a wing nut, they have a 25-wing sampler comprising five flavors, five wings each. Unfortunately, their beer selection is bottom-shelf.

Mama's Farmhouse (208 Pickel St., Pigeon Forge, 865/908-4646, www.mamas-farmhouse.com, 11am-9pm Sun.-Thurs., 11am-10pm Fri.-Sat., closed an hour earlier in winter) is the place for a family-style Southern meal. Every meal is all you can eat (adults $13 breakfast, $16 lunch, $20 dinner; kids 5-12 $6 breakfast, $8 lunch, $9 dinner). Once you put in your drink order, the food will arrive, and there's a whole lot of it. For dinner, you'll get three meats—fried chicken with meatloaf, turkey and stuffing, ham, country-fried steak, or turkey pot pie—and your choice of five sides, plus soup or salad, biscuits, and dessert. Try the peach butter on your biscuits; you can thank me later.

ACCOMMODATIONS

There are several chain hotels in Pigeon Forge and Sevierville, and for the most part they're all the same. However, the **Clarion Inn** (124 Waldens Main St., Pigeon Forge, 865/868-5300, www.pigeonforgeclarion.com, $55-180) is convenient to anything you'll want to do in Pigeon Forge, and it has a pool, lazy river, and slide for the kids. Plus, they have a pretty good breakfast.

Whispering Pines Condominiums (205 Ogle Dr., Pigeon Forge, 800/429-4361, www.whisperingpinescondos.com, $100-300) has a great location if you want a front-row seat for the action of Pigeon Forge, or you can opt for mountain views and unwind a little. The condos here are large, so they're ideal for families or small groups traveling together, especially if you don't want to break the bank.

The Inn at Christmas Place (119 Christmas Tree Lane, Pigeon Forge, 888/465-9644, www.innatchristmasplace.com, $150-349) is an outstanding place to stay. Given that the place is permanently festooned with Christmas decorations (they are somewhat subdued from January to October) and they play Christmas music on a constant loop, I was surprised at how great this property is. Impeccable landscaping; a beautiful, turreted building; a robust breakfast; an indoor and outdoor pool, complete with a 95-foot waterslide; and a game room are only a few of the reasons this inn is such a find.

RiverStone Resort and Spa (212 Dollywood Lane, Pigeon Forge, 877/703-3220, www.riverstoneresort.com, $145-460) has condos and cabins that are luxurious through and through. Add to that an on-site full-service spa, and you have a truly relaxing place to stay. A playground and a lazy river keep the youngest guests occupied outdoors. There is a game room indoors. This is a great hotel for golfers, as it's adjacent to the Gatlinburg Golf Course.

★ **Dollywood's DreamMore Resort** (2525 DreamMore Way, Pigeon Forge, 800/365-5996, www.dollywoodsdream-moreresort.dollywood.com, from $190) was inspired by Dolly's own family-filled front porch. Though it's just a little bigger than the tiny cabin where she grew up, DreamMore promises that same family focus in its 307 rooms, indoor and outdoor pools, storytelling stations, restaurant, and Smoky Mountain views. It's the first hotel on Dollywood property, and as such, staying here has its privileges, like a complimentary shuttle to the park.

TRANSPORTATION AND SERVICES

Car

The most-traveled route to Pigeon Forge and Sevierville is I-40, carrying visitors in from the east and west. Exit 407 puts you on US-66 southeast, which leads into Sevierville and then feeds into US-441, taking you to Pigeon Forge. Most travelers will be going north on US-441, following Newfound Gap Road from Great Smoky Mountains National Park and Gatlinburg.

Public Transit

It's surprising to see a well-organized public transit system in a town the size of Pigeon Forge, but the **Fun Time Trolley** (186 Old Mill Ave., 865/453-6444, www.pigeonforgetrolley.org, 8am-midnight daily Mar.-Oct., 10am-10pm daily Nov.-Dec., $0.50-0.75 or an all-day pass for $2.50) has more than 100 regular stops in Pigeon Forge, Sevierville, and Gatlinburg. Routes run on a regular schedule (as traffic allows), and stops include all of the high points in the area. Passes are available at the address listed.

Services

The **Pigeon Forge Welcome Center** (1950 Parkway, 800/251-9100, www.mypigeonforge.com, 8:30am-5pm Mon.-Sat., 1pm-5pm Sun.) is located at traffic light #0 on Parkway. Here, and at the **Pigeon Forge Information Center** (3107 Parkway, 8:30am-5pm Mon.-Fri.), you can find information on the area and volunteers ready to help you plan your time here.

The folks at the **Sevierville Chamber of Commerce Visitors Center** (3099 Winfield Dunn Parkway, 888/738-4378, www.visitsevierville.com, 8:30am-5:30pm Mon.-Sat., 9am-6pm Sun.) are ready to help with trip planning, or they can simply point you in the right direction and help you enjoy your vacation.

If you need a hospital, **LeConte Medical Center** (742 Middle Creek Rd., Sevierville, 865/446-7000, www.lecontemedicalcenter.com) is your best bet.

There are three police departments here: the **Sevier County Sheriff's Office** (106 W. Bruce St., 865/453-4668), the **Pigeon Forge Police Department** (225 Pine Mountain Rd., 865/453-9063), and the **Sevier County Police Department** (300 Gary Wade Blvd., 865/453-5506).

Knoxville

Perhaps best known among college football fans, Knoxville is the biggest city in East Tennessee and a major travel hub granting access to Great Smoky Mountains National Park and, beyond that, the Blue Ridge Parkway. Unlike Nashville and Memphis, which have national reputations as music towns, Knoxville's fame comes from University of Tennessee Volunteers athletics, but that's a bit unfair because the city is also home to the historic Tennessee Theatre and the Bijou Theatre, and has a very lively music scene of its own.

In the last decade or so, downtown Knoxville has undergone a significant revitalization. Knoxville's downtown had suffered as businesses and residents left in favor of suburbs, office parks, and strip malls. Then, in 1982, the World's Fair came along and reignited Knoxville's hometown pride. Throughout the preparation for the fair, for the six months it was here, and for the year afterward, the city rode this wave of positive energy. When that wave lifted many residents and business owners saw what Knoxville could become. Historic restoration projects, downtown revitalization initiatives, and awareness campaigns began to roll out, and slowly, Knoxville began to turn. By the early 2000s, downtown Knoxville resonated with businesses. Restaurants and shops began to open in spruced-up buildings from yesteryear.

Knoxville

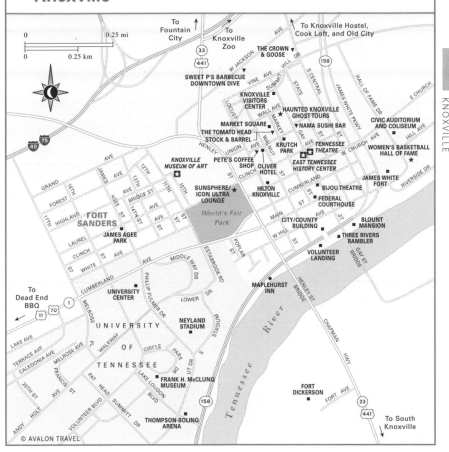

Bars followed, and boutiques began to flourish. Soon, downtown had turned into what it is today—a fun cultural center for the city and a place to visit rather than flee.

SIGHTS

★ East Tennessee History Center

In the heart of downtown, there's a great little museum telling the story of more than 200 years of East Tennessee's history. The **East Tennessee History Center** (601 S. Gay St., 865/215-8830, www.easttnhistory.org, 9am-4pm Mon.-Fri., 10am-4pm Sat., 1pm-5pm

Sun., adults $5, seniors $4, children 16 and under free, free admission on Sun.) has exhibits on the Cherokee, the local involvement in skirmishes and battles of the Civil War, notable slaves and former slaves from the region, the origins of country music, and many displays and scenes showing Knoxville throughout the years. There are also exhibits on logging and mining, two vocations important to the region, as well as Oak Ridge National Laboratory, where important work in World War II's Manhattan Project was conducted.

The museum itself is great, but also take

note of the wonderful neoclassical Italianate architecture of the building as you walk in. It's Knoxville's old Customs House, built in 1874. Since then, it has served several purposes—a courthouse, post office, TVA offices. Like many buildings around town, it's built from Tennessee marble.

★ Knoxville Museum of Art

The **Knoxville Museum of Art** (1050 World's Fair Park Dr., 865/525-6101, www. knoxart.org, 10am-5pm Tues.-Sat., 1pm-5pm Sun., free, donations accepted) is a three-story showcase of art and artists of East Tennessee. A huge exhibition, *Cycle of Life: Within the Power of Dreams and the Wonder of Infinity*, from renowned glass artist Richard Jolley, hangs on the walls and ceiling of the ground floor, and a colorful, impressive element of it—a nebula of colored glass orbs—can be seen as you walk through the museum doors. On the top level, two galleries show historic and contemporary works created by artists from or inspired by East Tennessee. The main level has another pair of galleries with rotating exhibits where they display national, international, and regional works, single-artist shows, and themed collections, like the assembly of more than a dozen pieces of amazing blown and cast glass sculptures.

★ Tennessee Theatre

The **Tennessee Theatre** (604 S. Gay St., 865/684-1200, www.tennesseetheatre.com, box office 10am-5pm Mon.-Fri., showtimes and ticket prices vary) is magnificent. In October 1928, this fabulous space opened its doors to rave reviews. The exterior features that classic marquee we just don't make today, and the inside puts any contemporary movie theater or music hall to shame. The Spanish-Moorish-style interior was painstakingly restored to its original grandeur in 2003 with a price tag north of $25 million, funded through public expenditures and private donations. Today, when you walk into the lobby, huge chandeliers twinkle high above. You follow the lines of the ceiling and the

patterns on the wall to the marble floor. Twin staircases lead to the balcony upstairs, and once in the theater, there's more ornate wood- and plasterwork. On stage, there's a gorgeous Wurlitzer organ from the same era as the theater. The best part is the theater actually has someone who knows how to play the organ, and play it well. Shows here vary from national and international musicians to plays and stage shows to a handful of films.

Sunsphere

When the World's Fair came in 1982, the city was transformed. The most dramatic change is one that has permanently transformed the skyline and become an easily recognizable symbol of the city. The **Sunsphere** (810 Clinch Ave., Fl. 5, 865/251-8161, www. worldsfairpark.org, 9am-10pm daily Apr.-Oct., 11am-6pm daily Nov.-Mar., free) is a 266-foot-tall tower topped by a huge golden ball. Inside the ball are private offices, a lounge, and a great observation deck that gives you a 360-degree view of Knoxville. It's a shame that the Sunsphere sat mostly unused from the end of the fair until 1999, when it was reopened briefly, then closed again just as suddenly. In 2005, Knoxville's mayor announced that the Sunsphere and the adjacent Tennessee Amphitheater (6am-midnight, showtimes vary), another World's Fair attraction, would be renovated and returned to public use. This is a great structure that symbolizes many things for this city, so it's good to see it in use again.

Knoxville Zoo

The **Knoxville Zoo** (3500 Knoxville Zoo Dr., 865/637-5331, www.knoxville-zoo.org, 10am-4:30pm daily, closed Christmas Day, adults $20, seniors and children 4-12 $17, parking $5) has more than 900 animals from all over the world including the expected zoo animals and some surprises. There are a number of red pandas here (the zoo is a breeding facility for them), a giraffe you can feed, and Budgie Landing, an enclosed aviary in the Clayton Family Kids Cove that's filled with what seems like a million budgies (a type of small parrot) flying around.

Women's Basketball Hall of Fame

Given the basketball prowess of the University of Tennessee Lady Vols and famed former coach Pat Summitt, Knoxville is a fitting place for the **Women's Basketball Hall of Fame** (700 Hall of Fame Dr., 865/633-9000, www.wbhof.com, 11am-5pm Tues.-Fri., 10am-5pm Sat. Labor Day-Apr., 10am-5pm Mon.-Sat. May-Labor Day, adults $8, seniors and children 6-15 $6). This facility, the only one devoted entirely to women's basketball achievements at all levels, opened in 1999 and celebrates the rich history of women's basketball. The exhibits here are more than just a plaque and write-up on Hall of Fame members; there are interactive areas like the court where you can practice passing and dribbling skills or shoot a few balls at baskets both contemporary and from the earliest days of the game. Other exhibits include displays honoring current NCAA national champions and a set of mannequins dressed in uniforms from over the years. There's also a gift shop where you can pick up basketballs autographed by Hall of Fame members. Oh,

and the building is hard to miss—one end has the world's largest basketball, which appears to be dropping into a net.

Haunted Knoxville Ghost Tours

Haunted Knoxville Ghost Tours (301 S. Gay St., 865/377-9677, www.hauntedknoxville.net, adults $40, children 9-12 $35, tour dates and times vary, reserve online) is more than just a person walking around telling some "scary" stories filled with local color—these guides offer one of the leading historical and investigation-based ghost tours. They've dug up some juicy, and creepy, stories that reveal a hidden side of this friendly city. And they continue to carry out investigations, bringing with them on every tour a host of tools used to gather information on the paranormal.

ENTERTAINMENT AND EVENTS

Nightlife

Hops & Hollers (937 N. Central St., 865/312-5733, www.hopsandhollers.com, noon-midnight Mon.-Thurs., 2pm-late Fri., noon-late Sat., 11am-10pm Sun.) is a fun little craft beer bar with 100 beers in bottles and

the Sunsphere in World's Fair Park

Tennessee's Unsung Music Town

Knoxville gets short shrift when folks talk about Tennessee music. Ever eclipsed by Nashville and overlooked by bluegrass and mountain string band lovers for spots like Gatlinburg and Pigeon Forge, Knoxville is often forgotten. But no more. The music scene in this hip Southern town is lively and growing livelier by the minute. Bands like The Black Lillies, with their mountain-influenced indie rock, and The Black Cadillacs, who take a more bluesy spin, have made a name for themselves nationally in recent years, playing at Bonnaroo and the Grand Ole Opry.

All across town you'll find buskers playing on the street, bands tucked into restaurants and bars, and free concerts on Market Square during the summer. Jam sessions pop up and musicians flow freely from one impromptu band to another until they find the perfect fit. Two historic venues—The Tennessee Theatre (the state's official theater, and a stunning place to see a band) and the Bijou Theatre—host concerts with clockwork regularity.

Music festivals, like Big Ears Festival (www.bigearsfestival.com), Smoky Mountain Music Fest (www.smmfestival.com), and Rhythm N Blooms Fest (www.rhythmnbloomsfest.com), celebrate the sounds of the city and bring in visiting bands and music fans from all over.

Make it a point while you're in town to take in one of the daily free shows at WDVX-FM, where their noontime Blue Plate Special concert series brings in local and regional acts to play for a live radio broadcast in front of a studio audience.

cans and 32 more on draft. Of those taps, 20 are dedicated to Tennessee brews, which will give craft beer connoisseurs a taste of some of the best beer the state has to offer. The bartenders know their brews and can make reliable recommendations (when in doubt, ask for a tasting pour). Musicians play here on a regular basis and food trucks stop by just about every night of the week.

Casual Pint (421 Union St., 865/951-2160, www.thecasualpint.com, 3pm-11pm Mon.-Thurs., 3pm-2am Fri., 11am-2am. Sat., noon-11pm Sun.) brews several beers in-house and always has a deep lineup on draft. Grab a sampler flight or the pint of your choice, or fill up a growler to take your brew home with you.

Club XYZ (1215 N. Central St., 865/637-4999, 7pm-3am nightly) is one of the best gay bars in Knoxville. They have drag shows, karaoke nights, dance parties, and great happy hour specials.

Icon Ultra Lounge (810 Clinch Ave., on the 5th fl. of the Sunsphere, 865/249-7321, www.knoxvilleicon.com, 4pm-midnight Tues.-Thurs., 4pm-2am Fri.-Sat.) has some fantastic views, good drinks, and a dinner and late-night menu. It's a great place to visit for

a drink or two before heading out for further adventures, or for stopping by for a nightcap and something to munch on before heading back to your hotel.

Performing Arts

The Bijou Theatre (803 S. Gay St., 865/522-0832, www.knoxbijou.com, ticket prices vary) is one of Knoxville's most important venues for live musical performances. Everyone from The Marx Brothers and Dolly Parton to The Ramones and Dave Matthews played here, and the audience at one time included President Andrew Jackson.

The Bijou (well, the building anyway) dates to 1817 and has been a hotel and tavern, a place for social gatherings, and an object of some consternation for its myriad owners until it finally opened as a theater in 1908. A vaudeville stage for a long time (with a rare-for-the-time policy of admitting black patrons to the gallery seating), the Bijou showed films on occasion, but that stopped when the Tennessee Theatre opened up the street. (The builders of the Tennessee bought the Bijou, then sold it with one caveat: the Bijou couldn't be used as a theater for the next five years.) After various incarnations, the Bijou reopened as a fully renovated theater in 2006.

Knox Comedy Live (www.knoxcomedy. com) isn't a comedy club, but rather a group of comedians living in the region who are helping to spread the word about smaller comedy shows and open mic opportunities. Check their website for upcoming shows. **The Pilot Light** (106 E. Jackson Ave., 865/524-8188, www.thepilotlight.com, 6pm-late nightly), a nightclub in Knoxville's Old City, hosts comedy shows as well as frequent musical acts.

Festivals and Events

Knoxville has great events going on throughout the year, including the **International Biscuit Festival** (865/238-5219, www.biscuitfest.com, mid-May), an annual spring gathering of foodies, food writers, and biscuit enthusiasts. **Big Ears** (www.bigearsfestival.com, weekend passes start at $135, day passes $50) brings all sorts of odd performers, films, and musical acts to Knoxville at the end of March. At the end of April, the **Scruffy City Film & Music Festival** (865/245-0411, www.knoxvillefilms.com, ticket prices from $8) invades downtown, filling it with musical performances and film screenings. There's

no telling what local and regional musical acts will show up, but it's guaranteed they'll be interesting and wide ranging in terms of genre and style. Films run the gamut from documentary shorts to music videos to full features, plus there are workshops designed to help filmmakers and musicians push their art to the limits. The very popular 24 Hour Film Festival is part of this six-day creative extravaganza.

Film is big in Knoxville and the **Knoxville Film Festival** (www.knoxville-filmfestival.com, festival pass $50, film blocks from $10) takes place in mid-September. In addition to excellent film screenings, there's a student filmmaking competition and a high-stakes seven-minute film competition. The 7-Day Shootout happens in August, when teams of filmmakers gather in Knoxville to develop their scripts and shoot them. The completed films are shown at the festival; the grand prize winner takes home $20,000 to turn their seven-minute film into a full feature.

SHOPPING

Market Square (865/524-2224) provides a center square (actually, a rectangle) around which people can gather. Just one block off

Knoxville's Market Square

Gay Street, this excellent little shopping and dining district is always busy. There are summer concerts, buskers, and a small fountain for the kids to play in, and the variety of people walking by and stores to peruse makes it easy to kill time while waiting for your table to be ready. There are a half-dozen restaurants on the square, and close to a dozen shops, including the **Mast General Store** (865/546-1336, www.maststoreknoxville, 10am-6pm Mon.-Wed., 10am-9pm Thurs.-Sat., noon-6pm Sun.), where you can buy everything from camping gear to home goods to penny candy; **Earth to Old City** (865/522-8270, www.earthtooldcity.com, 10am-9pm Mon.-Sat., noon-6pm Sun.) carries all sorts of odd and funky home decor (some of it may be more at home in a dorm room than your house); and twin shops **Bliss** (865/329-8868, www.shopinbliss.com, 10am-9pm Mon.-Thurs., 10am-10pm Fri.-Sat., 11am-8pm Sun.) and **Bliss Home** (865/673-6711, 10am-7pm Mon.-Sat., noon-5pm Sun.), selling home goods and lifestyle accessories. **Nothing Too Fancy** (435 Union Ave., 865/951-2916, www.nothingtoofancy.com, 10am-9pm Mon.-Fri., 9am-9pm Sat., 11am-6pm Sun.) has some very cool T-shirts and other silk-screened goods designed by local artists. Reflecting the culture, in-jokes, and vibe of Knoxville in their work, the shirts are fun, even for those not in the know.

The **Market Square Farmers Market** (www.marketsquarefarmersmarket.org, 11am-2pm Wed. and 9am-2pm Sat., May-Nov.) shows up in late spring, bringing with it dozens of farmers and craftspeople selling their wares, edible or not.

RECREATION

The unquestioned star of Knoxville's recreational scene is **Ijams Nature Center** (2915 Island Home Ave., 865/577-4717, www.ijams.org, 9am-5pm Mon.-Sat., 11am-5pm Sun.). This 300-acre urban wilderness is laced with hiking and single-track mountain biking trails, former quarries to explore on foot or even paddle around, and it's dog-friendly.

This vast, wild space is a strange thing so close to the city, but people love it. At any time of any day there are walkers, hikers, trail runners, bikers, families, couples, and singles on the trails here. From Ijams Nature Center, you can connect with a larger, nearly contiguous loop of some 40 miles. Grab a map when you come in or download one and plan your route ahead of time, or you could just bring some water and your camera and wander.

World's Fair Park (www.worldsfairpark.org) is the best city park in Knoxville. This 10-acre park has walking paths, a small lake, open grassy spaces, soccer fields, fountains, and a gorgeous stream running right down the middle of it. It's the home of the Sunsphere and Tennessee Amphitheatre, and at the north end of the park, past a fantastically large fountain, is a 4,200-square-foot playground. The playground and fountain get pretty crowded with kids, but there are other places you can go if you're traveling without a few of your own.

FOOD

Knoxville Food Tours (865/201-7270, www.knoxvillefoodtours.com, $99) shows off some of the best spots to drink and dine in downtown Knoxville. Tour dates are Friday and Saturday afternoons and evenings, but custom tours are available any day. The walk's not far—generally less than a mile—and you get to find a place to have dinner, all while under the tutelage of a local foodie.

The tiny shop **Just Ripe** (513 Union Ave., 865/851-9327, 8am-2pm Mon.-Sat., $1.50-10) sells coffee, a few baked goods, a pair of burritos, healthy grab-and-go lunch items, and these incredible biscuits and biscuit sandwiches. They're just the right mix of dense and fluffy, and with a little bacon or smoky tomato jam (or both) they are out of this world.

When a former rock musician opens a restaurant, you expect it to have a lot of personality, and ★ **Sweet P's Barbecue & Soul House** (3725 Maryville Pike, 865/247-7748, www.sweetpbbq.com, 11am-8pm

barbecuing over hardwood coals at Sweet P's

Tues.-Thurs., 11am-9pm Fri.-Sat., noon-7pm Sun., $4-22) delivers. Owner and Pitmaster Chris Ford ate in every barbecue joint he could find while on tour with his band and began developing recipes long before he had the idea for a restaurant. When the time came to open Sweet P's, he was ready. This is some fine barbecue, whether it's the ribs, the brisket, or the sides. The potato salad is good and the mac and cheese done just right, but the coleslaw is out of this world. Good news if you're going to stick to downtown Knoxville: **Sweet P's Downtown Dive** (410 W. Jackson Ave., 865/281-1738, www.sweetpbbq.com, 11am-9pm Tues.-Thurs., 11am-10pm Fri.-Sat., noon-9pm Sun., $5-20) lets you get your fix of 'cue without venturing far from the city's heart.

★ **Dead End BBQ** (3621 Sutherland Ave., 865/212-5655, www.deadendbbq.com, 11am-9pm Sun.-Thurs., 11am-10pm Fri.-Sat., $8-23) was started by a group of guys who would get together and make barbecue. Turns out they were onto something good. After their neighbors and wives praised them enough, they decided to enter a barbecue competition. They did well, very well, and entered another—and it wasn't long before they had accumulated a wall of trophies. Naturally, this little obsession turned into a restaurant, and a damn good one at that. Everything they do here is top-notch, so unless the brisket or ribs or some other dish catches your eye, get the sampler plate. They have one dish you don't see very often—beef brisket burnt ends. Far from being burnt, these succulent little morsels are trimmings off the brisket, and they go down easy. The sauce here is fantastic, and the sides outstanding. Save room for dessert; their banana pudding is so rich and thick that it's more like cheesecake.

Pete's Coffee Shop (540 Union Ave., 865/523-2860, www.petescoffeeshop.com, 6:30am-2:30pm Mon.-Fri., 7am-2pm Sat., $2-8) is a diner that's dirt cheap and super tasty. Their French toast is exceptional, as are their pancakes, and for lunch, Pete's Supreme (ham and melted Swiss on a hoagie) is excellent, as is the patty melt.

At **The Tomato Head** (12 Market Square, 865/637-4067, www.thetomatohead.com, 11am-9:30pm Mon.-Thurs., 11am-10:30pm Fri., 10am-10:30pm Sat., 10am-9pm Sun., brunch 10am-3pm Sat.-Sun., $3-28) you can sit outside, weather permitting, and watch the crowds on Market Square while you eat your pizza. The menu here features pizzas, sandwiches, burritos, and salads, but stick to the pizza—not because the other stuff is bad, but because the pizza is so good. You can build your own or choose one of their topping combinations. Odd combos like fresh spinach and black bean, lamb sausage and sundried tomato, and smoked salmon and pesto actually go down quite easily.

Stock & Barrel (35 Market Square, 865/766-2075, www.thestockandbarrel.com, 11am-late daily, $7-16) has an unparalleled bourbon selection, a list of burgers that are as tasty as they are creative, and a line out the door. Even if you make a reservation, you'll wait for a seat, but it's worth it because once you get in, you won't want to leave. Get a flight of bourbon and whatever burger pushes your buttons, and enjoy.

Nama Sushi Bar (506 S. Gay St., 865/633-8539, www.namasushibar.com, 11am-midnight Mon.-Thurs., 11am-2am Fri.-Sat., noon-midnight Sun., $4-24) is the best option for sushi in Knoxville. Their fish is always fresh and they serve both traditional rolls and rolls that are a little more inventive. The Moon Special Roll and the Orange Crush go pretty far afield from your basic roll and make for a delicious bite. This place gets crowded, especially on weekends or when Knoxville is hopping, so get there early or make a reservation.

The Crown & Goose (123 S. Central St., 865/524-2100, www.thecrownandgoose.com, 11am-11pm Mon.-Wed., 11am-midnight Thurs., 11am-1am Fri.-Sat., 11am-3pm Sun., $8-26) is a gastropub serving a fusion of traditional British and contemporary European dishes and techniques. Nothing here pushes the boundaries too far, but they do use some great ingredients in their interpretations of fish-and-chips and shepherd's pie, as well as in their small plates.

ACCOMMODATIONS

★ **The Oliver Hotel** (407 Union Ave., 865/521-0050, www.theoliverhotel.com, $160-265) is an outstanding boutique hotel. The service is impeccable and the rooms amazing—everything is done to a luxurious, but not ostentatious, level. When you first find it, you'll likely walk right past it—it blends in with the rest of the block almost seamlessly. Built in 1876 as a bakery, it was converted into a hotel for the World's Fair. There are 24 guest rooms with wet bars, coffee service, and fabulous bedding.

Maplehurst Inn (800 West Hill Ave., 865/851-8383, www.maplehurstinn.com, $125-175) is dated, but worth considering because of the friendly service and a pretty good breakfast. Your hosts make you feel at home and you can tell they care about your experience. Plus, it's a mansion in a truly lovely part of town.

Maple Grove Inn (8800 Westland Dr., 865/951-2315, www.maplegroveinn.com, $150-300) has seven rooms in one of the oldest residences in Knoxville. A popular spot for weddings, this full-service bed-and-breakfast sits on 15 acres of gardens, giving you the opportunity to truly check out of day-to-day life and relax in the moment.

Hilton Knoxville (501 W. Church Ave., 865/523-2300, www.hilton.com, $192-200) is only two blocks off Gay Street and has fantastic rooms. With on-site dining, a Starbucks right in the lobby, and parking next door, it's the best of the name-brand hotels you'll find.

There are a number of other chain hotels in town, including the **Hampton Inn Knoxville North** (5411 Pratt Rd., 855/271-3622, www.hamptoninn3.hilton.com, $120-170) and the **Country Inn & Suites Knoxville at Cedar Bluff** (9137 Cross Park Dr., 800/596-2375, www.countryinns.com, $120-185).

TRANSPORTATION AND SERVICES
Car

Driving to Knoxville is easy. If you've followed the Blue Ridge Parkway through Great Smoky Mountains National Park, just stay on US-441, which runs right into downtown. Coming from the east or west via I-40, take Exit 388 for Gay Street.

From Asheville, take I-40 West 116 miles (2 hours) to Knoxville. From Charlotte, where you'll find a major airport, take US-74 West to I-40 West into Knoxville, a four-hour drive. Alternatively, take the same route, but leave I-40 for US-19 into Cherokee, then take US-441/TN-71 through GSMNP and into Knoxville.

From the south, I-75 offers a direct route into Knoxville from Chattanooga, Tennessee (1 hour 45 minutes), and Atlanta, Georgia (3 hours). I-40 is likewise a direct route from Nashville to Knoxville (2 hours

45 minutes). From the north, Knoxville is accessible via I-81.

Air

McGhee Tyson Airport (2055 Alcoa Highway, Alcoa, 865/342-3000, www.flyknoxville.com) is located 20 minutes south of Knoxville in Alcoa, Tennessee. You can get there on US-129. From I-40, take Exit 386-B to US-129 south; it's 12 miles to the airport. Airlines serving McGhee Tyson include **Allegiant** (702/505-8888, www.allegiantair.com), **American Airlines** (800/433-7300, www.aa.com), **Delta** (800/221-1212, www.delta.com), **Frontier** (800/432-1359, www.flyfrontier.com), and **United** (800/525-0208, www.ual.com).

If you need taxi service between the airport and Knoxville, **A&B Ground Transportation** (865/389-0312), **Discount Taxi** (865/755-5143), **Odyssey Airport Taxi** (865/577-6767), and **Knoxville Taxi** (865/691-1900) are just a few of the car services you can call.

Public Transit

Once you're in town, there is plenty to walk to. **Knoxville Trolley Lines** (301 Church Ave., 865/637-3000, free), operated by Knoxville Area Transit, also runs throughout downtown. Check online or call for current schedules and routes.

Services

The **Knoxville Visitors Center** (301 S. Gay St., 800/727-8045, www.visitknoxville.com, 8:30am-5pm Mon.-Fri., 9am-5pm Sat., noon-4pm Sun.) is what visitors centers should be. They have the expected rack of maps and helpful volunteers on hand to answer questions, but what sets them apart is the gift shop filled with locally made art and foodstuffs, a kids' corner, coffee, and a radio station. This is the only visitors center I know of where you can watch a free concert every day at lunch or listen to it as a live radio broadcast.

The local public radio station, **WDVX-FM** (301 S. Gay St., 865/544-1029, www.wdvx.com) at 89.9 FM, is also the host of the Blue Plate Special concert series held on the stage in the Knoxville Visitors Center during lunch hour on weekdays. Listen to classic rock at **WIMZ** (103.5 FM). **WUTK** (90.3 FM) is a college station from the University of Tennessee. Tune in to public radio from UT at **WUOT** (91.9).

If you need medical care, there are more than a half-dozen clinics and hospitals in Knoxville. The **University of Tennessee Medical Center** (1924 Alcoa Highway, 865/305-9000, www.utmedicalcenter.org) is a 581-bed teaching hospital, and **Fort Sanders Regional Medical Center** (1901 Clinch Ave., 865/541-1111, www.fsregional.com) is conveniently located downtown.

North Carolina Gateways

A sense of otherworldliness and of magic rises up from these hills like the mist that evokes the Smoky Mountains.

Maybe it's the way the land is folded and rumpled like a quilt at the foot of the bed, or perhaps it's some element of Cherokee mythology come to life. After all, this is the ancestral home of the Cherokee people and the present home of the Eastern Band of the Cherokee Indians; it's possible that something in these hills and hollows remains, imprinted from their collective memories. In towns like Cherokee, the magic is thick, but it's also present in Bryson City, throughout the Nantahala National Forest, and along Maggie Valley, calling to visitors and enchanting them year after year.

The town of Cherokee sits on the Qualla Boundary at the edge of Great Smoky Mountains National Park. Make no mistake, this isn't a reservation; it's ancestral Cherokee land. They're quite proud of the small group of forefathers who refused relocation and the travesty of the Trail of Tears, choosing instead to hide in these hills, wage a guerilla war, and ultimately win the right to set up a Cherokee government.

Other towns here abut the national park or are just a few miles away, and the Cherokee influence is felt everywhere you go. An altogether lovely place, the mountains are tall, the roads winding, and the streams downright picturesque. It's a place people are proud to call home, whether their family has been here for 10 years or 10,000.

PLANNING YOUR TIME

To make the most of your time, spend **two days** in Cherokee, (one for the casino, one for the cultural sights), set aside at least **one day** to visit the national park, and use **one day** for exploring the small towns. If camping is your thing, there are plenty of campsites in the park and some very good ones on the outskirts; if it's not, there are lovely B&Bs and funky older hotels around. A more luxurious experience can be had at Harrah's Cherokee Casino.

When to Go

Autumn is prime time to visit the Smoky Mountains and the towns in this part of North

---

Previous: fall color on the mountains; bridge over the Nantahala River. **Above:** the Tuckasegee River in Bryson City.

Look for ★ to find recommended
sights, activities, dining, and lodging.

Highlights

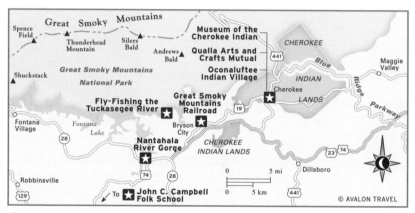

★ **Museum of the Cherokee Indian:**
The Cherokee people have lived in the Smoky
Mountains for thousands of years. This excellent
museum tells their unforgettable story (page 131).

★ **Qualla Arts and Crafts Mutual:**
Ancient craft traditions still thrive among
Cherokee artists here. Come see (and purchase)
the work of today's masters (page 132).

★ **Oconaluftee Indian Village:** Get
a glimpse into 18th-century tribal life at this
re-created Cherokee Indian village (page 132).

★ **Great Smoky Mountains Railroad:**
See the Blue Ridge on a rail tour departing from
the historic depot in Bryson City (page 141).

★ **Nantahala River Gorge:** This steep
gorge is an unbeatable place for white-water
rafting (page 141).

★ **Fly-Fishing the Tuckasegee River:**
Several outfitters can hook anglers up for a great
day on the river, which conveniently flows right
through Bryson City (page 142).

★ **John C. Campbell Folk School:** This
leading light in promoting American craft heritage, nurtures new generations of artists, secur-
ing the future of Appalachian artistic traditions
(page 148).

North Carolina Gateways

Fontana Village

Shuckstack 4,020ft

Pisgah National Forest

Robbinsville

129

NANTAHALA RIVER GORGE

Nantahala River Gorge

Nantahala

To JOHN C. CAMPBELL FOLK SCHOOL, Hayesville, Brasstown, and Murphy

28

19 74

Appalachian

Spence Field 4,900ft

Thunderhead Mountain 5,530ft

Fontana Lake

Trail

Cades Cove

RICH MTN

Rich MTN

321

Townsend

LITTLE RIVER RD

Little River

Great Smoky

Silers Bald 5,607ft

FLY-FISHING THE TUCKASEGEE RIVER

Andrews Bald 5,860ft

Clingmans Dome 6,643ft

Mountains

Bryson City

DEEP CREEK

19

MINGUS MILL

441

ELKMONT

To Knoxville

Sugarland Mtn

NEWFOUND

Newfound Gap 5,048ft

Mt LeConte 6,593ft

Charlie's Bunion 5,900ft

Gap

441 RD

Great Smoky Mountains National Park

Appalachian Trail

Mt Guyot 6,621ft

28

GREAT SMOKY MOUNTAINS RAILROAD

Pisgah National Forest

Dillsboro

CHEROKEE INDIAN LANDS

441

MUSEUM OF THE CHEROKEE INDIAN

OCONALUFTEE INDIAN VILLAGE

QUALLA ARTS AND CRAFTS MUTUAL

Cherokee

SMOKEMONT

INDIAN LANDS

Mingo Falls

CHEROKEE

BALSAM

BALSAM MOUNTAIN

BLUE

Mt Sterling 5,835ft

COVE CREEK RD

CATALOOCHEE

0   0

0   5 km

5 mi

Sylva

107

Cullowhee

281

© AVALON TRAVEL

23 74

RIDGE

PKWY

THE STOMPIN' GROUNDS

Maggie Valley

WHEELS THROUGH TIME MOTORCYCLE MUSEUM

19

To Lake Junaluska and Asheville

Carolina. As leaves on the trees change—first at the highest elevations, then creeping down the mountains week by week—the Blue Ridge Parkway sees heavy traffic and these little mountain towns bustle with people. Generally, this is during October, but it can start as early as mid-September and last as late as mid-November. Regardless of Mother Nature's schedule, it can be difficult to get a hotel room in October without advance reservations.

During **winter,** this area will see significant snowfall at times and correspondingly low temperatures. This is when Great Smoky Mountains National Park receives its lowest visitation levels and many businesses shutter for the season or reduce their hours. However, it's no less charming

a time to visit. Hiking the winter woods is a favorite of many an outdoors enthusiast. Some **roads may close** temporarily during winter, like the Blue Ridge Parkway and Newfound Gap Road, which bisects the national park and leads to Gatlinburg, Tennessee.

Spring sees the return of visitors as the mountains come alive with wildflowers and the year's first leaves. **Summer** brings on another flower show, with flame azaleas, mountain laurel, and rhododendron all blooming from April through July. Water activities like tubing and white-water rafting offer the chance to cool off after long hikes or a good ride on a mountain bike. Fly-fishing is popular year-round, with hundreds of miles of trout streams on the Qualla Boundary (where you'll need a tribal permit to fish).

Maggie Valley

Maggie Valley is a vacation town from the bygone era of long family road trips in wood-paneled station wagons. Coming down the mountain toward Maggie Valley you'll pass an overlook that, on a morning when the mountains around Soco Gap are ringed by fog, is surely one of the most beautiful vistas in the state.

SIGHTS

In a state with countless attractions for automotive enthusiasts, Maggie Valley's **Wheels Through Time Museum** (62 Vintage Lane, 828/926-6266, www.wheelsthroughtime.com, 9am-5pm Thurs.-Mon. Apr.-late Nov., $12 adults, $10 over age 65, $6 ages 5-12, free under age 4) stands out as one of the most fun. A dazzling collection of nearly 300 vintage motorcycles and a fair number of cars are on display, including rarities like a 1908 Indian, a 1914 Harley-Davidson, military motorcycles from both world wars, and some gorgeous postwar bikes. This collection, which dates mostly to before 1950, is maintained in working order—almost

every one of the bikes is revved up from time to time, and the museum's founder has been known to take a spin on one of the treasures.

Bluegrass music and clogging are a big deal in this town. The great bluegrass banjo player Raymond Fairchild is a Maggie native, and after his 50-year touring and recording career, he and his wife, Shirley, are now the hosts of the **Maggie Valley Opry House** (3605 Soco Rd., 828/926-9336, www.raymondfairchild.com, 8pm Mon.-Fri. June-Oct.). In season, you can find bluegrass and country music concerts and clogging exhibitions most every night.

RECREATION
Hiking
Near Maggie Valley, the mountains become rough. Located on the valley floor, the town of Maggie Valley is surprisingly short on trails, and what trails there are can be quite strenuous. There's the 2.6-mile stroll around **Lake Junaluska,** but other than that, the majority of the trails are found at the crest of the mountains, along the Blue Ridge Parkway. To the east of Maggie Valley, the mountains are a little

Maggie Valley

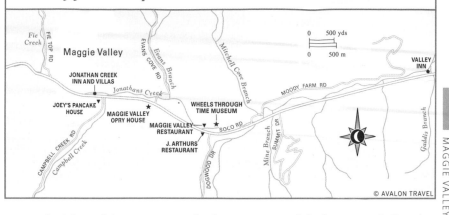

© AVALON TRAVEL

more forgiving and there are many trails of various intensities and lengths, but in the immediate area, you'll have to take the Heintooga Spur Road, a connector road between the Parkway and Great Smoky Mountains National Park, to a mile-high campground, picnic area with unparalleled views, and the **Flat Creek Trail.** On Heintooga Spur Road, you'll pass into Great Smoky Mountains National Park proper and be treated to no fewer than five stunning overlooks, the best of which is the Mile High Overlook, offering a glimpse of Clingmans Dome, Mount LeConte, Mount Kephart, and Mount Guyot.

FLAT CREEK TRAIL

Distance: 5 miles round-trip
Duration: 3 hours
Elevation gain: 250 feet
Difficulty: moderate
Trailhead: Heintooga Ridge picnic area off Heintooga Spur Road, accessible at MP 458.2

Though named the Flat Creek Trail, you will find a waterfall—the 200-foot Flat Creek Falls, a beautiful but difficult-to-see cascade—along the path. The main trail is easy, with little elevation gain or loss until you turn off onto the short spur trail that takes you to the falls. The falls trail is steep and slick, so be careful if you decide to explore in this area.

Heavy logging at the turn of the 20th century opened the forest up and allowed a thick swath of grass to grow here. Today, much of the grass remains and the forest seems to rise from it like an island in a sea of green. It's a strange sight.

Winter Sports

Maggie Valley's **Cataloochee Ski Area** (1080 Ski Lodge Rd., off US-19, 800/768-0285, snow conditions 800/768-3588, www.cataloochee. com, lift tickets $20-65, rentals $21-30) has slopes geared to every level of skier and snowboarder. Classes and private lessons are taught for all ages.

At Cataloochee's sister snow-sports area, **Tube World** (US-19, next to Cataloochee Ski Area, 800/768-0285, www.cataloochee.com, $25, must be over 42 inches tall, late Nov.-mid-Mar.), you can zip down the mountain on inner tubes, and there's a "Wee Bowl" area for children (call ahead, $5).

FOOD AND ACCOMMODATIONS

★ **Joey's Pancake House** (4309 Soco Rd., 828/926-0212, www.joeyspancake.com, 7am-noon Fri.-Wed., about $8) has been flipping flapjacks for travelers and locals alike since 1966. The pancakes, waffles, and country ham are so good that lines form on the weekends—get here early.

J. Arthurs Restaurant (2843 Soco Rd., 828/926-1817, www.jarthurs.com, lunch noon-2:30pm Fri.-Sun., early-bird dinner 4:30pm-6pm daily, early bird $17, dinner from 4:30pm daily, $15-25) is a popular spot locally for steaks, which are the house specialty; they've been serving them up for more than 25 years. The restaurant also has a variety of seafood and pasta dishes, but there are few vegetarian options.

A Maggie Valley dining institution that's been around since 1952 is **Maggie Valley Restaurant** (2804 Soco Rd., 828/926-0425, www.maggievalleyrestaurant.net, 7am-9pm daily May-Oct., breakfast $1-10, lunch and dinner $5-12). Expect comfort-food classics—meatloaf, meatloaf sandwiches, something called a chuck wagon, pork chops, biscuit sandwiches, grits, bottomless coffee, and even buttermilk—along with one of the best pieces of fresh fried trout you'll find in these mountains.

The main drag through Maggie Valley (Soco Rd./US-19) is lined with motels, including some of the familiar national chains. Among the pleasant independent motels are **The Valley Inn** (236 Soco Rd., 800/948-6880, www.thevalleyinn.com, in-season rates vary, from $39 off-season) and **Jonathan Creek Inn and Villas** (4324 Soco Rd., 800/577-7812, www.jonathancreekinn.com, from $90), which has creekside rooms with screened-in porches.

TRANSPORTATION

US-19 is the main thoroughfare in these parts, leading from Asheville to Great Smoky Mountains National Park. If you're taking your time between Asheville, Boone, or parts north, the Blue Ridge Parkway is a beautiful, but slow, drive to this part of the state. Maggie Valley is also a reasonably short jog off I-40 via exits 20, 24, and 27.

Cherokee and the Qualla Boundary

The town of Cherokee is a study in juxtapositions: the cultural traditions of the Cherokee people, the region's natural beauty, a 24-hour casino, and community-wide preparation for the future. Cherokee is the seat of government of the Eastern Band of the Cherokee, who have lived in these mountains for centuries. Today, their traditional arts and crafts, government, and cultural heritage are very much alive. The Qualla ("KWA-lah") Boundary is not a reservation, but a large tract of land owned and governed by the Cherokee people. Institutions like the Museum of the Cherokee Indian and the Qualla Arts and Crafts Mutual provide a solid base for the Eastern Band's cultural life. As you drive around, take a look at the road signs: Below each English road name is that same name in Cherokee, a beautiful script created by Sequoyah, a 19th-century Cherokee silversmith. This language, once nearly extinct, is taught to the community's youth and there is a Cherokee language immersion

school on the Qualla Boundary. However, this doesn't mean the language is not in danger; few Cherokee people speak it fluently.

The main street in Cherokee is a classic cheesy tourist district where you'll find "Indian" souvenirs—factory-made moccasins, plastic tomahawks, peace pipes, and faux bearskins. In a retro way, this part of Cherokee, with its predictable trinket shops and fudgeries, is charming; check out the garish 1950s motel signs with comic-book caricatures outlined in neon, blinking in the night.

Aside from its proximity to Great Smoky Mountains National Park and the Blue Ridge Parkway, the biggest draw in town is Harrah's Cherokee Casino, one of the largest casino-hotels in the state and home to a world-class spa. The 24-hour entertainment opportunities attract visitors from far and wide, some of whom stay on the property the whole time, while others take a break from the slap of cards and the flash of slot machines to

Cherokee

To
Great Smoky Mountains National Park and
Blue Ridge Parkway

TSALI BLVD

DR

WASHINGTON

OCONALUFTEE
INDIAN VILLAGE

JOSEPH

ACQUONI RD

QUALLA ARTS AND
CRAFTS MUTUAL

MUSEUM OF THE
CHEROKEE INDIAN
1361

Fair
Grounds

441

B'A HWY 1390

B'A HWY 316

Oconaluftee River

0   200 yds
0   200 m

441 19   19

TSALAGI RD

To
Harrah's Cherokee
© AVALON TRAVEL   Casino and Hotel

experience the natural and cultural wonders of Cherokee.

Take everything you see—the casino, the tacky tourist shops, and the stereotyping signs—with a grain of salt, as they don't represent the true nature of the Cherokee people and their long history.

SIGHTS
★ Museum of the Cherokee Indian

The **Museum of the Cherokee Indian** (589 Tsali Blvd., 828/497-3481, www.cherokeemuseum.org, 9am-7pm Mon.-Sat., 9am-5pm Sun. late June-Aug., 9am-5pm daily Sept.-May, $10,

$6 ages 6-12, free under age 5) was founded in 1948 and was originally housed in a log cabin. Today, it is a well-regarded modern museum and locus of community culture. In the exhibits that trace the long history of the Cherokee people, you may notice the disconcertingly realistic mannequins. Local community members volunteered to be models for these mannequins, allowing casts to be made of their faces and bodies so that the figures would not reflect an outsider's notion of what Native Americans should look like; the mannequins depict real people. The Museum of the Cherokee Indian traces the tribe's history from the Paleo-Indian people of the Pleistocene, when the ancestral Cherokees were hunter gatherers, through the ancient days of Cherokee civilization, and into contact with European settlers.

A great deal of this exhibit focuses on the 18th and 19th centuries, when a series of tragedies befell the Cherokee as a result of the invasion of their homeland. It was also a time of great cultural advancement, including Sequoyah's development of the script to write the Cherokee language. The forced relocation of Native Americans called the Trail of Tears began near here, along the North Carolina-Georgia border, in the early 19th century. A small contingent of Cherokees remained in the Smokies at the time of the Trail of Tears, successfully eluding, and then negotiating with, the U.S. military, who were trying to force most of the Native Americans in the Southeast to move to Oklahoma. Those who stayed out in the woods, along with a few others who were able to return from Oklahoma, are the ancestors of today's Eastern Band, and their history is truly remarkable.

A favorite part of the museum are the stories, legends, and myths described on placards throughout the museum. There's the story of a boy who became a bear and convinced his entire clan to become bears also. There's one about Spearfinger, a frightening creature that some say still lives in these woods. And there are tales about Selu, the corn mother, and Kanati, the lucky hunter. Cherokee member and contemporary writer Marilou Awiakta has written widely about Selu, tying the past and present together with taut lines of thought that challenge our views on culture and technology.

★ Qualla Arts and Crafts Mutual

Across the street from the museum is the **Qualla Arts and Crafts Mutual** (645 Tsali Blvd., 828/497-3103, http://quallaartsand-crafts.com, 8am-6pm Mon.-Sat., 9am-5pm Sun.), a community arts co-op where local artists sell their work. The gallery's high standards and the community's thousands of years of artistry make for a collection of very special pottery, baskets, masks, and other traditional art. As hard as it is to survive as an artist in a place like New York City, artists in rural areas such as this have an exponentially more difficult time supporting themselves through the sale of their art while maintaining the integrity of their vision and creativity. The Qualla co-op does a great service to this community in providing a year-round market for the work of traditional Cherokee artists, whose stewardship of and innovation in the arts are so important. The double-woven

baskets are especially beautiful, as are the carvings of the masks representing each of the seven clans of the Cherokee people (the Bird, Deer, Longhair, Blue, Wolf, Paint, and Wild Potato).

★ Oconaluftee Indian Village

Oconaluftee Indian Village (778 Drama Rd., 828/497-3481, http://visitcherokeenc. com, open Mon.-Sat. May-mid-Oct, gates open and tours begin at 10am, tours run every 15 minutes until 4pm when the box office closes, village closes after final tour, usually around 5pm, $19 adults, $11 children, free 5 and under) is a re-created Cherokee village tucked into the hills above the town. Here, you'll see how the tribe lived in the 18th century. Tour guides in period costumes lead groups on walking lectures with stops at stations where you can see Cherokee cultural, artistic, and daily-life activities performed as authentically as possible. From cooking demos to flint knapping (for arrowheads and spearpoints) to wood carving and clay work, you'll get a look at how the Cherokee lived centuries ago. The highlight of the tour is the ritual dance demonstration showing half a dozen dances and explaining their cultural significance.

Museum of the Cherokee Indian

The Story of the Cherokee

The Cherokee believe that the mountains of western North Carolina have been part of their homeland dating back to at least the last ice age (some 11,000 years ago). By the time Spanish soldiers encountered the Cherokee in the 1540s, the tribe controlled around 140,000 square miles across the southern United States, living in log cabins in towns and villages throughout their territory. They farmed corn, squash, and beans (known as "The Three Sisters"); hunted elk, deer, and bear; and prospered in peacetime and warred with other tribes periodically.

During the first two centuries of earnest European contact, the Cherokee were peaceful and hospitable with the colonists they encountered. Through the course of those 200 years, strings of broken treaties and concessions by the Cherokee had shrunk their once-vast empire dramatically. When President Andrew Jackson insisted that all Indians in the Southeast be moved west of the Mississippi, the real trouble began.

As Jackson's forced march and relocation of the Cherokee and other tribes, known as the **Trail of Tears,** pressed on, a small group of Cherokee avoided relocation by becoming North Carolina citizens. A band of resistance fighters stayed behind near modern-day Cherokee, hiding in the hills, hollows, and caves high in the mountains. These holdouts would become the core of the **Eastern Band of Cherokee Indians.** Unable to own any land, the Cherokee turned to an adopted tribe member to purchase and hold land in his name. He did so, and in 1870, the Cherokee formed a corporation and took control of that land, which they called the **Qualla Boundary.**

Today, the Eastern Band of the Cherokee Indians has nearly 15,000 members (their counterparts in Oklahoma number 10 times as many), many of whom live within the 82-square-mile Qualla Boundary. Tribe members are fiercely proud of their heritage, traditions, stories, and language. An afternoon spent at the **Museum of the Cherokee Indian,** the **Qualla Arts and Crafts Mutual,** and the **Oconaluftee Indian Village,** followed by an evening showing of *Unto These Hills,* will give you a more complete understanding of their history.

Harrah's Cherokee Casino

The Eastern Band of the Cherokee operates **Harrah's Cherokee Casino and Hotel** (777 Casino Dr., 828/497-7777, www. harrahscherokee.com, 24 hours daily). This full-bore Vegas-style casino has more than 3,800 digital games and slot machines along with around 150 table games, such as baccarat, blackjack, roulette, and a poker-only room. Inside the casino complex is a 3,000-seat concert venue where acts like Alicia Keys and the Black Crowes have performed, as well as a huge buffet and a grab-and-go food court next to the casino floor. Unlike in the rest of the state, smoking is allowed on the casino floor, though certain areas have been designated as nonsmoking. If you're a nonsmoker, it may take some patience. Inside the hotel portion of the casino are a restaurant, a Starbucks, and the **Mandara Spa,** which offers salon and spa services such as massages and facials.

ENTERTAINMENT

Of the several outdoor dramas for which North Carolina is known, among the longest running is Cherokee's *Unto These Hills* (Mountainside Theater, 688 Drama Rd., adjacent to Oconaluftee Indian Village, 866/554-4557, www.visitcherokeenc.com, 8pm Mon.-Sat. May 30-Aug. 15, $20-23 adults, $10-13 ages 6-12, free under age 6). For more than 60 summers, Cherokee actors have told the story of their nation's history, from ancient times through the Trail of Tears. Every seat in the house is a good seat at the Mountainside Theater, and the play is certainly enlightening. If you're gun-shy or easily startled, be warned: There is some cannon fire and gunfire in the play.

Hear stories, learn dances, and interact with Cherokee storytellers at the **Cherokee Bonfire** (Oconaluftee Islands Park, Tsalagi Rd. and Tsali Blvd., where US-19 and US-441

134

NORTH CAROLINA GATEWAYS
CHEROKEE AND THE QUALLA BOUNDARY

intersect, 800/438-1601, www.visitcherokeenc.com, 7pm and 9pm Fri.-Sat. May-Sept., free, including marshmallows). Bring your bathing suit and some water shoes to the bonfire; afterward, you may want to go for a wade or a quick dip in the Oconaluftee River, which is wide, rocky, and fun.

RECREATION

I'd be in trouble with my dad if I didn't mention that you can—no, must—ride go-karts at **Cherokee Fun Park** (1897 Tsali Blvd., 828/497-5877, www.cherokeefunparknc.com, 10am-10pm Sun.-Thurs., 10am-11pm Fri.-Sat. summer, hours vary seasonally, single rider $8, doubles $12). A family tradition for as long as I remember, we would strap ourselves into a go-kart and hurtle around a track—and, boy, do they have a track at Cherokee Fun Park. You can't miss it as you're driving to or from Great Smoky Mountains National Park; there's an insane three-level corkscrew turn on one track and a pro track inside where you can drive faster-than-usual carts. And there's mini golf ($8).

Fishing

Cherokee has more than 30 miles of streams, rivers, and creeks ideal for fishing. Add to that the fact that the Eastern Band owns and operates a fish hatchery that releases around 250,000 trout into these waters every year and you have the perfect mix for fantastic fishing. Unlike the rest of North Carolina, you don't need a North Carolina fishing license; you need a **Tribal Fishing Permit** (www.fishcherokee.com, 1 day $10, 2 days $17, 3 days $27, 5 days $47), sold at a number of outlets in Cherokee. You'll find brook, brown, golden, and rainbow trout, and it's fly-rod-only, so you have to have your cast down pat if you want to bring in a big one. There are both catch-and-release and catch-and-keep waters in the Qualla Boundary, but if you want to fish outside the boundary, where several streams and the Oconaluftee River have great fishing, you need a North Carolina or Tennessee fishing permit. Tennessee permits are only valid inside Great Smoky Mountains National Park boundaries in North Carolina.

Golf

The **Sequoyah National Golf Club** (79 Cahons Rd., Whittier, 828/497-3000, www.sequoyahnational.com, 18 holes, par 72, greens fees from $55), five miles south of Cherokee in Whittier, is a stunning mountain golf course. Making the most of the contours and elevation, the course offers tee boxes with breathtaking views of the fairways and the Smoky Mountains. The course record is 62, an impressive feat on a normal course, but here it's something else. Holes like number 12, a par 5 that plays uphill the whole way, present the usual par-5 difficulties combined with steep elevation gain, and number 15, a par 4 that entices golfers to play over aggressively and drop a ball short of the fairway and into the woods, test a golfer's club knowledge and course IQ. This is a tough course for first-timers because so many of the holes have blind approaches, doglegs, or both, but it's enjoyable enough.

Water Sports

For fun on the water, try **Smoky Mountain Tubing** (1847 Tsali Blvd., 828/497-4545, http://cherokeetubeandraft.com, 10am-6pm daily, weather permitting, $10). They do only one thing: rent tubes on which you'll drift down the river and splash your friends. Smoky Mountain Tubing has mountains of tubes, so rent one and float down the Oconaluftee River for two or three hours. They have a fleet of shuttle buses to pick you up a few miles downstream.

FOOD

The arrival and expansion of Harrah's Cherokee Casino (777 Casino Dr., 828/497-7777, www.harrahscherokee.com) brought with it a bevy of restaurants. **Ruth's Chris Steak House** (dinner 5pm-10pm Mon.-Thurs., 5pm-11pm Fri.-Sat., lounge 4pm-11pm Mon.-Thurs., 4pm-midnight Fri.-Sat., lounge and dinner 4pm-9pm Sun., $60) is here, and like its other locations, serves a variety of steaks and chops, a handful of seafood dishes, and more than 220 wines.

Brio Tuscan Grille (828/497-8233, 11:30am-10pm Sun.-Thurs., 11:30am-11pm Fri.-Sat., $20-40) is a fine Italian restaurant specializing in dishes from northern Italy. This isn't a spaghetti-and-meatballs kind of place; it's more refined, with dishes like lasagna Bolognese al forno, lobster and shrimp ravioli with crab insalata, Tuscan grilled pork chops, and bistecca alla Fiorentina. The ambience is nice, the wine list is nicer, and the food is great.

What's a casino without a buffet? Anyone can find something that satisfies at **Chef's Stage Buffet** (4:30pm-10pm Mon.-Thurs., 4:30pm-11pm Fri.-Sat., 1pm-10pm Sun., $26; seafood buffet Sun.-Fri., $32), where four chefs run four distinct micro-restaurants. There's everything here: Asian dishes, Latin, Italian, seafood, Southern, barbecue, a salad bar you could land an airplane on, and desserts for days. A second buffet option is the **Selu Garden Café** (7am-2:30pm daily, around $15), which offers up a hearty breakfast every day, a slightly more upscale brunch on weekends (11:30am-2:30pm Sat.-Sun.), and a bottomless soup and salad bar.

Downstairs in Harrah's, just off the casino floor, is an airport-style food court that includes the **Winning Streaks Deli** (11am-11pm daily, $10), a deli serving hot and cold sandwiches and panini made with Boar's Head meats and cheeses; grab-and-go sandwiches are available 24 hours daily. There is also **Pizzeria Uno Express** (11am-11pm Sun.-Thurs., 11am-2am Fri.-Sat., around $10), serving thin-crust pizza, calzones, and pasta dishes; **Noodle Bar** (6pm-2am Mon.-Thurs., 5pm-3am Fri.-Sat., 5pm-2am Sun., around $18), serving Asian dishes like ramen and dim sum options; **Johnny Rockets** (24 hours daily, around $10), serving burgers, sandwiches, fries, milk shakes, and breakfast; and a **Dunkin' Donuts Express** (24 hours daily, around $5) that has doughnuts and coffee. The food court also has a variety of snacks and drinks available 24 hours daily.

Just outside of the town of Cherokee is **Granny's Kitchen** (1098 Painttown Rd., 828/497 5010, www.grannyskitchencherokee. com, breakfast 7am-11am daily June-Aug. and Oct. and Fri.-Sun. Apr.-May, Sept., and Nov.; lunch and dinner 11am-8pm daily mid-Mar.-Nov., breakfast $8, lunch $8.50, dinner $12), a country-buffet restaurant where you can get some of the best fried chicken in

the Sequoyah National Golf Club

North Carolina. You won't find Granny here; Granny is actually a man who likes to joke, "no one wants to eat at grandpa's, so I became granny."

ACCOMMODATIONS

Cherokee has many motels, including a **Holiday Inn** (376 Painttown Rd., 828/497-3113, www.ihg.com, from $90) and an **Econo Lodge** (20 River Rd./US-19, 828/497-4575, www.choicehotels.com, from $70, pets allowed).

★ **Harrah's Cherokee Casino Resort** (777 Casino Dr., 828/497-7777, www. harrahscherokee.com, $100-500) is without a doubt the best place to stay in Cherokee. The rooms are spacious, comfortable, and well kept; there's the casino and a number of dining options an elevator ride away; and the spa provides an added layer of amenities you don't find at other hotels in town. At the higher floors, the view of the mountains is spectacular.

There's something about visiting a place and living where the residents live, and ★ **Panther Creek Cabins** (Wrights Creek Rd., 828/497-2461, www.panthercreekresort. com, cabins $100-150) gives you that chance with your choice of eight cabins, ranging from private two-person affairs to larger lodges that could easily sleep you and seven others in four beds. These quaint cabins are quiet, just outside of downtown Cherokee, and comfortable.

TRANSPORTATION AND SERVICES

Cherokee is located on a particularly pretty and winding section of US-19 between Maggie Valley and Bryson City, 2.5 miles south of the southern terminus of the Blue Ridge Parkway. From the cultural center of Cherokee, the Blue Ridge Parkway is only six minutes north along US-441, and Great Smoky Mountains National Park only a few minutes beyond. US-441—called Newfound Gap Road within the national park—bisects the park, connecting Cherokee with the Tennessee towns of Gatlinburg and Pigeon Forge; it's about a 45-minute drive to reach Gatlinburg.

The **Cherokee Welcome Center** (498 Tsali Blvd., 800/438-1601, www. visitcherokeenc.com, 8am-8pm daily) can help you with tickets, directions, and things to do and see.

There's one radio station in Cherokee, and that's **WNCC** (101.3), a country station, though you can pick up distant stations with a wider selection.

SYLVA

The small town of Sylva, about 15 miles south of Cherokee, is crowned by the pretty Jackson County Courthouse, a stunning building with an ornate cupola, kept under wistful watch by the requisite courthouse-square Confederate monument. Visitors should stop by the **Jackson County Visitor Center** (773 W. Main St., 800/962-1911, www.mountainlovers. com) or visit them online to learn more about the communities here.

Sights

Sylva's most photogenic, and therefore most-photographed, building is the **Historic Courthouse** (310 Keener St.). Perched on a hill overlooking West Main Street, it's a beautiful sight. A long white stairway leads to the classical revival building built in 1914; along the way is a fountain, statue, and beautiful view of downtown. In 1994, court operations moved to the Justice Center, and today the Jackson County Genealogical Society, the Jackson County Historical Association, the Jackson County Arts Council, and the Jackson County Public Library call the building home.

South of Sylva, the mysterious **Judaculla Rock** (off Caney Fork Rd., www. judacullarock.com) has puzzled folks for centuries. The soapstone boulder is covered in petroglyphs, estimated to be at least 500 years old. The figures and symbols and squiggles are clearly significant, but as of yet are not understood. I'm fascinated with petroglyphs, and these are some of the most mysterious

the Historic Courthouse in Sylva

In downtown Sylva is **Heinzelmannchen Brewery** (545 Mill St., 828/631-4466), which specializes in beer styles from brewmaster Dieter Kuhn's home region in Germany. Choices include a honey blonde ale, a delicious pilsner, a brown ale, and their Black Forest Stout, a dark, creamy draft. You may be wondering what a Heinzelmannchen is—they're helpful gnomes that live in the Black Forest. Around here, they stop by to help with the beer at night while everyone's asleep.

Shopping

Sylva's City Lights Bookstore (3 E. Jackson St., 828/586-9499, www.citylightsnc.com, 9am-9pm Mon.-Sat., 10am-3pm Sun.) is hardly a knockoff of the monumental Beat establishment in San Francisco with which it shares a name. Instead, it's a first-rate small-town bookstore with stock that has the novelty sought by vacationers and the depth to make regulars of the local patrons. In addition to the sections you'll find in any good bookstore, their books include regional interest, folklore, nature, recreation guides, history, and fiction and poetry by Appalachian and Southern authors.

Food

The North Carolina mountains are experiencing a booming organic foods movement, and you'll find eco-aware eateries throughout the area. ★ **Lulu's On Main** (612 W. Main St., 828/586-8989, www.lulusonmain.com, 11:30am-8pm Mon.-Thurs., 11:30am-9pm Fri.-Sat., $11-19) is one of the most acclaimed restaurants in the area. The menu is American gourmet at heart with splashes of Mediterranean and Nuevo Latino specialties. Try the walnut-spinach ravioli or the raspberry rum pork loin. There are plenty of vegetarian options.

At **Evolution Wine Kitchen** (506 W. Main St., 828/631-9856, www.evolutionwinekitchen.com, 9am-9pm Mon.-Wed., 9am-midnight Thurs.-Sat., $5-30), they have a full-service wine shop, a wine bar, and a little restaurant.

You can get a sandwich or salad, and they have a great charcuterie board if you want to linger over a glass or two. If you don't know wine that well, relax; they also have tastings and classes (check the schedule).

City Lights Café (3 E. Jackson St., 828/587-2233, www.citylightscafe.com, 8am-9pm Mon.-Sat., 9am-3pm Sun., breakfast $2-8, lunch and dinner $5-12), located downstairs from the bookshop of the same name, has some excellent crepes, a mighty good biscuit, and fun burritos, as well as wine and beer. It's a cool, casual spot to dine and relax with a book and a bottle of wine, or to see a small local play.

Soul Infusion (628 E. Main St., 828/586-1717, www.soulinfusion.com, 11am-late Mon.-Fri., noon-late Sat., $5-10) is a cozy hippie-gourmet teahouse in an old house on Main Street. You can get very good burritos, sandwiches, pizza, wraps, more than 60 kinds of tea, and even more selections of bottled beer. On weekends and some weeknights, local blues, folk, reggae, and experimental musicians put on a show. Seize the opportunity to hear some of the talent in this musical region.

Accommodations

The **Blue Ridge Inn** (756 W. Main St., Sylva, 828/586-2123, from $110) is a great place to stay in Sylva. Located at the far end of downtown, it's an eight-minute walk to the breweries at the other end of town and a three-minute walk to dining spots like Lulu's and City Lights Cafe. The rooms are comfortable and priced right, and the staff is exceptionally polite.

Transportation

Sylva lies 19 miles southwest of Waynesville along US-74, known as the Great Smoky Mountain Expressway; take exit 83 and you'll be in town in just over a mile. Asheville is an hour northeast along US-74 and I-40; Cherokee and the entrance to Great Smoky Mountains National Park is only 25 minutes north via US-74 and Highway 441.

DILLSBORO

Next door to Sylva is Dillsboro, a river town of rafters and crafters. **Dogwood Crafters** (90 Webster St., 828/586-2248, www.dogwoodcrafters.com, 10am-6pm daily Mar.-Dec., 11am-4pm Fri.-Sun. Jan.-Feb.), in operation for more than 30 years, is a gallery and co-op that represents around 100 local artists and artisans. While the shop carries some of the ubiquitous country-whimsical stuff, mixed in is the work of some very traditional Blue Ridge weavers, potters, carvers, and other expert artisans, making the shop well worth a visit.

In November, Dillsboro's population grows by approximately 5,000 percent when potters and pottery lovers descend on the town for the annual **Western North Carolina Pottery Festival** (828/631-5100, wwww.wncpotteryfestival.com). This juried pottery show features more than 40 potters, a street fair, and the Clay Olympics. The Clay Olympics are timed competitions to make the tallest cylinder or widest bowl, as well as blindfolded pot-making. It's odd, but the crowd and the artists get into it, making the one-day festival worth seeing.

Recreation

Dillsboro River Company (18 Macktown Rd., 866/586-3797, www.northcarolina-rafting.com, 10am-6pm daily May-Sept., last float trip 2:30pm, rentals $5-30, guided trips $22-40), across the river from downtown Dillsboro, will set you afloat on the Tuckasegee River, a comparatively warm river with areas of Class II rapids. (It's pronounced "tuck-a-SEE-jee" but is often referred to simply as "the Tuck.") Dillsboro River Company rents rafts, "ducks," and inflatable and sit-on-top kayaks. If you'd like to hire a river rat, guides will be happy to lead you on tours twice daily, and for an extra fee you can share a boat with the guide. There are minimum weight restrictions for these watercraft, so if you are traveling with children, call ahead to ask if the guides think your young ones are ready for the Tuckasegee.

Food

The ★ **Jarrett House** (100 Haywood St., 800/972-5623, www.jarretthouse.com, 11:30am-2:30pm and 4:30pm-7:30pm Tues.-Sun., under $15) is famous for its dining room, an extravaganza of country cooking based on the staples of country ham and red-eye gravy. You can order many other mountain specialties, including fried catfish, fried chicken, sweet tea, biscuits, and for dessert the daily cobbler or vinegar pie (a strange but tasty pie that's similar to a pecan pie without the pecans and with vinegar). There are few options for vegetarians, but if you like heavy Southern fare, you'll think you're in heaven. You can also eat at **Coach's Bistro** ($15-20), a little restaurant serving up more modern dishes in a more modern setting; menu items range from homey bites to roast beef and mashed potatoes.

Haywood Smokehouse (403 Haywood St., 828/631-9797, www.haywoodsmokehouse. com, 11am-9pm Tues.-Sat., $8-26) is a funky little barbecue shack serving some fine western North Carolina 'cue, craft beers, and house-made smoked barbecue sauces. The menu's small, but if it's pork or chicken and it can be barbecued, it's here. The Haywood Smokehouse is biker-friendly, so don't be surprised if you see a line of Harleys outside.

Accommodations

Of the many historic inns in this region, one of the oldest is Dillsboro's **Jarrett House** (100 Haywood St., 828/586-0265 or 800/972-5623, www.jarretthouse.com, from $129, includes full country breakfast). The three-story 1880s lodge was built to serve railroad passengers, and today it's once again a busy rail stop, now for the Great Smoky Mountains Railroad's excursion trains. The guest rooms have old-fashioned furniture, air-conditioning, and private baths, but the only TV is in the lobby.

The **Best Western Plus River Escape Inn & Suites** (248 WBI Dr., 828/586-6060, www.book.bestwestern.com, $95-210) is a surprisingly great hotel. While most chain hotels are nondescript, this one really steps it up with

The Fly-Fishing Trail

Jackson County is the home of the first and only Fly-Fishing Trail in the country; it includes 15 spots on some of the best trout waters in the Smokies where you can catch rainbow, brook, and brown trout, and even the occasional golden trout. Because of its proximity to many mountain communities, the Fly-Fishing Trail has become the epicenter of fly-fishing in the region. Easy access to these waters, convenient complimentary **maps** (available at www.flyfishingtrail.com and http://mountainloversnc.com), and the excellent support the trail receives make it a choice spot for trout fishing no matter which community you're visiting.

Top spots include **Panthertown Creek,** where a two-mile walk from the end of Breedlove Road (Hwy. 1121) leads you to what some have called the "Yosemite of the East" because of its picturesque rocky bluffs. You'll catch more brook trout than you may have thought possible on this three-mile stream, which is catch-and-release only.

For an "urban" fishing experience, try the **Tuckasegee River** as it passes through Dillsboro. You can park and fish at a number of places between Dillsboro Park and the Best Western River Escape Inn, and you run a good chance of catching a large rainbow or brown trout.

The **Lower Tuckasegee River,** running from Bakers Creek Bridge to Whittier along US-19/74, is around 10 miles of excellent fishing for rainbow and brown trout as well as smallmouth bass.

Fly-Fishing Trail cofounder Alex Bell, who knows the waters of western North Carolina intimately, operates **AB's Fly Fishing Guide Service** (828/226-3833, www.abfish.org, half-day wading trips $150/1 person, $225/2 people, $300/3 people, full day with lunch, $225/1 person, $300/2 people, and $375/3 people; full-day float trips with lunch $350/1 or 2 people). AB's supplies tackle and waders if you need them, as well as extensive lessons in proper casting, water reading, and fly selection, but you're responsible for securing your own North Carolina fishing license and trout stamp.

a well-kept, modern interior and rooms with balconies overlooking the river.

Transportation

Dillsboro is only 1.8 miles west of Sylva; you can get there by following West Main Street out of town. US-23/US-441 runs through Dillsboro and provides easy access to the region from the south (Atlanta, Georgia, is 2.5 hours away) and connects the town to US-74. From Exit 81 on US-74, Dillsboro is a mile away.

CULLOWHEE

The unincorporated village of Cullowhee ("CULL-uh-wee"), located on Highway 107 between Sylva and Cashiers, is the home of Western Carolina University (WCU). The university's **Mountain Heritage Center**

(Hunter Library, WCU campus, 828/227-7129, www.wcu.edu, 10am-4pm Fri.-Mon., 10am-7pm Thurs.) is a small museum with a great collection that will fascinate anyone interested in Appalachian history. The permanent exhibit *Migration of the Scotch-Irish People* is full of artifacts like a 19th-century covered wagon, wonderful photographs, homemade quilts, linens, and musical instruments. The Mountain Heritage Center also hosts two traveling exhibits in addition to the permanent installation as well as the annual **Mountain Heritage Day** (www.mountainheritageday.com, late Sept.) festival, which brings together many of western North Carolina's best and most authentic traditional musicians and artisans in a free festival that draws up to 25,000 visitors.

Cullowhee is only 6 miles south of Sylva along NC-107, a trip of about 10 minutes.

Bryson City and the Nantahala Forest

To look at the mountains here, you'd think that the defining feature in this part of North Carolina would be the surrounding peaks, but that is only half right. This is a land dominated by water. Smoke-thick fog crowds valleys in the predawn hours. The peaks stand ringed in clouds. Moss, ferns, and dense forests crowd the edges of rivers and streams. All of it—the mountains, the mist, the ferns, the fog—makes it feel like you've stepped into a fairy tale when you're in the Nantahala Gorge. According to Cherokee stories, a formidable witch called Spearfinger lived here, as did a monstrous snake and even an inchworm so large it could span the gorge.

The Nantahala River runs through the narrow gorge, attracting white-water enthusiasts to the rapids. Nearby Bryson City is a river town whose proximity to the cataracts makes it a favorite haunt for rafters, kayakers, and other white-water thrill seekers. If you approach Bryson City from the north on US-19, you're in for a strange sight: The banks of the Tuckasegee River are shored up with crushed cars.

SIGHTS
★ Great Smoky Mountains Railroad

The **Great Smoky Mountains Railroad** (GSMR, depots in Bryson City and Dillsboro, 800/872-4681, www.gsmr.com, from $50 adults, $29 children) is one of the best and most fun ways to see the Smokies. On historic trains, the GSMR carries sightseers on excursions from two to several hours long, through some of the most beautiful scenery in the region. Trips between Dillsboro and Bryson City, with a layover at each end for shopping and dining, follow the banks of the Tuckasegee River, while round-trips from Bryson City follow the Little Tennessee and Nantahala Rivers deep into the Nantahala Gorge. Many other excursions are offered,

including gourmet dining and wine- and beer-tasting trips. There are Thomas the Tank Engine and the Little Engine That Could trips for kids, and runs to and from river-rafting outfitters.

RECREATION
★ Nantahala River Gorge

The stunningly beautiful Nantahala River Gorge lies just outside Bryson City in the **Nantahala National Forest.** Nantahala is said to mean "land of the noonday sun," and there are indeed parts of this gorge where the sheer rock walls above the river are so steep that sunlight only hits the water at the noon hour. Eight miles of the Nantahala River flow through the gorge over Class II-III rapids. The nearby Ocoee River is also a favorite of rafters, and the Cheoah River, when there are controlled water releases, has some of the South's most famous and difficult Class III-IV runs.

OUTFITTERS AND TOURS

The Nantahala River Gorge supports scores of river guide companies, many clustered along US-19 west. Because some of these rapids can be quite dangerous, be sure to call ahead and speak to a guide if you have any doubts as to your readiness. If you are rafting with children, check the company's weight and age restrictions beforehand.

Endless River Adventures (14157 US-19 W., near Bryson City, 800/224-7238, www.endlessriveradventures.com) gives white-water and flat-water kayaking instruction, rentals, and guided trips on the Nantahala, Ocoee, and Cheoah Rivers. They'll be able to suggest a run suited to your skill level. **Carolina Outfitters** (715 US-19, Topton, 800/468-7238, www.carolinaoutfitters.com) has several package outings that combine river trips with horseback riding, bicycling, panning for gems, and riding on the Great Smoky Mountains Railroad. **Wildwater**

Rafting (10345 US-19 W., 12 miles west of Bryson City, 828/488-2384, www.wildwaterrafting.com) offers river guide services and leads **Wildwater Jeep Tours** ($50-110 adults, $40-90 children), half- and full-day Jeep excursions through back roads and wilderness to waterfalls and old mountain settlements.

You can explore the mountains around Bryson City with the **Nantahala Outdoor Center** (13077 US-19 W., Bryson City, 828/785-4836, www.noc.com, 9am-5pm daily, from $30), which offers a variety of adventure options that include white-water rafting, stand-up paddleboarding on the flat-water sections of the river, hiking, mountain biking, and zip-lining. Half-day, full-day, and overnight trips are possible, and excursions like the Rapid Transit combine a relaxing morning train ride with an afternoon rafting trip.

★ Fly-Fishing the Tuckasegee River

The Smoky Mountains, especially the eastern grade of the Smokies, are laced with streams perfect for fly-fishing. Anglers from all over come here to float, wade, camp, fish, hone their fly-tying craft, and learn the finer points of fly-fishing. The Tuckasegee River flows right through downtown Bryson City,

and many of its feeder streams and creeks are ideal spots to throw a line.

For fly-fishers who don't need a guide, a number of streams around are packed with fish, but be sure to inquire about regulations for individual streams; some may be catch-and-release, while a neighboring stream could be catch-and-keep. Some streams have regulations about the types of hooks you can use. Once you're ready to put your line in the water, try **Hazel Creek** on the north shore of Fontana Lake, where you'll find pristine waters and a good number of fish. Other nearby creeks, like **Eagle Creek** and any of the feeder creeks that empty into the lake, are prime spots as well.

GUIDES

Fontana Guide Service (3336 Balltown Rd., Bryson City, 828/736-2318, www.fontanaguides.com, $200-500 full-day trips, price depends on group size) has a number of options depending on season, interest, and skill level, including options to fish in the national park. In addition to fly-fishing excursions, they also offer kayak fishing, bass and lake fishing, as well as night fishing in select spots.

Fly Fishing the Smokies (Bryson City, 828/488-7665, www.flyfishingthesmokies.

fly-fishing on the Tuckasegee River

net) has a number of guides and options for a day or more of fishing. Wade the streams with them for a half-day (1 person $150, 2 people $175) or full-day (1 person $200, 2 people $250) outing, try a float trip (half-day $225 per boat, full-day $300 per boat), or go backcountry camping and fly-fishing in Great Smoky Mountains National Park ($500-850 per person). They also go bass fishing on nearby Fontana Lake (half day $225, full day $300).

A top fishing guide in the Bryson City area is **Steve Claxton's Smoky Mountain Adventures** (Bryson City, 828/736-7501, http://steveclaxton.com), who specializes in leaving civilization behind in favor of camping, catching wild mountain trout, and getting a true taste of the wilderness. Three-day, two-night camping trips for 5-7 people run around $400 per person, and four-day, three-night trips are $450-500 per person. They also offer daylong fishing trips (1 person $225, 2 people $250, 3 people $300).

Nantahala Fly Fishing Co. (Robbinsville, 828/479-8850 or 866/910-1013, www. flyfishnorthcarolina.com, guided trips and private lessons half day $150 1 angler, $75 per additional person, full day $300 1 or 2 anglers, $75 per additional person) provides guided trips for fly-rod fishing, but if you've never held one of these odd fishing rods in your hand, they also provide a fly-fishing school ($300 for 2 days) and private instruction. Best of all, they have a "No Fish, No Pay" guarantee.

Hiking

Great Smoky Mountains National Park has more than 800 miles of wilderness trails, and with around 40 percent of the park located in Swain County, more trails than you could hike in a week are within striking distance of Bryson City. **Deep Creek Loop** is a four-mile loop that passes two waterfalls on an easy, mostly flat, track. You can also take the strenuous **Deep Creek Trail** to Newfound Gap Road, a 14.2-mile one-way hike that will require a return ride. The **Noland Creek Trail**

is a fairly easy six-mile trail near the end of the Road to Nowhere (a failed road-building project from the 1930s and 1940s). At the end of the Road to Nowhere, just past the tunnel, is the **Goldmine Loop Trail,** a three-mile track that's beautiful and enjoyable.

Golf

Smoky Mountain Country Club (1300 Conleys Creek Rd., Whittier, 828/497-7622, www.carolinamountaingolf.com, 18 holes, par 71, greens fees 18 holes $59, 9 holes $35, includes cart, discounts for students, seniors, and off-peak play, club rentals $10) is a mountain golf course where nearly every hole has views that will distract you from the sport; an aggressive player will find rewards on several holes. While some of the greens are open, many are well guarded by bunkers and contours that make greenside chipping tricky, especially if you haven't played much in the mountains.

FOOD

The **Cork & Bean Bistro** (24 Everett St., 828/488-1934, www.theeveretthotel.com, 4:30pm-8pm Tues., 11am-8pm Wed.-Thurs., 11am-8:30pm Fri., 9am-8:30pm Sat., 9am-3pm Sun., $9-36) serves three excellent meals daily, using local and seasonal ingredients to create updated takes on familiar dishes or regional specialties. The trout cakes (or any preparation of locally sourced trout) are outstanding, as is any venison dish, but you can't go wrong with a burger either.

The Appalachian Trail passes only a few feet from **River's End Restaurant** (13077 Hwy. 19 W., 828/488-7172, www.noc.com, 8am-7pm Sun.-Thurs., 8am-7pm Fri.-Sat., $6-20) at the Nantahala Outdoor Center. Given its proximity to the trail (really a footbridge over the river, but on the trail nonetheless) and to the center's rafting, paddling, hiking nexus, it's a popular spot for outdoorsy sorts. The menu reflects this with dishes like the Sherpa bowls (rice, veggies, and optional meat) that are packed with protein, calories, and carbs to fuel you through a day on the trail.

For a hearty steak, check out **Jimmy Mac's Restaurant** (121 Main St., 828/488-4700, www.jimmymacsrestaurant.com, 11:30am-9pm daily, $8-30). In addition to steak, they serve beef, elk, and buffalo burgers and seafood. Service is fantastic; let them know you're there for a special occasion and they'll treat you even better.

ACCOMMODATIONS

The ★ **Folkestone Inn** (101 Folkestone Rd., 828/488-2730 or 888/812-3385, www.folkestoneinn.com, $120-169) is one of the region's outstanding bed-and-breakfasts, a roomy 1920s farmhouse expanded and renovated into a charming and tranquil inn. Each room has a balcony or porch. Baked treats at breakfast include shortcake, kuchen, cobblers, and other delicacies. An 85-year-old hotel listed in the National Register of Historic Places, the **Fryemont Inn** (245 Fryemont St., Bryson City, 828/488-2159 or 800/845-4879, www.fryemontinn.com, mid-Apr.-late Nov., $110-283 with meals, late-Nov.-mid-Apr. $115-225 no meal service) has a cozy, rustic feel with chestnut-paneled guest rooms and an inviting lobby with an enormous stone fireplace.

Some river outfitters offer lodging, which can be a cheap way to pass the night if you don't mind roughing it. The **Rolling Thunder River Company** (10160 US-19 W., near Bryson City, 800/408-7238, www.rollingthunderriverco.com, no alcohol permitted) operates a large bunkhouse with beds ($10-12 per person per night) for its rafting customers. **Carolina Outfitters** (715 US-19, Topton, 828/488-6345, www.carolinaoutfitters.com) has a number of accommodations available ($50-100), including two-room cabins, two-bedroom apartments, and three-bedroom cabins suitable for a large group. Many of the outfitters also offer camping on their properties.

Camping

Among the nicest camping options available in the Nantahala National Forest is **Standing Indian Campground** (90 Sloan Rd., Franklin, 877/444-6777, www.recreation.gov, Apr.-Nov., $16). Standing Indian has a nice diversity of campsites, from flat grassy areas to cozy mountainside nooks. Drinking water, hot showers, flush toilets, and a phone are all available on-site, and leashed pets are permitted. At 3,400 feet in elevation, the campground is close to the Appalachian Trail.

Deep Creek Tube Center and Campground (1090 W. Deep Creek Rd., Bryson City, 828/488-6055, www.deepcreekcamping.com, Apr. 3-Oct. 30, camping $23-50, cabins $69-195) has more than 50 campsites and 18 cabins, as well as access to Deep Creek, where you can go tubing (tube rentals $5 per day). The creek runs right by many campsites. You can also go gem "mining" here, a great mountain tradition; they sell bags and buckets of gem-enriched dirt in the camp store. The best part is that the facility is within walking distance of Great Smoky Mountains National Park.

TRANSPORTATION

Bryson City can be reached via US-19, if you're coming south from Maggie Valley and Cherokee. US-74 also passes close by for easy access from the east or the west. Since Bryson City is less than 20 minutes from Cherokee, it's a good base from which to explore the national park via Newfound Gap Road, the Blue Ridge Parkway, and the southwestern edge of GSMNP.

Robbinsville and the Valley Towns

Between Robbinsville and the Georgia state line is another region at the heart of Cherokee life. Snowbird, not far from Robbinsville, is one of the most traditional Cherokee communities, where it's common to hear the Cherokee language and the arts, crafts, and folkways are flourishing. The burial site of Junaluska, one of the Eastern Band's most prominent leaders, is here.

As moving as it is to see the memorial to one of the Cherokee heroes, the town of Murphy is forever linked to tragedy for the Cherokee people and a dark incident in American history—the Trail of Tears. Around 16,000 Cherokee people, including warriors and clan leaders, men, women, children, the elderly, and the infirm, were forced to leave their homes in North Carolina, Tennessee, and Georgia; they were arrested and marched under guard to Fort Butler, here in Murphy, and from Fort Butler they were forced to walk to Oklahoma. You'll find the names of these people, many of whom died along the way, inscribed in Cherokee on a memorial at the L&N Depot in Murphy.

In addition to places of historical significance in Cherokee culture, this far southwestern corner of North Carolina has other compelling sights. Brasstown, a tiny village on the Georgia state line, is the home of the John C. Campbell Folk School, an artists' colony nearly a century old, where visitors can stroll among studios and along trails and stop in to a gallery-shop for some of the most beautiful crafts you'll find in the region. Back up toward Robbinsville, the relentlessly scenic Cherohala Skyway crosses 43 miles of the Cherokee and Nantahala National Forests. This road is a major destination for motorcyclists and sports-car drivers as well as day-trippers and vacationers.

ROBBINSVILLE

The whole southwestern corner of North Carolina is rich with Cherokee history and culture, and the Robbinsville area has some of the deepest roots of great significance to the Cherokee people. In little towns and crossroads a few miles outside Robbinsville, several hundred people known as the Snowbird community keep alive some of the oldest Cherokee ways. The Cherokee language is spoken here, and it's a place where some of the Eastern Band's most admired basket makers, potters, and other artists continue to make and teach their ancient arts. If you're visiting and want to enjoy an adult beverage, you'd better bring your own, as Graham County is North Carolina's one and only dry county.

Sights

Outside Robbinsville in the ancient Stecoah Valley is an imposing old rock schoolhouse built in 1930 and used as a school until the mid-1990s. It has been reborn as the **Stecoah Valley Center** (121 Schoolhouse Rd., Stecoah, 828/479-3364, www.stecoahvalleycenter.com), home of a weaver's guild, a native plants preservation group, a concert series, several festivals, and a great **Gallery Shop** (828/497-3098, 10am-5pm Mon.-Sat. Mar.-Oct., 10am-5pm Mon.-Fri. Nov.-Dec., closed Jan.-Feb.) of local artisans' work. Concerts in the Appalachian Evening summer series, featuring area musicians, are preceded by community suppers of traditional mountain cuisine.

On Robbinsville's Main Street is the **Junaluska Memorial** (Main St., 0.5 miles north of the Graham County Courthouse, 828/479-4727, 9am-5pm Mon.-Sat. Apr.-Oct., call for hours Nov.-Mar.), where Junaluska, a 19th-century leader of the Eastern Band of the Cherokee, and his third wife, Nicie, are

Junaluska

One of the most important figures in the history of the Eastern Band of the Cherokee is Junaluska, who was born near Dillard, Georgia, in 1776. During the wars against the Creek Indians from 1812 to 1814, the Cherokee people fought beside U.S. forces, and it's said that the fierce young Junaluska saved the life of Andrew Jackson at the battle of Horse Shoe Bend in Alabama.

Twenty years later, Jackson, by then president, repaid Junaluska's bravery and the loyalty of the Cherokee people by signing the Indian Removal Act, which ordered that they, along with four other major Southern nations, be forced from their homelands and marched to the new Indian Territory of Oklahoma. Junaluska traveled to Washington and met with Jackson to plead for mercy for the Cherokee nation; his pleas were ignored, and in 1838, Junaluska joined 16,000 members of the Cherokee nation who were force-marched close to 1,000 miles to Oklahoma. Midway across Tennessee, he led a failed escape attempt and was captured and chained; he completed the march in leg irons and manacles. It was during this time that Junaluska supposedly said, "If I had known what Andrew Jackson would do to the Cherokees, I would have killed him myself that day at Horse Shoe Bend." In 1841 he was finally able to leave Oklahoma and made the 17-day trip to North Carolina on horseback.

He spent his final years in Cherokee County, on land granted to him by the state of North Carolina. He and his third wife, Nicie, are buried at Robbinsville, at what is now the Junaluska Memorial and Museum. His grave was originally marked according to Cherokee tradition—with a pile of stones—but in 1910 the Daughters of the American Revolution commissioned a marker for his gravesite. During the dedication ceremony, Reverend Armstrong Cornsilk delivered a eulogy in the Cherokee language:

> He was a good man. He was a good friend. He was a good friend in his home and everywhere. He would ask the hungry man to eat. He would ask the cold one to warm by his fire. He would ask the tired one to rest, and he would give a good place to sleep. Juno's home was a good home for others. He was a smart man. He made his mind think well. He was very brave. He was not afraid. Juno at this time has been dead about 50 years. I am glad he is up above [pointing upward]. I am glad we have this beautiful monument. It shows Junaluska did good, and it shows we all appreciate him together—having a pleasant time together. I hope we shall all meet Junaluska in heaven [pointing upward] and all be happy there together.

buried. The marker was dedicated in 1910 by the Daughters of the American Revolution, and the gravesite is maintained by the Friends of Junaluska, who also operate the **Junaluska Museum** (828/479-4727, 9am-5pm Mon.-Sat. Apr.-Oct., call for hours Nov.-Mar., free) on the same site. At the museum you'll find ancient artifacts from life in Cheoah thousands of years ago. There are also contemporary Cherokee crafts on display, and outside you can walk a path that highlights the medicinal plants used for generations in this area.

Down a winding country road 14 miles outside Robbinsville, **Yellow Branch Pottery and Cheese** (136 Yellow Branch Circle, Robbinsville, 828/479-6710, www. yellowbranch.com, noon-5pm Tues.-Sat. Apr.-Nov. or by appointment) is a beautifully rustic spot for an afternoon's excursion. Bruce DeGroot, Karen Mickler, and their herd of Jersey cows produce prizewinning artisanal cheeses and graceful, functional pottery. Visitors are welcome at their farm and shop.

Entertainment and Events

Every year on the Saturday of Memorial Day weekend in late May, the Snowbird Cherokee host the **Fading Voices Festival** in Robbinsville. The festival features a mound-building ceremony along with typical festival attractions—music, dancing, storytelling, crafts, and lots of food—but in the deeply traditional forms carried on by the Snowbird community. Contact the Junaluska Museum (828/479-4727) for more information.

Recreation

The **Joyce Kilmer Memorial Forest** (Joyce Kilmer Rd., off Hwy. 143 west of Robbinsville, 828/479-6431, www.grahamcountytravel.com) is one of the largest remaining tracts of virgin forest in the eastern United States, where 450-year-old tulip poplar trees have grown to 100 feet tall and 20 feet around. The forest stands in honor of Joyce Kilmer, a soldier killed in action in France during World War I. His poem, "Trees," inspired this living memorial. The only way to see the forest is on foot, and a two-mile loop or two one-mile loops make for an easy hike through a remarkable forest.

The Joyce Kilmer Memorial Forest abuts the Slickrock Wilderness Area, and **Slickrock Creek Trail** is one of its longest trails. This 13.5-mile (one-way) trail starts out easy, but the final 5-5.5 miles are fairly strenuous. *Backpacker* magazine has named this one of the toughest trails in the country, in part because the hike can be made into a 21.7-mile loop by connecting with the **Haoe Lead, Hangover Lead,** and **Ike Branch** trails.

Be forewarned that this is a big trip, but it's rewarding, with views of waterfalls (the first is only a few miles in, on the easy part) and rhododendron thickets. Its name is apt: The rocks here can be incredibly slick.

The trailhead for the **Hangover Lead South Trail** is adjacent to the parking area at Big Fat Gap (off Slick Rock Rd., about 7 miles from US-129). The trail is only 2.8 miles long, but it's strenuous. The payoff is the view from the Haoe Lead summit at 5,249 feet. There are backcountry campsites here, and the rule is to keep campsites 100 yards from streams and follow Leave No Trace guidelines.

A handy collection of trail maps for Joyce Kilmer Memorial Forest, Slickrock Creek, Snowbird Back Country, and Tsali Recreation Area are available from the Graham Chamber (http://grahamchamber.com). The maps provide a rough idea of the locations and routes of these trails, but they are not a replacement for topographic maps, which you should have with you while on any of these rugged or isolated trails.

Food and Accommodations

The **Snowbird Mountain Lodge** (4633 Santeetlah Rd., 11 miles west of Robbinsville, 800/941-9290, http://snowbirdlodge.com,

Joyce Kilmer Memorial Forest

$240-470) was built in the early 1940s, a rustic chestnut-and-stone inn atop a 3,000-foot mountain. The view is exquisite, and the lodge is perfectly situated amid the Cherohala Skyway, Lake Santeetlah, and the Joyce Kilmer Forest. Guests enjoy a full breakfast, picnic lunch, and four-course supper created from seasonal local specialties.

Another pleasant place to stay near Robbinsville is the **Tapoco Lodge Resort** (14981 Tapoco Rd., 15 miles north of Robbinsville, 828/498-2800, www.tapocolodge.com, Thurs.-Sat. Nov.-Sept., daily Oct., rooms and suites $239-329, cabins $149-249). Built in 1930, the lodge is in the National Register of Historic Places, and it has the feel of an old-time hotel. Guest rooms in the main lodge and surrounding cabins are simple but comfortable, and the resort overlooks the Cheoah River, a legendary run for rafters when occasional controlled releases of water form crazy-fast rapids. The on-site **Jasper's Restaurant** (dinner from 5:30pm Thurs.-Sat., $26-46) serves fine Appalachian food, while the pub **SlickRock Grill** (11am-late daily, $9-23) is perched over the river.

Angels Landing Inn Bed & Breakfast (94 Campbell St., Murphy, 828/835-8877, www.angelslandinginn.wordpress.com, $88-105) is one of the only B&Bs in town. Fortunately, the folks are friendly and the price is right. **Mountain Ivy Rentals** (56 Airport Rd., 2.5 miles east of Robbinsville, 8258/735-9180, www.mountainivy.com, 2-night minimum, $125) has one log-sided cabin that sleeps six and is steps away from great trout fishing in the stream that runs alongside the cabin. An indoor fireplace and a space outside for a campfire help make it cozy in any season. The garage is handy for motorcycle travelers, as it gives them a place to secure trailers, bikes, and other gear.

CAMPING

At the **Simple Life Campground** (88 Lower Mountain Creek Rd., 828/788-1099, www.thesimplelifecampground.com, Mar.-Nov., cabins $28-108, RVs $24-42, tents $14) the cabins, RV sites, and tent sites have access to hot showers and Wi-Fi. This campground is near the Cherohala Skyway, Joyce Kilmer Memorial Forest, and Lake Santeetlah.

If you're RVing your way through the Smokies, the six-acre **Teaberry Hill RV Campground** (77 Upper Sawyers Creek Rd., 828/479-3953, http://teaberryhill.com, $45) is one of the nicest campgrounds you'll find, with large pull-through sites to accommodate any size RV. Amenities include 50-amp electrical hookups, water and sewer, and Wi-Fi access.

HAYESVILLE, BRASSTOWN, AND MURPHY

Between Hayesville and Brasstown, you can get a really good sense of the art that has come out of this region over the years. These three small towns are along the Georgia border on US-64.

Murphy River Walk

The **Murphy River Walk** in Murphy is a three-mile trail along the Hiwassee River and Valley River, winding from Konehete Park to the Old L&N Depot. A beautiful walk (and a great way to stretch your legs after a long ride) through this charming, tiny town, the River Walk gives you the chance to see Murphy up close and personal.

After your walk along the river, take a look at some of the antique stores in Murphy. A popular stop is **Linger Awhile Antiques and Collectibles** (46 Valley River Ave., 321/267-2777, 10am-5pm Tues.-Sat.).

★ John C. Campbell Folk School

One of North Carolina's most remarkable cultural institutions, the **John C. Campbell Folk School** (1 Folk School Rd., Brasstown, 800/365-5724, www.folkschool.org) was created by Northern honeymooners who traveled through Appalachia 100 years ago to educate themselves about Southern highland culture. John C. and Olive Dame Campbell, like other high-profile Northern liberals of their day, directed their humanitarian impulses toward the education and economic betterment of Southern mountain dwellers. John Campbell died a decade later, but Olive, joining forces with her friend Marguerite Butler, set out to establish a "folk school" in the Southern mountains that she and John had visited. She was inspired by the model of the Danish *folkehøjskole*, workshops that preserved and taught traditional arts as a means of fostering economic self-determination and personal pride in rural communities. Brasstown was chosen as the site for this grand experiment, and in 1925, the John C. Campbell Folk School opened its doors.

Today, thousands of artists travel every year to this uncommonly lovely remote valley, the site of an ancient Cherokee village. In weeklong and weekend classes, students of all ages and skill levels learn about the traditional arts of this region, such as pottery, weaving, dyeing, storytelling, and chair caning, as well as contemporary and exotic crafts such as photography, kaleidoscope making, bookmaking, and paper marbling. The website outlines the hundreds of courses offered every year, but even if you're passing through the area on a shorter visit, you can explore the school's campus. Visitors are asked to preserve the quiet atmosphere of learning and concentration when viewing the artist studios, but you can have an up-close look at some of their marvelous wares in the school's **Craft Shop** (bottom floor of Olive Dame Campbell Dining Hall, 8am-5pm Mon.-Wed. and Fri.-Sat., 8am-6pm Thurs., 1pm-5pm Sun.), one of the nicest craft shops in western North Carolina. Exhibits about the school's history and historic examples of the work of local artists of past generations are on display at the **History Center** (8am-5pm Mon.-Sat., 1pm-5pm Sun.), next to Keith House.

There are several nature trails on campus that thread through this lovely valley. Be sure to visit the 0.25-mile **Rivercane Walk,** which features outdoor sculpture by some of the greatest living artists of the Eastern Band of the Cherokee. In the evenings you'll often find concerts by traditional musicians, or community square, contra, and English country dances. A visit to the John C. Campbell Folk School, whether as a student or a traveler, is an exceptional opportunity to immerse yourself in a great creative tradition.

Clay County Historical and Arts Council Museum

Hayesville's Old Clay County Jail, built in 1912, is now home to the **Clay County Historical and Arts Council Museum** (21 Davis Loop, Hayesville, 828/389-6814, www.clayhistoryarts.org, 10am-4pm Tues.-Sat. late May-early Sept., call for hours early Sept.-late May). This is a small and extremely interesting museum with varied collections, including the medical instruments of an early country doctor; an original jail cell complete with a file hidden by a long-ago prisoner, discovered during renovations; an old moonshine still; a collection of beautiful Cherokee masks; and a remarkable crazy quilt embroidered with strange and charming illustrations.

Food

Herb's Pit Bar-B-Que (15896 W. US Hwy. 64, Murphy, 828/494-5367, www.herbspitbarbque.com, 11am-8pm Wed., Thurs., and Sun., 11am-9pm Fri. and Sat., $2-24) is the western terminus of the North Carolina Barbecue Trail and should be your first (or last) stop on it. Here you can sample more than the 'cue that pitmasters in the deep mountains make—you can also order plates of tasty fried trout and chicken.

Tiger's Department Store (42 Herbert St., Hayesville, 828/389-6531, 9:30am-6pm Mon.-Sat., under $10) may be a surprise as a dining option, but in addition to clothing and gear, this store has an old-fashioned soda counter that provides some tasty refreshments.

The Copper Door (2 Sullivan St., Hayesville, 828/389-8460, http://thecopperdoor.com, 5pm-10pm Mon.-Sat., $16-48) is an upscale joint serving a nice selection of seafood, steaks, and other meat-centric dishes, but they can accommodate vegetarians and vegans. This elegant restaurant is run by a chef from New Orleans, and his influence is all over the menu, from crawfish to mussels to other French- and creole-inspired creations. In 2011 and 2012 they received *Wine Spectator* magazine's Award of Excellence.

Accommodations

Harrah's Casino in Cherokee opened a sister location here in Murphy in late 2015. **Harrah's Cherokee Valley River Casino & Hotel** (777 Casino Pkwy., Murphy, 828/422-7777, www.caesars.com, from $179) has 300 rooms in a seven-story hotel, and a huge gaming floor: 50,000 square feet containing 70 table games and more than 1,000 slot machines. As the rooms go, they're quite comfortable (borderline luxury), but remember that smoking is permitted at the casino, so be sure to request a non-smoking or smoking room, based on your preference.

At time of publication, the dining options were limited to **Nathan's Famous Hot Dogs** (open 24 hours), **Panda Express** (11am-11pm Sun.-Thurs., 11am-2am Fri.-Sat.), **Earl of Sandwich** (11am-11pm Sun.-Thurs., 11am-2am Fri.-Sat.), **Papa John's Pizza** (11am-11pm Sun.-Thurs., 11am-2am Fri.-Sat.), and **Starbucks** (6am-11pm Sun.-Thurs., 6am-1am Fri.-Sat.). Still, who comes to a casino to eat? The table games are fun and it's going to be interesting to watch this casino grow.

TRANSPORTATION

This is the southwestern-most corner of North Carolina, in some places as close to Atlanta as to Asheville. Robbinsville is located on US-129 about 30 miles (40 minutes) southwest of Bryson City. Hayesville and Brasstown are easily reached via US-64, which closely parallels the Georgia border. Robbinsville, Hayesville, and Brasstown are all less than a two-hour drive from Asheville.

Asheville

Asheville's proximity to Great Smoky Mountains National Park (it's a little more than an hour to the south and west) makes it a convenient travel hub. Use Asheville as a starting or ending point, or as a base of operations. The city also offers diverse dining and lodging options.

FOOD

Asheville is a town that clearly loves its food, with 13 active farmers markets, more than 250 independent restaurants, and 21 microbreweries in a city of fewer than 100,000 residents.

One of the best meals you'll eat in Asheville is at **Rhubarb** (7 SW Pack Sq., 828/785-1503, www.rhubarbasheville.com, 11:30am-9:30pm Mon. and Wed.-Thurs., 11:30am-10:30pm Fri., 10:30am-10:30pm Sat., 10:30am-9:30pm Sun., shared plates $5-19, full plates $18-32).

The Admiral (400 Haywood Rd., West

Asheville, 828/252-2541, www.theadmiralnc.com, 5pm-10pm daily, small plates $10, entrées $28) serves some distinguished and much-lauded New Southern food that keeps the kitchen on its toes with interesting techniques and seasonal ingredients.

At **Buxton Hall Barbecue** (32 Banks Ave., 828/232-7216, www.buxtonhall.com, 11:30am-3pm and 5:30pm-10pm Tues.-Sun., $5-16) Chef Elliott Moss serves up a blend of old-school barbecue at its best. Chicken bog (rice, chicken, and sausage) from the South Carolina low country is right beside eastern North Carolina whole-hog barbecue and South Carolina barbecue hash and smoked sausages. All are accompanied by an excellent selection of classic barbecue sides.

Mela (70 Lexington Ave., 828/225-8880, www.melaasheville.com, lunch 11:30am-2:30pm daily, dinner 5:30pm-9:30pm

Sun.-Thurs., 5:30pm-10pm Fri.-Sat., $10-15) is one of the best Indian restaurants in North Carolina. **Cúrate** (11 Biltmore Ave., 828/239-2946, www.curatetapasbar.com, 11:30am-10:30pm Tues.-Thurs., 11:30am-11pm Fri.-Sat., 11:30am-10:30pm Sun., small plates $5-20) features a Spanish tapas-style menu.

ACCOMMODATIONS

The **Asheville Bed & Breakfast Association** (www.ashevillebba.com) has a constantly growing membership of inns and B&Bs in the area that band together to promote getaways, tours, and seasonal packages. Check with them for any current specials.

ASIA Bed and Breakfast Spa (128 Hillside St., 828/255-0051, www.ashevillespa.com, $189-279) is one of my favorite places to stay in town. Just off the Blue Ridge Parkway north of Asheville is the **Sourwood Inn** (810 Elk Mountain Scenic Hwy., 828/255-0690, www.sourwoodinn.com, $155-200 inn rooms, $200 separate cabins). Situated on the end of a ridgeline, the view is nearly 270 degrees from every balcony and bedroom window. There's no Wi-Fi or cell service, so you can truly unplug.

TRANSPORTATION

Car

From Asheville it's easy to get to Great Smoky Mountains National Park (GSMNP). In just over an hour you can be in Cataloochee, at the north end of the park, to camp, hike, and watch for elk in a serene mountain cove; to get there take I-40 west to Exit 20 and follow the signs. You can also take I-40 west into Tennessee, then follow the Foothills Parkway to US-321 and skirt the edge of Great Smoky Mountains National Park to **Gatlinburg,** Tennessee, and the entrance to the park (a trip of about 90 minutes). From Gatlinburg, you can make a loop back to Asheville by taking Newfound Gap Road across Great Smoky

Mountains National Park to Cherokee, North Carolina (about 2.5 hours), and then back to Asheville via US-441 to US-19 to I-40, a total loop of about 3.5 hours and some 175 miles.

You can also head straight to **Cherokee** from Asheville and enter Great Smoky Mountains National Park via Newfound Gap Road there. It's an hour drive following I-40 west to exit 27, then taking US-19 south to US-441, which carries you right into Cherokee.

Alternately, you can take the more scenic, but much longer, route and get to Cherokee via the **Blue Ridge Parkway.** This route is only 83 miles, but it takes 2-2.5 hours. If you want to go this way, head south out of Asheville along US-25 and pick up the Blue Ridge Parkway about 5.5 miles out of town; turn south on the Parkway and drive it until you reach Cherokee and Great Smoky Mountains National Park. And, of course, you can reverse the course if you're making that grand loop; you can return to Asheville via the Blue Ridge Parkway by picking it up in Cherokee and driving north.

Air

The **Asheville Regional Airport** (AVL, 61 Terminal Dr., 828/684-2226, www.flyavl.com) is located south of the city in Fletcher, a 20-minute drive on I-26. Several airlines offer flights to Atlanta, Charlotte, and other U.S. cities. Asheville's public bus system connects the airport with downtown Asheville. A taxi from the airport will run about $45.

Bus

There is a **Greyhound station** (2 Tunnel Rd., 828/253-8451, www.greyhound.com) in Asheville. Asheville's extensive public bus system, **ART** (www.ashevillenc.gov, 6am-11:30pm Mon.-Sat., $1, $0.50 seniors), connects most major points in the metropolitan area, including the airport, with downtown. Check online for routes and schedules.

Background

The Landscape

GEOGRAPHY

The Mountain Region forms the western border of North Carolina. The ridges of the Blue Ridge and Great Smoky Mountains, both subranges of the Appalachian Mountain chain, undulate like the folds of a great quilt, running northeast-to-southwest from Virginia along the border with Tennessee and into the southwestern corner where the inland tip of North Carolina meets Georgia. This is a land of waterfalls, rivers, and fast-flowing creeks, and rugged, beautiful peaks of smaller mountain configurations. Hemmed in among the peaks and hollows of the Blue Ridge and the Smokies are the Black Mountains, the Pisgah Range, and the Unka Range. The Black Mountains are only about 15 miles wide and are confined mostly to Yancey County, but they're the highest in the state, and six of the ten highest peaks in the eastern United States are here, including Mount Mitchell, the highest at 6,684 feet.

This is a region rich in resources, with coal seams, limestone and marble quarries, natural gas deposits, and, surprisingly, pockets and veins of precious and semiprecious gems. The rivers here are old, with the ironically named New River, one of the oldest in the world, flowing northward from North Carolina's Blue Ridge through Virginia and into West Virginia.

CLIMATE

The mountains are much cooler than either the Piedmont or the coast, and winter lasts longer. North Carolina towns like Asheville and Boone can be blanketed in snow while less than 100 miles away the trees in Piedmont towns aren't even showing their fall colors. The coldest temperature ever recorded in

North Carolina, -34°F, was recorded in 1985 on Mount Mitchell. Spring and fall can bring cool to temperate days and chilly nights, while summer days can hit the 80s, and the evenings bring a welcome relief. The Piedmont, on the other hand, can be brutally hot during the summer and quite warm on spring and fall days, though winter is milder. The coast sees long, hot summers and cool—not cold—winters with rare snowfall.

The Smoky Mountains experience four distinct seasons, with temperatures and microclimates that can vary wildly depending on elevation and sun exposure. Temperatures can swing drastically with those elevation shifts, changing as much as 15 or 20 degrees as you go from the lowest elevations to the highest. That means on warm summer days, when cities like Asheville might see temperatures in the 80s, Mount Mitchell, 6,000 feet above sea level, will be in the low 50s and possibly cooler, depending on wind.

During spring, temperatures in this region range from the low 40s to the mid- or upper 60s, and rain or even an early-spring snowfall is common. Summer sees higher temperatures, reaching 80 degrees with some regularity, higher on rare occasions; summer lows can dip down into the 60s and may be even lower at high elevations along the Blue Ridge Parkway. In fall, temperatures are similar to spring, with daytime temperatures in the 40s to 60s, and nights plunging to 30 degrees on occasion. Winter is cold, with ranges from the low 30s to the high 40s; nighttime temperatures, and temperatures in the deepest hollows, can fall into the teens and single digits. Temperatures that low are possible across the region during the coldest periods of winter, even lower at elevations

Geographical Vocabulary

This region has some unusual landscapes and environments, and some unusual vocabulary to describe them. As you explore, you may encounter the following terms.

HOLLER

Here's a term that's really more of a regional pronunciation than a unique word. A holler is what is on paper termed a "hollow"—a mountain cove. It's just that in the South we aren't much for rounding words that end in "ow." If you don't believe me, just beller out the winda to that feller wallering in yonder meada.

BALD

An ecological mystery, the Appalachian bald is a mountaintop area on which there are no trees, even though surrounding mountaintops of the same elevation may be forested. Typically, a bald is either grassy or a heath. Heaths are more easily explained, as they are caused by soil conditions that don't support forest. Grassy balds, though, occur on land where logically trees should be found. Some theories hold that grassy balds were caused by generations of livestock grazing, but soil studies show that they were grassy meadows before the first cattle or sheep arrived. Grazing may still be the answer, though: The balds may originally have been chomped and trampled down by prehistoric megafauna—ancient bison, mastodons, and mammoths. Today, in the absence of mammoths or free-ranging cattle, some balds are gradually becoming woodland, except where deliberately maintained.

SANDHILLS

If you're in Wilmington or Southport, or somewhere else along the state's southeastern coast, take note of what the soil beneath your feet looks like. Now, turn your back to the ocean and head inland. Travel 100 miles west and then look down again. What you'll see is very similar— sandy, light-colored ground, wiry vegetation (and a few carnivorous plants), maybe even some scattered shells. About 20 million years ago, during the Miocene Epoch, the areas of present-day Fayetteville, Southern Pines, and Sanford were sand dunes on the shores of an ocean that covered what is now North Carolina's coastal plain. Imagine the landscape millions of years ago, when the Uwharrie Mountains, just west of the Sandhills, towered 20,000 feet over an ocean that swirled at their feet.

POCOSIN

Pronounced "puh-COH-sin," the word is said to come from the Algonquin for "swamp on a hill." A pocosin is a moist peat bog of a sort unique to the Southeast and particularly associated with eastern North Carolina. The peat layer is thinnest around the edges and usually supports communities of pine trees. Moving toward the center of the bog, the ground becomes slightly higher, and the peat thicker, more acidic, and less welcoming to plant species. Because the soil is so poor and leached of nutrients, carnivorous plants, which have their meals delivered rather than depending on the soil's bounty, are particularly well suited to life in pocosins.

CAROLINA BAY

The word *bay* here refers not to an inlet on the coast but to another kind of upland swamp. The bays' origins are mysterious, and their regularity of form and commonness in this region is uncanny. If you look down at eastern North and South Carolina from an airplane, or in a satellite image, the bays are unmistakable. They're oval-shaped depressions, varying in size from Lake Waccamaw to mere puddles, and are always aligned in a northeast-to-southwest configuration. Unlike ponds and regular swamps, bays are usually unconnected to any groundwater source but are fed solely by rainwater. Like pocosins, bays attract colonies of carnivorous plants, which love to establish their dens of iniquity in such unwholesome soil.

The weather changes in an instant at high elevations.

once or twice each winter and the occasional dusting of snow. Outside the mountains, most North Carolinians are woefully inexperienced snow drivers, and the state Department of Transportation doesn't have the equipment in coastal counties to handle much more than a little snow.

ENVIRONMENTAL ISSUES

The parklands and forests along the routes through the Smoky Mountains are preserved so future generations can enjoy nature in as pristine a state as possible. That's why there's no gas available on the Blue Ridge Parkway. It also explains the constant reminders to adhere to **Leave No Trace** (www.LNT. org) principles. Leave No Trace principles are similar to the Boy Scouts of America teachings: plan ahead and prepare, travel and camp on durable surfaces, dispose of waste properly, leave what you find, minimize campfire impacts, respect wildlife, be considerate of other visitors. These easy rules can improve the outdoor experience for everyone.

If you pack something in, pack it out, and consider carrying a **trash bag** on trails to pick up after less responsible hikers. If each of us would make this a habit, we could clean up a lot of litter that clutters up our view and is detrimental to the environment.

Dogs are allowed on some trails throughout this route, though they must be on leash or under physical control at all times. If you have Fido out on the trail or let him use the grassy facilities at an overlook or wayside, be sure to pick up what he's putting down.

You'll pass several ponds and lakes as you travel this region, but unless there's a designated **swimming** area, going for a dip isn't cool. There are exceptions, but those exceptions are noted near the potential swimming hole. When in doubt, ask before you dive in.

You'll spot lots of **wildlife** on your trip. Common animals include white-tailed deer, raccoons, opossums, turtles, bobcats, and even black bears. Coyotes are becoming a

where it's not uncommon to experience a few freezing days.

This is a wet place, with regular snowfall from late fall through early spring, and rains common any time of year. Winter storms can dump a few inches of wet snow on the mountains here, or they can dust it with some fine, powdery snow. Thunderstorms in spring, summer, and fall can be heavy, though the worst of the weather is only occasional; regular rain showers contribute to the 50-80 inches of precipitation falling annually.

Tornadoes, most common in the spring, can cause trouble any time of year. A rare November twister touched down in 2006, smashing the Columbus County community of Riegelwood, killing eight people and leaving a seven-mile swath of destruction. Even plain old **thunderstorms** can be dangerous, bringing lightning, flash flooding, difficult driving conditions, and even hail. **Snowstorms** are rare, and usually occur in the mountains. The Piedmont sees more snow than the coast, which sees flurries more frequent sight along the way, and in certain areas of the Smoky Mountains, you can even see the occasional elk. Many times, a herd of deer will be in a pasture off the Parkway. If you see deer (or any other animal), and you want to get a photograph, keep a safe distance from the animal and don't offer them any food; this makes them grow accustomed to people and can have negative impacts on their health.

Plants

In the early 1700s, John Lawson, an English explorer who would soon be one of the first victims of the Tuscarora War, wrote of a magnificent tree house somewhere in the very young colony of North Carolina. "I have been informed of a Tulip-Tree," he wrote, "that was ten Foot Diameter; and another, wherein a lusty Man had his Bed and Household Furniture, and liv'd in it, till his Labour got him a more fashionable Mansion. He afterwards became a noted Man, in his Country, for Wealth and Conduct." Whether or not there was ever a tulip poplar large enough to serve as a furnished bachelor pad, colonial forests must have seemed miraculous to the first Europeans to see them.

FORESTS

Today, after generations of logging and farming across the state, few old-growth forests exist. In the Smoky Mountains, stands of old-growth timber, like the Joyce Kilmer Memorial Forest, are a sight to behold, and some of the trees almost validate Lawson's anecdote. Across the state, scores of specialized ecosystems support a marvelous diversity of plant and animal life. In the east, cypress swamps and a few patches of maritime forest still stand; across the Sandhills are longleaf pine forests; in the mountains are fragrant balsam forests and stands of hardwoods.

Because the state is so geographically and climatically varied, there's a greater diversity in tree species than anywhere in the eastern United States. More than half of the land in the Piedmont and eastern North Carolina is forested. Coastal forests are dominated by hardwoods—**oaks** of many varieties, **gum,** **cypress,** and **cedar**—and the barrier islands have a few remaining patches of maritime forest where the branches of **live oak** trees intertwine to shed storm wind and their roots sink deep to keep islands stable. The best and largest remaining example of a pristine maritime forest is on Bald Head Island, where the Bald Head Island Conservancy provides education and studies the form, function, and future of barrier islands, including these important maritime forest ecosystems. In the Piedmont, oak and **hickory** dominate the hardwoods alongside bands of piney woods. In the mountains oak and hickory are also the rule, but a number of conifers, including **pine** and **balsam,** appear.

The science and profession of forestry were born here: In the 1880s and 1890s, George W. Vanderbilt, lord of the manner at Biltmore, engaged Fredrick Law Olmsted, who designed New York City's Central Park, to plan a managed forest of the finest, healthiest, and hardiest trees. Vanderbilt hired Gifford Pinchot and later Carl Schenck to be the stewards of the thousands of wooded acres he owned in the Pisgah Forest south of Asheville. The contributions these men made to the nascent field are still felt today and are commemorated at the Cradle of Forestry Museum near Brevard.

Longleaf Pine

The longleaf pine, sometimes called the pitch pine, is something of a rare sight today, as the vast stands of longleaf pines that formerly blanketed the eastern part of the state were used extensively in the naval stores industry in the 18th and 19th centuries, providing valuable turpentine, pitch, tar, and lumber. The

rhododendron blooms

overharvesting of this tree has a lot to do with the disappearance of North Carolina's once-legendary pine barrens, but an unanticipated ancillary cause is the efficiency of modern firefighting. Longleaf pines depend on periodic forest fires to clear out competition from the underbrush and provide layers of nutrient-rich singed earth. In the 20th century the rule was to put out forest fires, cutting down on smoke but disturbing the natural growth cycles of these trees. In some longleaf-harboring nature preserves today, controlled burns keep the woods alive and healthy as crucial habitats for several endangered species, including the red-cockaded woodpecker and the Pine Barrens treefrog.

FLOWERS

Some of the region's flora puts on great annual shows, drawing flocks of admirers—the gaudy **azaleas** of springtime, the **wildflowers** of the first warm weather in the hills, the **rhododendrons** and **mountain laurel** of the Appalachian summer. The Ericaceae family, a race of great woody bushes with star-shaped blossoms that includes azaleas, rhododendrons, and laurel, is the headliner in the floral fashion show.

The **flame azalea** makes a late-spring appearance on the mountainsides of the Blue Ridge and Great Smokies, joined by its cousins the mountain laurel and Catawba rhododendron in May and June. The ways of the rhododendron are a little mysterious; not every plant blooms every year, and there's no surefire way of predicting when they'll put on big shows. The area's widely varying elevation also figures into bloom times. If you're interested in timing your trip to coincide with some of these flowering seasons, your best bet is to call ahead and speak with a ranger from Great Smoky Mountains National Park to find out how the season is coming along.

Around the end of April and into May, when spring finally arrives in the mountains but the forest floor is not yet sequestered in leafy shade, a profusion of delicate flowers emerges. **Violets** and **chickweed** emerge early on, as do the white **trillium** and the wake-robin, a trillium that looks something like a small poinsettia. Every year since 1950, around the end of April, Great Smoky Mountains National Park has hosted the **Spring Wildflower Pilgrimage,** a weeklong festival featuring scores of nature walks that also reveal salamanders, birds, and wild hogs, along with workshops and art exhibits. Visit www.springwildflowerpilgrimage.org for a schedule of events.

Surprisingly, one of the best places to view displays of wildflowers is along the major highways. For more than 20 years the state Department of Transportation has carried out a highway beautification project that involves planting large banks of wildflowers along highways and in wide medians. The displays are not landscaped but are allowed to grow up in unkempt profusion, often planted in inspired combinations of wildly contrasting colors that make the flowerbeds a genuinely beautiful addition to the environment. The website of the state's **Department of**

Horticultural Havens

North Carolina's natural scenery provides inspiration for landscapes of almost equal beauty. Asheville is the home of the **North Carolina Arboretum,** a garden of more than 400 acres that borders the Pisgah National Forest and the Blue Ridge Parkway. Special collections include the National Native Azalea Repository and more than 200 bonsai. You can tour the arboretum on foot, by Segway, or on your bike, and you can even bring your dog on some of the trails.

At the **Biltmore Estate,** Frederick Law Olmsted created formal gardens of beauty to match the opulent mansion, and architect Richard Morris Hunt designed the conservatory where young plants are still raised for the gardens. Self-guided tours of the conservatory—and the walled, shrub, Italian, vernal, and azalea gardens—are all included in admission to the estate.

Asheville is also an excellent home base for excursions to other garden spots in the mountains. Don't miss the **Rivercane Walk** at the John C. Campbell Folk School in Brasstown, where modern Cherokee sculpture lines a path along Little Brasstown Creek. The **Mountain Farm Museum** at the edge of Great Smoky Mountains National Park demonstrates gardening methods used on the early mountain homesteads. The **Cradle of Forestry** in Pisgah National Forest explains how the science of modern forestry was born here in western North Carolina.

Transportation (www.ncdot.org) offers a guide to the locations and seasons of the wildflower beds.

FALL FOLIAGE

Arriving as early as mid-September at the highest elevations and gradually sliding down the mountains through late October, autumn colors bring a late-season wave of visitors. Dropping temperatures change trees' sugar production, resulting in a palette of colors, while simple fatigue causes the green to fade in others, exposing underlying hues. Countless climatic factors can alter the onset and progress of leaf season, so the mountains blush at slightly different times every year. The latter weeks of October tend to be the peak; during those weeks it can be difficult to find lodging in the mountains, so be sure to plan ahead. Some of the best places for leaf peeping are along the Blue Ridge Parkway and in Great Smoky Mountains National Park.

CARNIVOROUS PLANTS

There are many species of **pitcher plants,** a familiar predator of the plant world. Shaped like tubular vases with a graceful elfin flap shading the mouth, pitcher plants attract insects with an irresistible brew. Unsuspecting bugs pile in, thinking they've found a keg party, but instead find themselves paddling in a sticky mess from which they're unable to escape, pinned down by spiny hairs that line the inside of the pitcher. Enterprising frogs and spiders that are either strong or clever enough to come and go safely from inside the pitcher will often set up shop inside a plant and help themselves to stragglers. Another local character is the **sundew,** perhaps the creepiest of the carnivorous plants. Sundews extend their paddle-shaped leaf-hands up into the air, hairy palms baited with a sticky mess that bugs can't resist. When a fly lands among the hairs, the sundew closes on it like a fist and gorges on it until it's ready for more.

Animals

Among the familiar wildlife most commonly seen in the state, **white-tailed deer** are out in force in the countryside and in the woods; they populate suburban areas in large numbers as well. **Raccoons** and **opossums** prowl at night, happy to scavenge from trash cans and the forest floor. **Skunks** are common, particularly in the mountains, and are often smelled rather than seen. They leave an odor something like a cross between grape soda and Sharpie markers. There are also a fair number of **black bears,** not only in the mountains but in swamps and deep woods across the state.

In woods and yards alike, **gray squirrels** and a host of familiar **songbirds** are a daily presence. Different species of **tree frogs** produce beautiful choruses on spring and summer nights, while **fireflies** mount sparkly shows in the trees and grass in the upper Piedmont and mountains.

The Carolina woods harbor colonies of **Southern flying squirrels.** It's very unlikely that you'll see one unless it's at a nature center or wildlife rehabilitation clinic because flying squirrels are both nocturnal and shy. They're also almost unspeakably cute. Fully extended, they're about nine inches long snout to tail, weigh about four ounces, and have super-silky fur and pink noses, and like many nocturnal animals have comically long whiskers and huge, wide-set eyes that suggest amphetamine use. When they're flying—gliding, really—they spread their limbs to extend the patagium, a membrane that stretches between their front and hind legs, and glide along like little magic carpets.

Also deep in the Smokies are some herds of **wild hogs,** game boar brought to the area about 100 years ago and allowed to go feral. The official line among wildlife officials is that **mountain lions**—in this region called panthers—have been extinct in North Carolina for some time. But mountain dwellers claim there are still panthers in the Blue Ridge and Smokies, and most people here have seen or heard one—their cry sounds like a terror-filled scream. There are even tales of a panther in the inland woods of Brunswick and Columbus Counties on the southeast coast.

BACKGROUND
ANIMALS

Deer graze in a field at Cades Cove.

REINTRODUCED SPECIES

In the 1990s and early 2000s a federal program to reestablish **red wolf** colonies in the Southeast focused its efforts on parkland in North Carolina. Red wolves, thought to have existed in North Carolina in past centuries, were first reintroduced to Great Smoky Mountains National Park. They did not thrive, and the colony was moved to the Alligator River National Wildlife Refuge on the northeast coast. The packs have fared better in this corner of the state and now roam several wilderness areas in the sound country.

The Smokies proved a more hospitable place for the reintroduction of **elk.** Now the largest animals in Great Smoky Mountains National Park, elk, which can grow up to 700 pounds, are most often observed in the Cataloochee section of the park, grazing happily and lounging in the mist in the early morning and at twilight.

AMPHIBIANS

Dozens of species of **salamanders** and their close kin, including **mudpuppies, sirens,** and **amphiumas,** call this region home, and Great Smoky Mountains National Park harbors so many of them that it's known as the Salamander Capital of the World. Throughout the state, **frogs** and **toads** are numerous and vociferous, especially the many species of dainty **tree frogs.** Two species, the gray tree frog and the spring peeper, are found almost everywhere, and beginning in late winter they create the impression that the trees are filled with ringing cell phones.

Hellbenders are quite possibly the strangest animal. They are enormous salamanders—not the slick little pencil-thin five-inch salamanders easily spotted along creeks, but hulking brutes that grow to more than two feet long and can weigh five pounds. Rare and hermetic, they live in rocky mountain streams, venturing out from under rocks at night to gobble up crayfish and minnows. They're hard to see even if they do emerge in the daytime because they're lumpy and mud-colored, camouflaged against streambeds. Aggressive with each other, the males often sport battle scars on their stumpy legs. They've been known to bite humans, but as rare as it is to spot a hellbender, it's an exponentially rarer occurrence to be bitten by one.

REPTILES

Turtles and **snakes** are the state's most common reptiles. **Box turtles,** found everywhere, and **bog turtles,** found in the Smokies, are the only land terrapins. A great many freshwater turtles inhabit the swamps and ponds, and on a sunny day every log or branch sticking out of fresh water will become a sunbathing terrace for as many turtles as it can hold. Common water turtles include **cooters, sliders,** and **painted turtles. Snapping turtles** can be found in fresh water throughout the state, so mind your toes. They grow up to a couple of feet long and can weigh more than 50 pounds. Not only will they bite—hard!—if provoked, they will actually initiate hostilities, lunging for you if they so much as disapprove of the fashion of your shoes. Even the tiny hatchlings are vicious, so give them a wide berth.

The vast majority of snakes are shy, gentle, and totally harmless to anything larger than a rat. There are a few species of venomous snakes that are very dangerous. These include three kinds of **rattlesnake:** the huge diamondback, whose diet of rabbits testifies to its size and strength; the pigmy; and the timber or canebrake rattler. Other venomous species are the beautiful mottled **copperhead** and the **cottonmouth or water moccasin,** famous for flinging its mouth open in hostility and flashing its brilliant white palate. The **coral snake** is a fantastically beautiful and venomous species.

Most snakes are entirely benign to humans, including old familiars such as **black racers** and **king snakes** as well as **milk, corn,** and **rat snakes.** One particularly endearing character is the **hognose snake,** which can be found throughout North Carolina but is most common in the east. Colloquially known as a spreading adder, the hognose snake compensates for its total harmlessness with amazing displays of histrionics. If you startle one, it will first flatten and greatly widen its head and neck and hiss most passionately. If it sees that you're not frightened by plan A, it will panic and go straight to plan B: playing dead. The hognose snake won't simply lie inert until you go away, though; it goes to the dramatic lengths of flipping onto its back, exposing its pitiably vulnerable belly, opening its mouth, throwing its head back limply, and sticking out its tongue as if it had just been poisoned. It is such a devoted method actor that should you call its bluff and poke it back onto its belly, it will fling itself energetically back into the mortuary pose and resume being deceased.

Local Culture

TOURISM

In the mountains, the main industries have been mining and logging, agriculture, and tourism. As the way we care for our environment has evolved, mining and logging have largely fallen by the wayside and been replaced by small pockets of manufacturing from national and international companies or larger local companies. Through this, the importance of tourism has increased.The region has always drawn visitors to its mountains, waters, and cities, and as the economy evolves, the tourism sector has become vital to the state's well-being. In the mountains, **Great Smoky Mountain National Park** is a recognizable, even marquee, name for visitors, and **Asheville**, with its superb dining and much-lauded craft beer scene, is atop many visitors' lists. Heritage tourism is helping small towns as visitors follow quilt and craft trails across rural counties. This is helping grow interest in lesser-known cities and small towns throughout the mountains.

INDIGENOUS CULTURES

In the Great Smoky Mountains, the town of Cherokee on the Qualla Boundary, which is Cherokee-administered land, is the governmental seat of the Eastern Band of the Cherokee. The Eastern Band are largely descended from those Cherokee people who escaped arrest during the deportation of the Southeast's Native Americans on the Trail of Tears in the 19th century, or who made the forced march to Oklahoma but survived and walked home to the mountains.

The early 19th century in North Carolina was a good deal more peaceful than the previous hundred years had been. Yet despite the relative peace, there was also conflict. Andrew Jackson's administration presided over the passage of the Indian Removal Act in 1830, which assigned reservations in the Indian Territory of present-day Oklahoma to the "Five Civilized Tribes" of the southeastern United States—the Cherokee, Choctaw, Creek, Chickasaw, and Seminole. Thousands of Cherokee people were forced out of western North Carolina, northern Georgia, eastern Tennessee, and Alabama and marched west on the Trail of Tears. About 4,000 died along the way. Another 1,000 or so Cherokee people, through hiding, fighting, and negotiation, managed to win the right to stay in North Carolina—an act of resistance that was the birth of the modern Eastern Band of the Cherokee, still centered on the town of Cherokee on the Qualla Boundary in North Carolina's Great Smoky Mountains.

The Cherokee people depict emblematic episodes in their history in the outdoor drama *Unto These Hills,* in production since 1950. It's especially important to note that among the characteristics of outdoor drama in North Carolina is the fact that the cast, crew, and often the producers and playwrights are members of the communities whose stories the plays tell.

Understanding Local Lingo

Regional speech features delightful and sometimes perplexing regional vocabulary and grammar. Following are some of the common phrases most likely to stump travelers.

- **Bless your/his/her heart:** A complex declaration with infinitely varied intentions, interpreted depending on context or tone. In its most basic use, "Bless your heart," is a sincere thank-you for a favor or a kindness paid. It's also an exclamation of affection, usually applied to children and the elderly, as in, "You're *not* 92 years old! You are? Well, bless your heart." Frequently, though, hearts are blessed to frame criticism in a charitable light, as in, "Bless his heart; that man from New York don't know not to shout."

- **buggy:** a shopping cart, as at a grocery store.

- **carry:** convey, escort, give a ride to. "I carried my mother up to the mountains for her birthday."

- **cattywampus:** topsy-turvy, mixed up. Used especially in the Piedmont and farther west.

- **Coke:** any soft drink; may be called "pop" in the mountains.

- **come back:** often uttered by shopkeepers as a customer leaves, not to ask them to return immediately, but simply an invitation to patronize the establishment again someday.

- **dinner:** the midday meal.

- **evening:** not just the twilight hours, but all the hours between about 3pm and nightfall.

- **ever-how:** however; similarly, "ever-when," "ever-what," and "ever-who."

- **fair to middling:** so-so, in response to "How you?"; a holdover term from North Carolina's moonshining days, the term originally applied to grading 'shine by examining bubbles in a shaken mason jar.

- **fixing:** about to or preparing to do something. "She's fixing to have a baby any day now."

- **holler:** hollow, a mountain cove.

- **mash:** press, as a button. "I keep mashing the button, but the elevator won't come."

Throughout the town of Cherokee, North Carolina, you'll see many street and commercial signs written in English and a set of pretty, twisty symbols that look like a cross between Khmer or Sanskrit and Cyrillic. This is Cherokee, written in the alphabet famously devised by Sequoyah in the early 19th century. Cherokee also survives as a spoken language, though typically among the elders in traditional communities. To combat the slow death of the language, Eastern Band of Cherokee leadership has started a program to teach tribal youth to speak and write the language, though the pool of fluent speakers is very small.

ARTS AND CRAFTS

Several communities are known worldwide for their local traditions, and countless individual artists, studios, and galleries can be found across the region.

Cherokee craft is an important aesthetic school comprising a wide range of techniques and media such as wood and stone carving, fiber arts, traditional weaponry, and avant-garde sculpture and painting. **Qualla Arts and Crafts Mutual,** located in the town of Cherokee, has a wonderful sales gallery that will dazzle lovers of fine craft.

Asheville is an epicenter of the arts, the heart of a vast community of artists that

- **mess:** discombobulated, in a rut, not living right. "I was a mess until I joined the church."

- **might could/should/would:** could/should/would perhaps. "Looks like it's fixing to rain. You might should go roll up your car windows."

- **piece:** a vague measure of distance, as in, "down the road a piece" (a little ways down the road) or "a fair piece" (a long way).

- **poke:** a bag, such as a paper shopping bag. Used especially in the mountains.

- **reckon:** believe, think. Often used in interrogative statements that end in a falling tone, as in, "Reckon what we're having for dinner." (That is, "What do you suppose is for lunch?")

- **right:** quite, very. Variations include "right quick" (soon, hurriedly), "right much" (often), and "a right many" or "a right smart of" (a great quantity).

- **sorry:** worthless, lame, shoddy. "I wanted to play basketball in college, but I was too sorry of an athlete."

- **speck so:** "I expect so," or, "Yes, I guess that's correct."

- **supper:** the evening meal (as opposed to "dinner," the midday meal).

- **sy-goggling:** see *cattywampus*. Used especially in the mountains.

- **ugly:** mean or unfriendly, spiteful. Sometimes referred to as "acting ugly." "Hateful" is a common synonym. The favorite Southern injunction that "God don't like ugly" does not mean that God wants us to be pretty, but rather that we should be nice.

- **wait on:** to wait for.

- **y'all:** pronoun used to address any group of two or more people.

- **yonder:** over there.

- **y'uns:** mountain variation of *y'all*.

stretches throughout western North Carolina and includes such major folk schools as **John C. Campbell** in Brasstown, near the Georgia state line, and **Penland,** close to Tennessee in the northeastern mountains. In Asheville you can see and purchase an infinite variety of crafts that include handmade baskets, quilts, furniture, clothing, jewelry, and iron architectural elements. The **Southern Highland Craft Guild** (www.southernhighlandguild. org), an old and accomplished organization, deserves a lot of the credit for the thriving craft movement. Its website has a great deal of information about contemporary master crafters and their work.

As people become more accustomed to a world where almost every object we see and use was mass-produced far away, we develop an ever-deeper appreciation for the depth of skill and aesthetic complexity that went into the production of everyday objects in past generations. The artists of this region have always been great crafters of utilitarian and occupational necessities. As you travel, keep an eye out for objects that you might not immediately recognize as art—barns, fishing nets, woven chair bottoms—but that were made with the skill and artistry of generations-old traditions.

MUSIC

Asheville's a music-loving town if ever there was one. And the music scene revolves around the lauded, almost legendary, **Orange Peel Social Aid and Pleasure Club**. Everyone who's anyone in rock and improvisational music has played or will play here. The cool downtown venue offers shows just about every night of the week, including local and regional acts in addition to major players and the "next big thing" bands. The **Grey Eagle Tavern and Music Hall** is another of Asheville's long-running spots to catch a show. One of the biggest annual shows in Asheville is the **Warren Haynes Christmas Jam**, an all-star concert fund-raiser featuring a lineup of some of the top rock musicians playing with their bands, with one another, and in any mix imaginable.

If there is an epicenter of traditional Appalachian music, it may just be Gatlinburg and Pigeon Forge. Traditional music has been played here since the first European settlers arrived. As tourism increased and the towns grew into that "aw-shucks, we're hillbillies" character, traditional music also played a role. Today, you can hear everything from very strict traditional music to bluegrass covers of modern pop songs being played and sung on the streets and in any number of small theaters and shows. There's no marquee venue; the closest thing is Dollywood, which draws a big crowd and will do a lot to get a musician or band's name out there.

Knoxville has a busy college music scene; major musical acts roll through town, but smaller, no-less-talented bands come through as well. Traditional music is heard throughout the city; musicians from novices to virtuosos saw on fiddles, pluck banjo strings, and slap out bass rhythms on the street, in bars, and in concert halls like the **Tennessee Theatre** and **Bijou Theatre**.

FOOD

Up in the Great Smoky Mountains, the early spring is the season for **ramps,** sometimes called skunk cabbage—very pungent wild onions that grow along creek beds in the deep mountains. They're another of those foods passionately defended by those who grew up eating them but are greeted with trepidation by outsiders. The reason they're feared by the uninitiated is their atomically powerful taste, which will emanate from every part of your body for days if the ramps are too strong or not prepared correctly. Ramps taste like a cross between regular onions, garlic,

The Orange Peel Social Aid and Pleasure Club is one of the top music halls in the southeast.

leeks, shallots, and kryptonite. When they're young, they're perfectly pungent—not too overwhelming, but still powerful enough to let you know they're in the dish. Folks skillet-cook them, fry them up in grease, boil them with fatback, or just chomp on them raw. For a special treat and a gentle introduction to ramps, stop in at the Stecoah Valley Center near Robbinsville and pick up a bag of the Smoky Mountain Native Plants Association's special cornmeal mix with dried ramps, and make yourself a skillet of deliciously tangy cornbread. You can also try them at the local ramps festivals held in Robbinsville and Cherokee in spring. A growing number of restaurants from Asheville to Wilmington are buying ramps and **morel mushrooms** from mountain foragers and preparing them every way from skillet fried to pickled, so ramp lovers can get a taste of this springtime mountain delicacy even on the coast.

Vegetarians and devotees of organic food, fear not; most places are unusually progressive state when it comes to healthy and home-grown grub. Nevertheless, if you want to avoid meat, you have to be cautious when ordering at a restaurant: Make sure the beans are made with vegetable oil rather than lard, ask if the salad dressing contains anchovies, and beware of hidden fish and oyster sauce. Traditional Southern cooking makes liberal use of fatback (cured pork fat) and other animal products; greens are often boiled with a strip of fatback or a hambone, as are most soups and stews. Even pie crusts are still made with lard in many old-time kitchens.

You'll find organic grocery stores in the major cities. Earth Fare and Whole Foods are the most common chains, but there are also plenty of small independent markets. Farmers markets and roadside stands are so plentiful that they almost have to fight for space.

Essentials

← Big Creek   16
  Cosby   28
↑ Interstate 40   10

Transportation

GETTING THERE

Car

The north-south interstates of I-81 and I-75 meet in Knoxville, Tennessee, just 30 miles northwest of the western entrance to Great Smoky Mountains National Park. Coming from the south, I-75 is a natural feeder from Chattanooga, Tennessee, and Atlanta, Georgia; I-81 cuts a south-southwest diagonal through Virginia along the Shenandoah Valley, passing by or through Winchester, Lexington, Roanoke, Blacksburg, and Radford, Virginia, before hitting Bristol and Johnson City, Tennessee, and finally Knoxville.

Running east-west, I-40 carries westbound visitors directly by Asheville, across the Tennessee border just north of the national park, and to Knoxville; eastbound drivers will find Little Rock, Arkansas, and Memphis and Nashville, Tennessee, on the route.

To enter Smoky from Gatlinburg, follow I-40 to Exit 407 for Sevierville, which connects to Highway 66 south. Upon reaching the Sevierville junction, stay straight to continue on US-441 south, which becomes Newfound Gap Road on its way into the park.

From Cherokee, North Carolina, I-74 connects with US-441 north into the park, where it becomes Newfound Gap Road.

CAR RENTAL

Rental cars are available at every airport, and if you take a train to your departure point, you'll find rental agencies in or near the station. Since many bus and train stations share a facility or are near one another, the same is true if you take a bus in. The major rental players—Hertz, National, and Enterprise, among others—will be readily available with their standard fleet of cars, but if you are looking for a specific vehicle (like a 4WD or convertible), check availability with the agencies and reserve your vehicle. Most of these vehicles will be available for one-way rental, allowing you to rent a car at one end and drive it to another, returning it there before boarding a plane, or hopping a bus or train back home. Before you embark on a long, one-way trip with a rental vehicle, be sure you can return it at the other end. Check with your car rental agency about additional fees for one-way rentals, because some charge hefty fees for this type of rental.

Air

Most visitors to Great Smoky Mountains National Park arrive by car, but for those flying in, several airports offer reasonably convenient access to the surrounding regions.

Asheville Regional Airport (61 Terminal Dr., NC, 828/684-2226, www.flyavl. com) is located south of the city in Fletcher. The next-closest airport in North Carolina is **Charlotte-Douglas International Airport** (5501 Josh Birmingham Pkwy., 704/359-4910, www.charmeck.org), two hours away. Charlotte-Douglas is the 10th-largest hub in the United States, with nonstop flights to and from more than 125 destinations worldwide.

The **Greenville-Spartanburg International Airport** (2000 GSP Dr., Greer, SC, 864/848-6254, www.gspairport.com) is 80 minutes south of Asheville. Airlines serving Greenville-Spartanburg include Allegiant, American Airlines, Delta, Southwest, and United. It's a drive of a little over an hour from Greenville-Spartanburg to Asheville.

The **McGhee Tyson Airport** (2055 Alcoa Hwy., Alcoa, TN, 865/342-3000, www.tys.

---

org) in Alcoa, Tennessee, is about two hours from Cherokee and about 20 minutes south of Knoxville. Airlines serving McGhee Tyson include Allegiant, American Airlines/ American Eagle, Delta, Frontier, and United. Gatlinburg and the western entrance to Great Smoky Mountains National Park is just over one hour away; Knoxville is closer, a drive of 20 minutes without traffic.

Bus

You can take a **Greyhound bus** (800/231-2222, www.greyhound.com) to Knoxville and Asheville, but other than those two cities, service is limited. Once you arrive, you'll need a rental car because meaningful public transportation in this region is virtually nonexistent. The **Knoxville Greyhound station** (100 E. Magnolia Ave., 865/525-9483) is not far from downtown, and some public transit options (taxis, Uber, other rideshare services) make it easy to get from the bus station to your accommodations. To get to the national park or North Carolina's Smoky Mountains, you'll need a rental car. The **Asheville Greyhound station** (2 Tunnel Rd., 828/253-8451) is also far from the real heart of downtown, and again, you'll need transportation once you arrive.

GETTING AROUND
Driving
SEASONAL CONSIDERATIONS

From where the Blue Ridge Parkway crosses the North Carolina line through to Gatlinburg, Tennessee, the weather can slow and stop traffic or even shut down sections of the route. Generally, though, the weather is quite pleasant and **winter** is the only time when there are widespread closures of the Blue Ridge Parkway. This route is high and exposed, making it vulnerable to ice and snow; that combined with the expense of the equipment necessary for proper snow and ice removal make wintertime closures an inevitability. Newfound Gap Road through Great Smoky Mountains National Park is a public highway and is maintained throughout the year. It may still close if heavy snowfall is expected or is more than road crews can cope with, but closure is rare. More often you'll be delayed as crews clear the road. Road conditions are available by contacting the **National Park Service** (865/436-1200).

Spring generally brings a good amount of rain. During the earliest months, and even toward the first part of April in the highest elevations, you can experience road closures if a spring snowstorm visits the high passes. The rest of the season, it may rain, but it doesn't impede traffic.

In the **summer,** there is a chance of thunderstorms, and on rare occasions hail. Most likely, you'll encounter a rain shower or fog. The fog can be quite dense, so slowing down or even pulling off at a socked-in overlook is advisable.

In the **autumn,** there are occasional rainstorms, and in the latest part of the season, the rare high-altitude snowstorm that dusts the tops of the mountains white. Autumn sees the highest number of visitors to Great Smoky Mountains National Park, and leaf-lookers often slow down well below the speed limit, causing some congestion on the roadway. Autumn color seekers also fill overlooks and line the sides of the road to snap pictures and take in the views, slowing traffic in these busy areas.

SPEED LIMIT

On Newfound Gap Road in Great Smoky Mountains National Park, the speed limit is 45 miles per hour, though it does slow in areas. Please observe the posted speed limit. Maintaining the speed limit allows you time to stop or avoid wildlife, debris, or other hazards on the road surface as well as pedestrians or other vehicles. Since long sections of the road are unprotected—read: no guardrails to break up the view—obeying the speed limit has the added benefit of keeping you and your passengers safe from leaving the roadway on an unexpected downhill trip.

Getting There

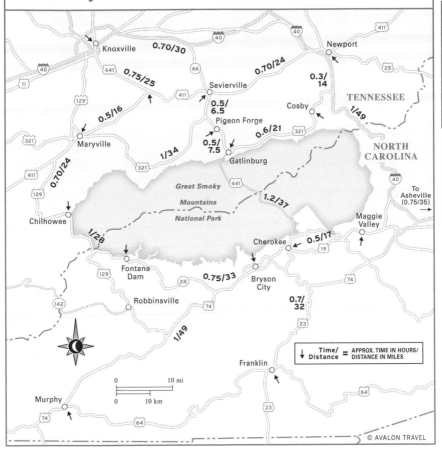

And if you think you can speed on the parkway or in the national park because rangers can't pull you over, think again: they can, and they will, delivering hefty fines to reckless drivers.

One reason for the low speed limits along this scenic drive is to keep wildlife free from harm. You'll see a number of woodland creatures on your drive, and as your route cuts through the forests where they live, you'll see many animals on or near the roadway. Be extra vigilant at dawn and dusk, when wildlife is most active. If you must stop in the road to allow an animal to cross, use your hazard flashers to alert other drivers, and try not to stop in blind curves or just over the crest of a hill where you'll be difficult to see.

PARKING

In Great Smoky Mountains National Park, parking is usually limited to designated parking areas at overlooks and trailheads; parking is permitted along the road shoulder, provided all four wheels are off the road surface and your vehicle doesn't impede traffic. On interstates and other highways, stop only when necessary, and when you do, be sure to pull fully off the road so you're not a danger to passing motorists and so you don't put yourself in harm's way.

FUEL

You won't find any fuel inside Great Smoky Mountains National Park, but you will find it in Cherokee and the other towns on the North Carolina side. Gas stations are plentiful on the Tennessee side once you leave the national park.

Recreation

BACKPACKING

To go backcountry camping anywhere in the park, you'll need a permit and a reservation from the **Backcountry Information Office** (Sugarlands Visitor Center, 1420 Old TN-73 Scenic, Gatlinburg, TN, 865/436-1297, https://smokiepermits.nps.gov, 8am-5pm daily, backcountry permits $4/night). The office can answer any questions about backcountry campsites, trail access, and trail shelters.

The **Appalachian Trail** (AT) runs nearly 2,200 miles from Georgia to Maine. The AT has 71.6 miles of trail in Great Smoky Mountains National Park and stepping foot on it is a highlight for thru-hikers, segment hikers, and day hikers.

There are no fees or permits required to hike the Appalachian Trail; however, there are requirements when you hike the AT in Great Smoky Mountains National Park. Thru-hikers are defined as those who begin and end their hike at least 50 miles from the border of the park and only travel on the AT while in the park. Thru-hikers are eligible for a **thru-hiker permit** (www.smokiespermits.nps.gov, $20). Segment hikers must get a permit from the Backcountry Information Office. Day hikers do not require a permit.

For information about the Appalachian Trail, contact the **Appalachian Trail Conservancy** (www.appalachiantrail.org) or visit the **National Park Service's AT website** (www.nps.gov/appa) for trip planning information, maps, trail reports, and more.

For AT thru-hikers there's only one place to stay in Great Smoky Mountains National Park: Appalachian Trail shelters. Four spots are reserved for thru-hikers at all trail shelters, but they're first-come, first-served. If you're thru-hiking and a shelter is full, you can to pitch your tent next to the shelters. Segment hikers and backpackers can reserve spots in AT shelters or at any of the numerous backcountry campsites along and near the Appalachian Trail.

FISHING

There are 2,900 miles of streams within Great Smoky Mountains National Park, and some 600 miles of waterways are ready for anglers to come wet a line and see what they catch. While many think of these mountain streams as perfect for trout fishing with fly rods (these anglers are not mistaken, the Smokies are perfect for fly-fishing), just as many forget that smallmouth bass and rock bass are fairly abundant in these waters.

Smallmouth bass like a rocky-bottomed stream with lots of nooks and crannies where they can hide, so roots, boulders and rock formations, and debris fields are ideal; they also like deep pools where slow-moving currents make it easier to feed. In this region of the Smokies, look for smallmouth along the West Prong of the Little Pigeon River near Gatlinburg and the park's western entrance. You'll also find them in the Little Pigeon River near Greenbrier. Other places you'll find smallmouth and rock bass in the park include the Little River on the way to Cades

Cove, Abrams Creek, and Fontana Lake, specifically the feeder creeks like Noland, Hazel, and Eagle Creek.

Fishing in the park is year-round, 30 minutes before sunrise to 30 minutes after sunset, and you can fish any stream in the park provided you have a license. Since Great Smoky Mountains National Park is in both North Carolina and Tennessee, a valid license from either state is accepted within the park and there's no trout stamp requirement. A special permit is required to fish in Cherokee and Gatlinburg. **License requirements** for North Carolina can be found at hwww.ncwildlife.org; requirements for Tennessee can be found at www.tn.gov/twra. Though both states offer online license sales, a license can be obtained in person at most sporting goods stores near the park.

As for daily possession limits you're able to possess five fish—brook, rainbow, or brown trout; smallmouth bass; or a combination—in total. Rock bass are the only exception; you're allowed to possess 20 of these in addition to the five-fish limit. There's no minimum size on rock bass, but smallmouth and trout are required to be at least 7 inches.

With regard to tackle, you're allowed one handheld rod and can only use single-hook artificial flies or lures. That means no fish bait, no liquid scents, and a healthy list of prohibited baits (including minnows, worms, corn, cheese, bread, and even natural baits you find alongside the stream). A full list of fishing provisions for Great Smoky Mountains National Park can be found online (www.nps.gov/grsm).

WATER SPORTS

Swimming and inner tubing is not recommended in the park due to a number of serious injuries and hazards. (Drowning is a leading cause of death in Smoky.) Deep Creek (in the southern section of the park, near Bryson City, NC) permits tubing on its waters.

White-water rafting outfitters are located in Gatlinburg, Tennessee. In North Carolina, Smoky Mountain Tubing in Cherokee rents tubes on the Oconaluftee River, while Dillsboro River Company will float you on the Tuckasegee River.

Your best option for white-water rafting, however, is the beautiful Nantahala River Gorge just outside Bryson City in the Nantahala National Forest. Several outfitters and guide services can get you out into this stunning gorge.

Travel Tips

INTERNATIONAL TRAVELERS

Visitors from other countries must present a valid **passport** and **visa** issued by a U.S. consular official to enter the United States; visas are not necessary for citizens of countries eligible for the Visa Waiver Program (such as Canada). For more information on traveling to the United States from a foreign country, visit www.usa.gov.

Foreign visitors who wish to drive should obtain an **International Driving Permit,** which is available from the nation that issued your driver's license. Driver's licensing rules vary from state to state. It's a good idea to familiarize yourself with the driving rules in the states that you'll be visiting (you can do this at www.usa.gov). Throughout the United States, drivers drive on the right side of the road, and distance and speed is measured in miles. Speedometers display both miles and kilometers; road signs display only miles.

If you're traveling to the United States from a foreign country, you'll need to exchange your currency at the airport or at a bank or currency exchange in your destination city; every attraction, restaurant, and lodging on the route accepts U.S. dollars only. Credit

Leave No Trace

PLAN AHEAD AND PREPARE

- Know the regulations and special concerns for the area you'll visit.
- Prepare for extreme weather, hazards, and emergencies.
- Schedule your trip to avoid times of high use.
- Visit in small groups. Split larger parties into groups of 4-6.
- Repackage food to minimize waste.
- Use a map and compass to eliminate the use of marking paint, rock cairns, or flagging.

TRAVEL AND CAMP ON DURABLE SURFACES

- Durable surfaces include established trails and campsites, rock, gravel, dry grasses, or snow.
- Protect riparian areas by camping at least 200 feet from lakes and streams.
- Good campsites are found, not made. Altering a site is not necessary.

  In popular areas:
- Concentrate use on existing trails and campsites.
- Walk single file in the middle of the trail, even when wet or muddy.
- Keep campsites small. Focus activity in areas where vegetation is absent.

DISPOSE OF WASTE PROPERLY

- Pack it in, pack it out. Inspect your campsite and rest areas for trash or spilled foods. Pack out all trash, leftover food, and litter.
- Deposit solid human waste in catholes dug 6-8 inches deep and at least 200 feet from water, camp, and trails. Cover and disguise the cathole when finished.
- Pack out toilet paper and hygiene products.
- To wash yourself or your dishes, carry water 200 feet away from streams or lakes and use small amounts of biodegradable soap. Scatter strained dishwater.

LEAVE WHAT YOU FIND

- Preserve the past: examine, but do not touch, cultural or historic structures and artifacts.

---

cards are widely accepted, but for moments when you need cash, there are plenty of ATMs along the route. Though ATMs are limited in Great Smoky Mountains National Park, you will find them at some visitors centers.

TOURIST INFORMATION
What to Bring

Depending on the season, you'll need slightly different clothing, and your supplies will depend on the activities you plan to include as part of your trip. No matter what, you'll want sunscreen and bug spray if you're traveling in the spring, summer, or fall, and sunscreen if you're visiting in winter (especially for skiers). Bring your binoculars and a camera with a zoom lens so you can enjoy the wildlife up close without disturbing it, keeping all parties involved safe and sound.

If you plan to hike, dress in layers so you

- Leave rocks, plants, and other natural objects as you find them.

- Avoid introducing or transporting non-native species.

- Do not build structures, furniture, or dig trenches.

MINIMIZE CAMPFIRE IMPACTS

- Campfires can cause lasting impacts to the backcountry. Use a lightweight stove for cooking and enjoy a candle lantern for light.

- Where fires are permitted, use established fire rings, fire pans, or mound fires.

- Keep fires small. Only use sticks from the ground that can be broken by hand.

- Burn all wood and coals to ash, put out campfires completely, then scatter cool ashes.

RESPECT WILDLIFE

- Observe wildlife from a distance. Do not follow or approach them.

- Never feed animals. Feeding wildlife damages their health, alters natural behaviors, and exposes them to predators and other dangers.

- Protect wildlife and your food by storing rations and trash securely.

- Control pets at all times, or leave them at home.

- Avoid wildlife during sensitive times: mating, nesting, raising young, or winter.

BE CONSIDERATE OF OTHER VISITORS

- Respect other visitors and protect the quality of their experience.

- Be courteous. Yield to other users on the trail.

- Step to the downhill side of the trail when encountering pack stock.

- Take breaks and camp away from trails and other visitors.

- Let nature's sounds prevail. Avoid loud voices and noises.

This copyrighted information has been reprinted with permission from the Leave No Trace Center for Outdoor Ethics. For more information or materials, please visit https://lnt.org or call 800/332-4100.

can easily regulate your temperature, and have a sturdy pair of hiking boots on hand; trekking poles or a hiking staff isn't a bad idea either. Throw in some rain gear and a day pack with your first-aid kit, extra water, and some snacks and you're good to go.

Many visitors enjoy water activities here, whether it's white-water rafting, wading in the streams, or going for a float on the river, and so you'll want a bathing suit. Since the white-water rivers can be cold even in summer, you'll want something warm, preferably a lightweight wool shirt; wool dries quickly and keeps you quite warm.

Other than these basics, you should pack any specialty gear that caters to your wants, needs, and plans—golf clubs, disc golf gear, skis, maps, rock-climbing gear, whatever it may be.

Maps

One of the best resources for exploring a new region is a good map. DeLorme's atlas and gazetteers are indispensable. The detail provided is enough to plan short day hikes or longer expeditions, and they point out everything from trailheads and boat launches to campgrounds, hunting and fishing spots, and back roads of all types. Look for the *North Carolina Atlas & Gazetteer* (Yarmouth, ME: DeLorme, 2012) and the *Tennessee Atlas & Gazetteer* (Yarmouth, ME: DeLorme, 2014). If you're doing any backcountry camping, these guides will give you a good overview, but you may want to get quadrant maps for greater detail. Excellent guides are available from any good outdoor retailer, and since Great Smoky Mountains National Park is the most visited national park, quality guidebooks are always on hand.

Accommodations and Camping

In Great Smoky Mountains National Park, no unauthorized backcountry camping is allowed. Reserve a spot at a backcountry shelter or campground, or get a spot at a front-country campground. Please adhere to Leave No Trace principles, and absolutely follow regulations and restrictions for campfires. Due to the hazard of fire, campfires are generally only permitted in front-country campsites. If you are front-country camping, be aware that you can't bring in your own firewood; you'll need to purchase or gather it on site. This rule is to prevent the spread of insect infestations, parasites, and disease that may harm local plants.

For much of the year, you should be able to travel without reservations, though even in the off-season you may not be able to get into your first choice of campgrounds, lodges, hotels, or B&Bs. During peak seasons, namely October and late summer, you'll need reservations because visitors flood the area to see the autumn color show or squeeze in one more summer getaway. For some of the most popular campgrounds and lodging along the route, you should book months in advance.

ACCESS FOR TRAVELERS WITH DISABILITIES

The overwhelming majority of trails in Great Smoky Mountains National Park are not accessible for travelers with disabilities, particularly those that impede mobility. The one exception is the Sugarlands Valley nature trail (on Newfound Gap Rd.). Luckily, a huge number of attractions, accommodations, and restaurants are accessible. All visitors center restrooms are wheelchair-accessible.

TRAVELING WITH CHILDREN

There's no shortage of kid-friendly activities in Great Smoky Mountains National Park. Along the route, there are kid-friendly hikes, Junior Ranger programs, animals galore, and visitors centers and gift shops where you can pick up a little something to keep the youngest traveler occupied while in transit. In the cities, you'll find children's museums, parks, zoos, and playgrounds.

SENIOR TRAVELERS

Aside from stubble-faced and bearded bikers, one of the most common sights is the gray-haired couple tooling about in their Subaru, RV, or truck towing an RV. Many attractions, accommodations, and dining options offer senior discounts, so flash that AARP card and save a few bucks. Overall, the driving routes described in this guide are safe and leisurely ones for seniors and solo travelers.

GAY AND LESBIAN TRAVELERS

LGBTQ travelers may be pleasantly surprised at how tolerant the region is, despite being rural and, in some areas, part of the Bible Belt. In Asheville and Knoxville, you'll find open and active gay cultures, and in most spots along the way the culture is open and accepting. This isn't to say everyone you meet is open to every lifestyle choice made, but it is to say that those closed-off individuals are fewer and farther between with each passing year.

HEALTH AND SAFETY

For the most part, your trip should be unremarkable as far as health and safety are concerned, provided you're attentive to your situation and surroundings, but there are a few things you should know. Those going on long hikes would also be wise to familiarize themselves with the **10 essentials** (www.rei. com/learn/expert-advice/ten-essentials.html).

Emergencies

For emergencies anywhere in the United States, dial **911** on your phone for immediate assistance. In North Carolina, dialing ***77** connects you to the state police and ***67** puts you in contact with the highway patrol. In Tennessee, dial ***847** for police assistance. If you have to call, try to note your mile marker or a nearby exit or landmark as a reference point for any assistance that's headed your way.

Wilderness Safety

Hikers should beware of **ticks,** some of which can transmit Lyme disease. An insect repellant and some thorough body checks (use a partner for more fun) should keep you tick-free after a jaunt through the woods. If you do get a bite or if you notice a red circular rash that's similar to a bull's-eye, consult a physician; Lyme disease can be life-threatening in the worst cases.

You'll encounter woodland animals including bees, wasps, yellow jackets, and hornets, so if you're allergic, be sure to have an **EpiPen** on hand. A number of **snakes,** including rattlesnakes and copperheads, live in these woods. Be alert and keep an ear open for that warning rattle, and if you unexpectedly smell cucumbers in the woods, you may be near a copperhead; in either case, back away slowly and detour around. **Spiders** can be a concern in places, namely woodpiles and some backcountry shelters. Most are harmless, though the brown recluse is seen from time to time, and the more commonly seen black widow spider is easily identifiable by the red hourglass on the female's abdomen.

Along the trails and roadsides you'll likely encounter **poison ivy, poison oak,** and **poison sumac,** all of which deliver an itchy blister when you come in contact with the oils they secrete. These oils are active for several months, so if you walk through a field of poison ivy, be sure to wash your pants, socks, and boots well lest you inadvertently get poison ivy a month later. You may also come upon **stinging nettles,** which leave itchy welts akin to mosquito bites; these are harmless and generally go away quickly.

Resources

Suggested Reading

HIKING AND FISHING

Adams, Kevin. *Hiking Great Smoky Mountains National Park*. Guilford, CT: Globe Pequot Press, 2013. An excellent hiking-only guide to trails and on-foot sights in Great Smoky Mountains National Park, from Falcon Guides.

Brewer, Carson. *Day Hikes of the Smokies*. Gatlinburg, TN: Great Smoky Mountains Natural History Association, 2002. This pocket-sized guide covers the 34 day hikes in the park, with maps, elevation profiles, and photos.

Johnson, Randy. *Hiking the Blue Ridge Parkway: The Ultimate Travel Guide to America's Most Popular Scenic Roadway*. Guilford, CT: Globe Pequot Press, 2010. A thorough trail guide to the Blue Ridge Parkway from Falcon Guides.

Rutter, Ian. *Great Smoky Mountains National Park Angler's Companion*. Portland, OR: Frank Amato Publications, 2002. Everything you need to know about fishing Smokie's creeks and steams, as well as fishing methods and seasons, written by a volunteer for the fisheries division.

Wise, Ken. *Hiking Trails of the Great Smoky Mountains*. Gatlinburg, TN: Great Smoky Mountains Natural History Association, 2001. This hike guide includes an overview of more than 125 trails in the park, with trailhead directions, maps, and points of interest along the way.

HISTORY AND CULTURE

Fisher, Noel C. *The Civil War In the Smokies*. Gatlinburg, TN: Great Smoky Mountains Natural History Association, 2005. How the Civil War impacted the park, written by the winner of the Peter Seaborg Award for the best nonfiction Civil War book.

Hall, Karen J. *Building the Blue Ridge Parkway*. Charleston, SC: Arcadia Publishing, 2007. Narrative and archival photos combine to tell the story of the early days of the Blue Ridge Parkway including construction, folkways, and cultural tidbits.

Pegram, Tim. *The Blue Ridge Parkway by Foot: A Park Ranger's Memoir*. Jefferson, NC: McFarland & Company, 2007. A fascinating story of a former park ranger who decided to hike the Parkway—not the trails along the Parkway, but along the roadside, experiencing the 469-mile drive on foot.

TRAVEL

Duncan, Barbara, and Brett Riggs. *Cherokee Heritage Trails*. Chapel Hill, NC: UNC Press, 2003; online companion at www.cherokeeheritage.org. A fascinating guide to both the historical and present-day home of the Eastern Band of the Cherokee in North Carolina, Tennessee, and Georgia, from ancient mounds and petroglyphs to modern-day arts co-ops and sporting events.

Fussell, Fred, and Steve Kruger. *Blue Ridge Music Trails of North Carolina: A Guide to Music Sites, Artists, and Traditions of the Mountains and Foothills.* Chapel Hill: UNC Press, 2013. A guide to destinations—festivals, restaurants, oprys, church singings—in North Carolina, where authentic bluegrass, old-time, and sacred music rings through the hills and hollers. An accompanying CD gives you a chance to hear some tunes rather than just read about them.

Maynard, Charles. *Going to Great Smoky Mountains National Park.* Helena, MT: Farcountry Explorer Books, 2008. A kid-friendly guide to the plants and animals in the park.

North Carolina Atlas and Gazetteer. Yarmouth, ME: DeLorme, 2012. Since I was in Boy Scouts, I have always been partial to DeLorme's state atlases. This series represents in great detail the topography and other natural features of an area, providing users with far more useful and comprehensive information than the standard highway map.

Simmons, Nye. *Best of the Blue Ridge Parkway: The Ultimate Guide to the Parkway's Best Attractions.* Johnson City, TN: Mountain Trail Press, 2008. Beautiful photography of some of the most iconic and picturesque spots along the Parkway is accompanied by write-ups of some of the highlights.

Internet Resources

GENERAL TOURIST INFORMATION
North Carolina
North Carolina Division of Tourism
www.visitnc.com
This comprehensive guide contains trip itineraries in each region, including a dedicated section on the Blue Ridge Parkway. The site is rich with photos and videos, and it contains a wide-ranging index of accommodations, attractions, and more.

Tennessee
Knoxville Tourism & Sports Corporation
www.visitknoxville.com
The official website for Knoxville, with lists of restaurants, hotels, and an online visitors guide.

Tennessee Department of Tourist Development
www.tnvacation.com
The official site of Tennessee's state tourism office is user-friendly, allowing you to narrow your focus on one region with just a

couple of clicks. Resources for the Smokies and East Tennessee include interactive maps that provide a great overview of the region's offerings from natural sights to man-made attractions.

NATIONAL PARK INFORMATION
Great Smoky Mountains National Park
Great Smoky Mountains National Park
www.nps.gov/grsm
An extensive history of the park, with details on flora, fauna, and natural features and downloadable maps and contact information for rangers and park offices.

Friends of the Smokies
www.friendsofthesmokies.org
Friends of the Smokies works to raise funds for park initiatives, trail maintenance and improvement, and a variety of other needs. They accept donations of time and money, so if you had a good time in the Smokies, consider lending them a hand or a few bucks.

Great Smoky Mountains Association
www.smokiesinformation.org
A nonprofit partner of Great Smoky Mountains National Park, the group operates retail stores in and benefiting the park; provides guidebooks, maps, logo-emblazoned clothing and gear, and other gifts; and helps with expenses associated in promoting the park.

OUTDOORS
Appalachian Trail
Appalachian Trail Conservancy
www.appalachiantrail.org
The Appalachian Trail Conservancy provides support to the Appalachian Trail, which parallels and even crosses the Blue Ridge Parkway in many places.

Hiking
www.gatlinburg.com
This website includes a brief list of hikes and waterfalls in the region of the park near Gatlinburg.

www.nchikes.com
All things hiking-related in North Carolina, including trails, books, and trip recommendations.

Sierra Club
http://nc.sierraclub.org
http://www.sierraclub.org/tennessee
Find information about upcoming hikes and excursions as well as an overview of each state's natural areas and environmental issues.

State Parks
www.ncparks.gov
http://tnstateparks.com
A number of state parks provide alternative camping options near Great Smoky Mountains National Park. Many travelers use the parks' campgrounds and facilities as resources and waypoints along their journey.

Wildlife
North Carolina Wildlife Resources Commission
www.ncwildlife.org
Information on fishing, and boating in North Carolina, including easy-to-understand hunting and fishing regulations and online license procurement.

Tennessee Wildlife Resources Agency
www.tn.gov/twra
Need-to-know information regarding hunting and fishing regulations and licenses.

Index

P

QR

S

T

Tennessee Gateways: 92-123; map 95
Tennessee Museum of Aviation: 109
Tennessee Theatre: 116, 118
Thunderhead Mountain: 72
Titanic Pigeon Forge: 109
Tom Branch Falls: 77
Tonic Craft Beer Market: 137
tourism: 161
Trail of Tears: 133
transportation: 167-170
TriCorner Knob Shelter: 91
Trillium Gap Trail: 46, 47, 49, 50
Tuckaleechee Cove: 74
Tuckasegee River: 140, 142-143
Tunnel Branch: 78
Tunnel Bypass Trail: 78
Twentymile: 19, 82-83
Twentymile Loop Trail: 82
Twentymile Trail: 82-83

UVWXYZ

Unto These Hills: 133
visas: 171

visitors centers: 28-30
Walker Camp Prong: 42
Walnut Bottoms: 55
waterfalls: 42, 45-47, 49-50, 51-52, 55, 65, 67, 68, 72, 75, 77
water sports: 171
weather: 153, 155
weddings: 100
Welch Ridge Trail: 40
Western North Carolina Pottery Festival: 139
West Prong Little Pigeon River: 42, 43
Wheels Through Time Museum: 128
wildfire of 2016: 31
Wildflower Pilgrimage: 84
wildlife/wildlife-watching: 70, 159-161
winter sports: 129
Wolf Ridge Trail: 82
Women's Basketball Hall of Fame: 117
Women's Work Festival: 84
WonderWorks: 109-110
Woody House: 18, 61
World's Fair Park: 120
zip lining: 102, 111
zoo: 116-117

List of Maps

Photo Credits

All photos © Jason Frye except page 1 © Thomas Fikar /123rf.com; page 6 © sean pavone /123rf.com; page 7 © Dfikar /Dreamstime.com; page 8 © daveallenphoto /123rf.com; page 9 (top) © daveallenphoto /123rf.com, (bottom right) © Dndavis /123rf.com; page 16 © alexandr grichenko /123rf.com; page 23 © Sayran /Dreamstime.com; page 66 © Anthony Heflin /Dreamstime.com; page 75 © Anthony Heflin /Dreamstime.com; page 80 © Alex Grichenko /Dreamstime.com; page 92 © sean pavone /123rf.com; page 98 © Brenda Kean /123rf.com; page 107 © Cynthia Mccrary /Dreamstime.com; page 109 © Anthony Totah /123rf.com; page 124 © Susan Leggett /123rf.com; page 125 © Jill Lang /123rf.com; page 142 © Shester171 /Dreamstime.com; page 147 © Jilllang /Dreamstime.com; page 159 © Barry Beard /123rf.com

Also Available

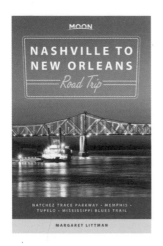

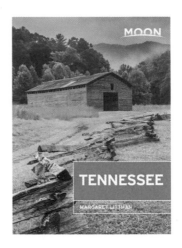

MOON GREAT SMOKY MOUNTAINS NATIONAL PARK

Avalon Travel
An imprint of Perseus Books
A Hachette Book Group company
1700 Fourth Street
Berkeley, CA 94710, USA
www.moon.com

Editor and Series Manager: Sabrina Young
Copy Editor: Mary Duffy
Production and Graphics Coordinator: Rue Flaherty
Cover Design: Faceout Studios, Charles Brock
Interior Design: Domini Dragoone
Moon Logo: Tim McGrath
Map Editor: Kat Bennett
Cartographers: Brian Shotwell, Stephanie Poulain,
    Lohnes + Wright, and Kat Bennett
Proofreader: Rachael Sablik
Indexer: Greg Jewett

ISBN-13: 978-1-61238-716-1
ISSN: 2475-0824

Printing History
1st Edition — May 2017
5 4 3 2

Front cover photo: Little River, Great Smoky Mountains National Park. © Don Johnston / All Canada Photos
Back cover photo: Hyatt Lane, Cade's Cove, Great Smoky Mountains National Park. © daveallenphoto/123rf.com

Printed in Canada by Friesens

MAP SYMBOLS

▭▭▭	Expressway	○	City/Town	✈	Airport	♨	Golf Course
▭▭▭	Primary Road	◉	State Capital	✈	Airfield	🅿	Parking Area
▭▭▭	Secondary Road	⊛	National Capital	▲	Mountain	▱	Archaeological Site
┄┄┄	Unpaved Road	★	Point of Interest	✛	Unique Natural Feature	▮	Church
───	Feature Trail	•	Accommodation	🌿	Waterfall	⛽	Gas Station
┄┄┄	Other Trail	▾	Restaurant/Bar	♠	Park		Glacier
··········	Ferry	■	Other Location	❶	Trailhead		Mangrove
▭▭▭	Pedestrian Walkway	Λ	Campground	⛷	Skiing Area		Reef
▥▥▥	Stairs						Swamp

CONVERSION TABLES

°C = (°F - 32) / 1.8
°F = (°C x 1.8) + 32
1 inch = 2.54 centimeters (cm)
1 foot = 0.304 meters (m)
1 yard = 0.914 meters
1 mile = 1.6093 kilometers (km)
1 km = 0.6214 miles
1 fathom = 1.8288 m
1 chain = 20.1168 m
1 furlong = 201.168 m
1 acre = 0.4047 hectares
1 sq km = 100 hectares
1 sq mile = 2.59 square km
1 ounce = 28.35 grams
1 pound = 0.4536 kilograms
1 short ton = 0.90718 metric ton
1 short ton = 2,000 pounds
1 long ton = 1.016 metric tons
1 long ton = 2,240 pounds
1 metric ton = 1,000 kilograms
1 quart = 0.94635 liters
1 US gallon = 3.7854 liters
1 Imperial gallon = 4.5459 liters
1 nautical mile = 1.852 km

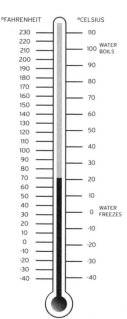

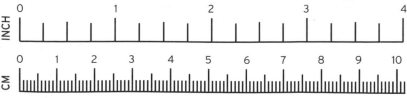